Terry Pilchick

J A I
BHIM!

*Dispatches
from a peaceful
Revolution*

Terry Pilchick

J A I
BHIM!

*Dispatches
from a peaceful
Revolution*

Windhorse Publications
in association with
Parallax Press

Windhorse Publications in association with Parallax Press

Windhorse Publications
136 Renfield Street
Glasgow G2 3AU

Parallax Press
P.O.Box 7355
Berkeley, California CA 94707

Printed by Richard Clay (The Chaucer Press) Ltd,
Bungay, Suffolk

Typeset by Budget Typesetting, Bromley, Kent

Cover photographs by Terry Pilchick and Framework
Portrait of the author by David Runnacles
Calendar reproduced with the kind permission of Lomte Calendars,
Poona, India

Cover design by Dhammarati and Paramabodhi

ISBN 0 904766 36 5 (Windhorse edition)

ISBN 0 938077 15 5 (Parallax edition)

These pages are warmly dedicated
to the people who live in them

I

Visions

one

At four o'clock this afternoon, Subhash and Madhu Parthay made an offering to the bizarre deity who has taken up residence on their land: they brought me a table. I think they are going to let me stay here after all.

'Here' is the box-like holiday bungalow the Parthays are building in a corner of their estate, a couple of miles up the road from Panchgani. When complete, the structure will boast another floor, but the delivery of my table suggests that that part of the project has been shelved until next year.

Balasaheb took it upon himself to accept my offer for one of the ground floor rooms at a time when construction work had come to a respectful halt. Old Narayan, the master of 'Parthay Sadan', and of the twenty-five souls who live in it, was seriously ill. When, just a week later, he died, a couple of his more canny sons allowed themselves to hope that I would not appear on the appointed day. That way they would be able to get back to their building work. My arrival therefore came as something of a blow and, so far as I can see, the family has been locked in dispute ever since.

Balasaheb must have saved me. But I doubt whether he could have prevailed without his mother's help. Narayan's grieving widow saw my arrival as an omen of unknown significance, and insisted that it would be recklessly impious, so soon after a death, to turn me away. Who was to know, perhaps I had been sent by the gods? Luckily for me, her view seems to have carried the day. It doesn't seem to bother anyone, or their gods, that I have a Buddhist name—Nagabodhi. The four brothers show every sign of finding it hilarious rather than disturbing, and call

Jai Bhim!

me 'Mr Terry'.

* * *

From where I stood on the sidelines, the initial negotiations for my room seemed terrifying. Heads shook dismissively, contemptuous exclamations split the air, and eyes flashed death. But as we strolled back to his downtown fish-stall, Mr Nizar assured me that everyone was quite happy with the deal.

'But we've got nothing in writing! They wouldn't even take any money in advance. How am I to know it's definite? I could come back in a couple of weeks and find they've let the place to somebody else.'

Mr Nizar—'Nizar' to his friends—fresh and trim in blue jeans and designer shirt, leaned against the iron frame of his stall. Removing Hollywood sunglasses he squinted manfully, observing my anxiety with god-like amusement. Behind, an old worthy in white robes and white fez, drowning in a sea of white facial hair, squatted on the counter, fanning tubes of silvery fish meat and launching fists of angry flies into the clammy air.

Nizar offered an indulgent smile. 'This is Maharashtra! Here it is enough that a man gives his word! Of course everything is definite!'

At a neighbouring stall, two women argued with the merchant while prodding a fat brown hen that sat, abristle with indignation, in one dish of a set of scales. In this country one never knew what was waiting round the corner. I was not to be placated easily.

'But what about that extra floor they want to build on the place? Are they really going to hold that over until next year?'

In his impatience, Nizar was prophetic: 'Listen! Nobody is going to do anything with that building until after the rains. You will be all right.'

And so it was that, some weeks later, I rattled through the burnt Maharashtran landscape in sympathy with the old bus that ran the haul from Poona to Mahabaleshwar. I was returning to Panchgani, this time to stay.

I was not alone.

'What is Knowledge without College? What is Life without a Wife?'

My fellow passenger, and self-appointed guide to India's mysteries, was one Abdul Farouqui, a youthful, leather-jacketed forty-one-year-old, who worked in the shareholders' department of the 'Bombay Dyeing and Suiting Company'. We had met at Poona bus station, where he chided me in the way that strangers often do for straying more than six feet from my suitcase. He had spent the first stage of our trip trying to convert me to Islam, and the second urging me to try for a job with an Indian advertising agency—if only to satisfy his curiosity as to whether such a thing might be possible. Now he was concluding, with some rhetorical flourish, an hour-long sermon on the delights of the married state. Hearing that I intended to spend my three months in Panchgani alone, he had seen it as his urgent duty to talk me into getting myself a spouse—if only for the duration.

'You will walk there, and you will see, in the evening at sunset, so many couples. They are going there for their honeymoons. And you will also want to *enjoy!*'

Abdul had a way with the word 'enjoy'. He could take hold of it, stretch it between his tongue and cheeks, roll it around his mouth, throat, and stomach, smooth and lubricate it, until it carried a hint of every form of pleasure, vice, and titillation know to man, woman, or beast.

But to be honest I was hardly listening. My mind was on other things. Above all I was noting that the closer we came to Panchgani, the fuller the bus was getting. Beyond the dust-grimed windows stretched an unbroken vista of rice fields and mango groves, sleepy villages, and the grey-gold slopes of looming ghats. Inside, things were different. The bus was packed to capacity with a boisterous cross-section of Indian society, squeezed onto the torn, green plastic seats, standing crushed together in the gangway. From here and there came the bleats and clucks of stifled animals; children moaned.

And I was thinking about my bag.

I had managed to stop worrying about the suitcase, rammed precariously into the luggage rack above, and now had every faculty free to ponder the exquisite problems posed by the voluminous travelling bag stowed under my seat. It was too bulky to come out of its lair any other way than sidewards, straight into the gangway. But taking a look at my fellow passengers, assessing their various qualities and temperaments, I wondered how many of them would understand the situation when the time came for a hurried exit. Would they get out of the way? Would anyone help?

Considerations such as these tend to mar one's experience of travel in India.

Creaking with effort, the old bus heaved its way round and up the dizzying hairpins of the final ghat. I tried to distract myself from my cares by taking in the panorama of baked hills and fields that danced in at me through the window. I had almost succeeded when a young girl bent forward, almost casually, and was sick on the precise spot in the gangway over which I would soon be dragging my holdall. Ice-cold sweat erupted from the pores of my back.

'An Indian girl! An Indian girl! You will see her—no more than that on the first occasion. But then you will see her again another day. She will smile! So you will keep seeing her, again and again. And . . . why not?—In time a love will grow between you. Then you will want marriage. Then you will want to *enjoy!*'

What I actually wanted at that precise moment was a friend: someone to share my troubles with. Perhaps we would have found something to laugh about. It crossed my mind that I could involve Abdul in my plight. But that didn't seem fair; I hardly knew the man. And anyway, would he be able to understand how that mess on the floor, now, represented an impending catastrophe? Only I, who had been obsessed by that bag since we'd boarded the bus at Poona, could fully appreciate the frightful difficulties ahead.

Minutes later, the bus came to a slurring halt on the road beside the bus station. Bedlam erupted.

'Come on! Come on!' Abdul was on his feet and calling from the gangway with practised urgency. 'Quickly now, pass me that bag!' He held out his arms, level with my head. I tugged and squeezed the holdall in a last hope that it might come out vertically after all.

'Yes! Yes! Quickly! Pass it to me!'

'It's no good, I'll have to . . .' My words petered out as I looked up to face him. It was unbelievable. The bus was under siege, and terrifying numbers of folk were forcing their way on. Nobody, absolutely nobody—except Abdul and myself—seemed to be getting off. Meanwhile, the driver impatiently massaged the accelerator and feathered the clutch, keeping the bus inching along the road. Steeling myself for the worst, I edged my body into the gangway, stooped down, and began to tug at the bag. Swathes of dhoti material flapped around my ears, and calloused feet battered my shoulders and elbows.

'No, no! Not like that! There is something on the floor there. Very dirty.'

'I know,' I snapped, 'but there is no other way!'

Abdul was being sucked away by the pressure of the crowd.

'Quickly!' he pleaded, 'Give it to me now, or it will be too late!' Numb with confusion, I watched him disappear from view, like a man in quicksand. Soon there was nothing left, not even an outstretched arm, to mark where he had once stood.

Soon the bus was on its way again. Since the Parthay home was two miles further on, I held on to a hope that the conductor might stop the bus for me as we passed by.

Having at last freed the bag, I steered its defiled bulk through the densely packed gangway, excusing myself, apologising, and cursing in close rotation. When, eventually, I made it to the door, there was Abdul. He had waited for me: a man I'd met just four hours ago.

'When you see your destination, tell the conductor. It is his *duty* to let you off. He *must* let you off. He *will* let you off!'

The conductor sat in his place beside the door looking as if his sole duty in the world would be to continue counting ticket stubs and filling in sheets of paper-work. I was not hopeful. Worse, in my struggle to get down the gangway I had lost all sense of space and time. I could have been at it for moments, minutes, or hours. I had been to Parthay Sadan only once, and hardly knew the surrounding landmarks at all. With an abrupt motion, Abdul jerked the bell-string and the bus skidded to a halt.

'I will get off here. If you like, we can strike out and find your place together: the two of us! What do you say?' He backed down onto the earthen verge, his eyes aflame with brotherly zeal. 'I am at your entire disposal! You can accept, or you can reject. I await your decision!'

But before I could say a word, the bus roared off, demonstrating an unprecedented power of acceleration. I took a last sight of Abdul; he stood proud and loyal, aiming his valedictory gaze at the departing vehicle, drenched in fine red dust.

I peered and strained over heads, through arm-pits, and under chins, but saw nothing through the windows that I remotely recognized. In the end, knowing for sure that we had come too far, I suggested to the conductor, as politely as I could, that he might like to let me off. His response was to give the rope a contemptuous pull, and a full half-mile later we glided to a sedate rest.

As I watched the bus disappearing round a bend, a semblance of silence began to settle, enriched by the chirrups of birds and crickets, washed by the continuous swish of a light breeze in sparse foliage. Three monkeys made a chattering appearance from a nearby field, loped on hands and feet across the road, and sprang into the branches of a banyan tree, hotly pursued by a slavering yellow dog. Behind a bush, a little way off, almost hidden in its leaves, three women paused from their illicit wood-chopping, and crouched motionless, watching me. A conveniently placed sign-post suggested that I had overshot my target by two miles. Clamping my hands around the bag handles, I set off down the road.

Squatting in the shadow of the crumbling, Victorian bungalow, Vasant Narayan Parthay watched as I finally entered the grounds of Parthay Sadan and staggered to the door of 'my' room. Looking astonishingly like Lee Marvin, and even sounding a little like him— give or take the occasional Indian intonation in his sparse English—he invited me to step over and join him. 'Are your belongings still at a hotel in town?' he enquired.

I felt on my guard. 'No. These are the only bags I've brought. I came straight here from Poona. I've arranged—with one of your brothers I think—to take that room for a few months. . . . Yes?'

Vasant could not conceal a certain calculation. 'Ah yes. My little brother did say something about a foreign guest. Unfortunately, there is a problem here. You are most welcome to move into the room, but after some few days there will begin some work which may cause botheration for you. But there is another place we can look at. Maybe you will be happier there. . . .'

By now, ten children and a small host of women had gathered round, eyeing me with undiluted curiosity, handing out glasses of water and offering tea. I was almost too despondent to look at them.

'Come!' said Vasant after a few strained minutes, 'Let us go and look at the other place. Then, if you like it we can go into town and find Nizar to discuss terms.'

'Of course,' he continued, 'the other place is not quite like the room you saw before . . .'

This was an understatement. Fifteen minutes later we scrambled down from the road and entered a crude wooden shack. For windows there were just a few roughly gouged gaps in the wooden wall-slats, partly covered by scraps of sacking. Because there was no electric light, and precious little illumination of any kind, it took me a while to make out the dim outlines of the room's contents: a mud and dung floor, an iron bed, some metal water pots, and a sizeable family.

'There is no lighting or water at the moment . . . But we can have that arranged in a few days if you like. We are also going to make windows. They are sitting outside, just waiting to be fitted into place. What do you think?'

'I think that light, water, and windows would be a sort of minimum requirement. I don't know whether your brother said anything about me, but I was rather hoping to do some writing.'

'Ah, well then, there is no problem at all. You can bring your writing table outside, and then you will have all the light you need! And there is a very good view for you to look at when you are thinking.'

That, at least, was true. I stood in the doorway and let my gaze tumble down an immense, curving sweep of terraces to a plain some fifteen hundred feet below. With one glance, as though from an aeroplane, I could take in ten distinct villages and a thousand fields of yellow, brown, red, and—occasionally—green. Beyond the fields and villages sparkled the waters of a man-made lake. In the far distance rose the valley's opposite wall in layers of silver, gold, and smoke.

I stood admiring the prospect, wondering how I was going to break it to Vasant that the place was completely unsuitable and—barring a complete refurbishment—would most likely remain so. For his part, Vasant had already entered into negotiations with the family who lived there. Speaking in soft, funereal murmurs, they cast scowls in my direction. From time to time Vasant would pause, slap his legs with drooping arms, and sigh: *'Kai Karaitsa?'*—'What to do?'

There really wasn't much *to* do. For one thing, I had no intention of displacing a family under any circumstances. Yet Vasant seemed equally determined to see me installed here. Soon he was demonstrating how close the latrine was to my hut, and insisting that the family in the neighbouring bungalow would not mind at all if I used it for an occasional ablution.

Launching sympathetic smiles towards the family, hoping they would appreciate my innocence, I steered Vasant towards the door, and suggested we proceed to the market. There we might find Nizar, who would either help me get the room I had originally booked, or suggest another place altogether.

But Nizar was not to be found at the market, and, instead, Vasant proposed a visit to the charcoal depot for a cup of tea. Tea at a charcoal depot? Why not? My estate agent was a fishmonger. There was nothing for it but to surrender the initiative for a while, and see where events led.

It turned out that the charcoal depot was the Parthay family business, and from where Vasant had placed me in the dingy reception office I could make out, through a gap in the wall, a cavernous, black chamber with a deep sunken floor. In the gloom of the pit a couple of labourers clambered about on ladders, bringing forth tin drums loaded with charcoal. Billowing clouds of acrid, black dust filled the air.

A dark-skinned young man sat at the soot-grimed desk, directing frankly amused looks in my direction as he discussed me with Vasant. I closed my eyes and pondered my fate. When I next looked up, Vasant was gone. I waited five minutes, ten, fifteen . . . I thought of returning to the house, to Poona, to England. . . .

But then Balasaheb burst in from the street. A wiry, fierce-eyed man, he looked busy, serious, and harassed. He also seemed surprised to see me.

'Hello! How are you?' he blustered.

'Not at all happy.' I returned. It seemed pointless to play social games.

He stopped and looked at me directly, his eyes brimming with genuine concern. 'Why is this?'

'Because I have just arrived, as we agreed, and I've been told that I can't have the room.'

His face darkened. 'Who is telling you this?'

'Your brother Vasant.'

A sharp exchange erupted between Balasaheb and the lad at the desk. In time Balasaheb turned back, and spoke with slow deliberation.

'There is no problem. You will have the room for as long as you want.'

'Yes, but what about the building work?'

'Do not worry about that. You will stay there and there will be no trouble for you. Now go to the bazaar. Buy whatever you are needing, and go back. Everything will be all right.'

A couple of hours later I was back at Parthay Sadan placing newspaper-wrapped parcels of sugar, tea, eggs, and bread on the room's shelves, working quickly, trying to establish a measure of squatter's rights on the territory. Through open windows I could enjoy a view almost identical to the one I'd admired from the shack. A delightful, cooling breeze fanned the room and rustled the leaves of the silver-oak and mango trees outside. I could be happy here.

By the time the brothers returned from work, and came tumbling into my room for a visit, I was completely unpacked, and even had some books lined up along a wall. Subhash, the young man I'd seen at the reception desk, picked his way through them.

'*Arre Barpré!* What have you come here to write about?'

I kept things vague. 'Well, I'm still thinking about that. It will be something about India, something about myself and my friends, something about the Buddha . . . and something about Dr Ambedkar. . . .'

'*Arre Barpré!*' he repeated, now with an edge of bewildered sympathy. He turned towards the others, holding up my books, talking quickly.

'*Arre Barpré!*' said the brothers, each in turn: Balasaheb, Madhu, Shankar, and Vasant. Each had his own way of saying it; it seemed to mean something like 'Blow me down!', or 'Holy smoke!' The unearthing of my typewriter and tape-recorder, however, saved me from further interrogation. By the time everyone had tapped a few keys, and listened to some bars from Mozart's 'Sinfonia Concertante', any reason I might have for being there had become irrelevant.

Later that night, doubtless after a family council which had given him grounds for hope, Balasaheb paid another visit.

'This is your home,' he announced. 'You will stay here for as long as you want. Do you want to stay?'

I let him know immediately how delighted I would be to spend the rest of my days there, but felt obliged to mention that Madhu and

Vasant were still hinting that I might have to move. Although I didn't say so, I had not failed to notice that they were both older than him. In India, such things count.

His eyes flashed fire. 'Look, you are to stay. This my home. It is also your home!'

'Then that must make *us* brothers too,' I said.

Balasaheb liked that. He laughed and offered his hand.

A couple of nights later, Subhash took me on a tour of the family bungalow, leading me from one simple room to another, explaining which brother's wife I was now meeting as we disturbed each in turn from her cooking routine. Of the five brothers, only Madhu had left home. He lived with his wife and children in a nearby town where he worked for the Bank of Maharashtra, but returned to the bosom of the wider family most weekends. All the brothers were married, except Subhash, and soon his time would come. His wedding was due to take place in May, at the height of the marrying season—a prospect he viewed with alarm, not because neither he nor any of his brothers yet knew who the bride would be, but because he was due to begin his own career at that time. He therefore planned to enlist the aid of a local Brahmin, and see if he couldn't get a stay of sentence for a few years. The trouble was, at twenty-three, he was getting a bit long in the tooth to delay things much further.

The biggest room in the house was really an extension of the veranda. At night it served as a communal sleeping area for the children. Alone, in a shadowy corner, sat the recently bereaved matriarch of the family, surrounded by a few personal possessions. Ignoring me, ignoring everyone, she stared into the gloom.

Subhash led me over to the family shrine, a sort of open-fronted doll's house, inhabited by the clay forms of tiny, misshapen creatures, each daubed with blots of ochre.

'What gods are these?' I asked. 'Do you know their names?'

Subhash laughed. 'They are gods, only. I do not know them. They are not for me. Just gods.'

As we made our way back to the veranda, the mother turned my way, raised her hands and folded them in salutation. Loudly, clearly, and deliberately, she enunciated the greeting, '*Namaskar!*', her voice thick with tears. There was a curious, impersonal formality to this act, but at the time I had no way of knowing that she was seeing me not so much as a person, but as a talisman.

Later, when Balasaheb paid his nightly call, I told him about my visit to the shrine. Like Subhash, he dismissed the gods with a shrug. Casually, I asked to which caste his family belonged.

'Maratha!' he declared with   pride, 'We are *Kshatriyas*: warriors, like

Shivaji Maharaj!'

I told him I had seen many of Shivaji's forts during the past months. Balasaheb was pleased, and asked whether I had ever seen a statue of Shivaji himself. I remarked that it was hard to spend any time in Maharashtra without bumping into one. Mounted on an archetypal charger, he cut an impressive figure with his tall turban, dense beard, and deadly sword.

The conversation subsided. Balasaheb lit a bidi and searched the room with his eyes, all the while jiggling his feet on the floor to keep mosquitoes at bay. His gaze came to rest on a small bronze statuette of the Buddha I'd put on the shelf.

'Boudd-HA!'

He vented the word like an exhalation, 'You like this Boudd-ha?'

'Yes,' I said, 'I am very interested in the Buddha. I know a lot of Buddhists in India.'

'Very *poor* people.' His face betrayed a curious blend of compassion and revulsion. 'There are Buddhists in your country also?'

'Yes. A few. But not as many as you have in Maharashtra. Perhaps a few thousand.'

There was a lengthy silence. Balasaheb's brow creased in speculation. It was his turn to seem casual.

'Do you have caste in England, also?'

I laughed. 'No. No we don't.'

t w o

A few nights later I met one of those 'very poor people'.

I was just returning from my evening stroll when I noticed a tall, slim young man standing in the narrow road beside 'Parthay Sadan'. To my surprise, he seemed to be waiting for me, and stepped forward a little timidly as I drew near.

'I am sorry to disturb you. We have heard that there is an Englishman staying here, so I was asked to come and meet you. They said you are writing something about Dr B. R. Ambedkar. Is this so?'

In the gathering dusk it was hard to tell his age—anything from seventeen to twenty-five. He was dark skinned, quite smartly turned out, and spoke impeccable English.

I couldn't understand his rather formal interest in me, and wondered who it was that had sent him. At that moment I wanted nothing less than to become a sort of local attraction, and had already felt the need to launch a friendly offensive against the Parthay tribe, whose regular visits were making it hard to get down to work. I was also bit wary about revealing too much of my book's theme.

Perhaps because he sensed my hesitation, he quickly introduced himself.

'My name is Sanjay Kamblay.'

—Which explained everything.

'Ah! A Buddhist?'

He nodded. Our eyes met as we laughed with something like relief. Then we set off for the first of many walks together.

* * *

It probably wouldn't strike many people as being at all strange that I should have met a Buddhist so soon after arriving in Panchgani. The Buddha, after all, was an Indian, as were his original disciples. The Buddhist scriptures are full of stories set in India; and there was a time, during the reign of king Ashoka, when most Indians would have been Buddhist. India was the cradle of Buddhism, the base from which it spread throughout the East.

So when I told my non-Buddhist friends that I was about to make my first trip to India, none of them seemed at all surprised. They just wondered why I had left it so long. I had been a Buddhist for ten years, after all; it was high time I went 'home', and saw the real thing. Like many people, they assumed that Buddhism was alive and well in its birthplace.

A few days after flying in, though, I had gone for a walk in Bombay with a Buddhist monk. Wherever we went he was consistently mistaken for a Hindu *sadhu*, or holy man, and greeted with cries of 'Hare Krishna! Hare Ram!' Later, in Poona, kids chucked pebbles and taunted him with cries of 'Rajneesh! Rajneesh!'

'But don't they realize you're a Buddhist?' I asked.

'Why should they? How many Buddhist monks do you think they've seen here before? I'm probably the first one that's ever walked through this locality.'

A few weeks later I joined the monk on a 'retreat'—a weekend of meditation, chanting, and study—out in the country, between Bombay and Poona. The exact location of the retreat was almost in the shadow of the Karla Buddhist cave-temples, and just a couple of miles from a similar complex at Bhaja. This part of India had once supported a

19

flourishing Buddhist community; those temples could never have been built without tremendous dedication, nor without formidable resources of money and manpower.

At one point we were circumnambulating our little shrine, chanting an age-old salutation to the Buddha: '*Namo Tassa; Bhagavato Arahato; Samma Sambuddhassa. . . .*' Fifty yards away, in a neighbouring field, some labourers were unloading hay from a bullock cart. After a while they began to take notice of our voices, which travelled easily through the unglazed windows. Shrugging their shoulders, they squatted down and spent the next twenty minutes gawping at us, scratching their heads in bewilderment. They hadn't the faintest idea what we were doing.

In the West, any public exhibition of religious zeal would attract attention. Even a modest procession of clergymen on the streets of a country village, and certainly on the highways of a major city, would be enough to stop the traffic and turn every head. But in India I had already seen any number of religious processions, complete with colourful bands, elephants, and dancers, proceeding along busy roads, causing nothing more than a temporary inconvenience. One day, in a small town in the Maharashtran sugar-cane belt, I had been the only person to look more than once as a dignified procession of middle-aged men walked down the main street, stark naked.

Religion, religious ritual, and religious excess are a commonplace of Indian life. There are the processions, the ubiquitous, gaudy temples whose tinkling bells fill the towns with noise, and the mosques from which *muezzin* sing out to the faithful across the roof-tops; tea-stalls, tailors' shops, and grocery stores are named after deities; holy men wander city streets bearing tridents and ash-smeared faces; beggars roll and writhe in the middle of walkways, calling out to their gods; and respectable businessmen pause in the bazaar to venerate passing cows. It is impossible to walk the residential side-roads of any town without coming upon some rite or ceremony in mid-performance: a baby-naming, a pregnancy blessing, the reading of a horoscope, even the sanctification of a building project. Religion is an integral part of Indian street life; it is everywhere, all around you wherever you look, and even beneath your feet as you tread on pavements colourfully daubed with swastikas and images of Sai Baba. And yet our simple Buddhist ritual was enough to bring that hay-making crew to a dumb-struck halt.

I knew that Buddhism had declined in India; I'd never really expected to find monks everywhere, mindfully prowling the pavements—except perhaps in the north where the Tibetan refugees were established; I knew that most of the temples and shrines were ruins. But I had not been ready for this. It was quite incredible. So far as I could see, Buddhism was as alien to the average Indian as would be a Navajo rain-dance on the streets of New York or London.

How could it have happened? How could an entire branch of idealism and culture, one so strongly established as Buddhism had been in India, simply disappear more or less without trace?

Naturally enough, one hears any number of explanations. But here is the one I heard most frequently:

Two-and-a-half-thousand years ago, when Gautama the Buddha was first wandering the highways and byways of Northern India expounding the 'good life', the priests of the old religion—the Brahmins—developed a powerful dislike for him and his doctrine. He was telling people that they could become like the gods, even become Buddhas—Enlightened beings—and outshine the gods. He was urging them to be 'lamps unto themselves', to take responsibility for their own spiritual lives, rather than depending on priests. He was teaching the notion of equality and discouraging caste discrimination. And for blasphemies such as these, kings and rulers were prepared to treat him with respect and veneration.

As Buddhism prospered, Brahminism suffered a decline. Soon, it was the Buddha's community of monks, or *sangha,* and not the Brahmins, who were being treated as the pampered elite of an established national religion.

So what could have gone wrong? What kind of mistake did the Buddhists make? For they must have got something wrong somewhere along the line. As was plain to see, the Brahmins were back on top—and had been for a very long time.

Although Buddhism is usually classed as one of the world's great religions, it has no place for any kind of all-seeing, all-judging God. This is one of its great strengths and attractions, for what it does have to offer is an ideal of human perfection and a body of teachings whose only concern is the potentiality of human life and consciousness. However, a religion that has no God-figure lurking in the background to fill its followers with awe and dread—bestowing absolute authority on its priesthood—is in an extremely vulnerable position as an institution.

Anyone who really believes in a god, and in the kind of powers that gods are supposed to have, would be a fool not to make some effort to observe the demands of his religion; he is not really free to do otherwise. His sincerity may of course be little more than a reflex of his capacity to experience fear; but for all that, he will still keep the faith and do his duty.

The Buddha argued that there is no one 'up there'—or anywhere else

21

for that matter—watching and judging us, expecting us to render worship in the correct way. There are no eternities of paradise or hell at stake either. People are essentially free to become 'Buddhists'—or not, free to practise the 'Buddha-Dhamma'—or not, entirely as they choose. The Buddha left a treasury of precepts and insights for the benefit of those who wished to follow him, but left it entirely up to his followers whether those teachings would be seized upon and used to the full, half-heartedly espoused, or merely toyed with.

In fairness to the monks of old, it must be said that the Buddha-Dhamma was hardly a matter of life or death for many of them. Once Buddhism had started to enjoy the patronage of the nobles, a great many of the full-time monks would have been young men sent away to well-endowed monasteries and academies by families eager for status. Naturally, there would have been some inspired, spiritually motivated people around too, but they were becoming increasingly rare, and incongruous, in that heady, ecclesiastical world.

As the monasteries grew bigger and richer, and as the monk's 'career' grew more clearly defined, a gulf began to develop between the monks and the 'laity'. For the lay folk, the practice of Buddhism came to mean little more than acquiring 'merit' by supporting the monks. In return, the monks were expected to conduct just a few simple ceremonies, perform their chants on festival days, and perhaps dispense a handful of basic teachings.

Having no faith in rules, the Buddha had always preferred to offer moral guidance in the form of precepts, or 'training principles'; but now, as the rules began to proliferate, it was the letter and not the spirit of those rules that took priority. It was not particularly easy to observe so many rules, but even so, coping with them had little to do with spiritual effort or attainment. There would have been plenty of monks able to conduct themselves impeccably, while at the same time making themselves quite comfortable in a very worldly way. In doing so, they let the Buddha's real teaching slip through their fingers, and with it the fate of Buddhism in India.

Carefully, almost methodically, the Brahmins got to work. With a masterly propaganda drive they enticed the neglected lay people back to the excitement and divine 'certainties' of the Hindu fold—depriving the Buddhist monks of their major source of material support. Buddhist rituals, icons, and even philosophical viewpoints, were incorporated into the old religion—transforming it, in the process, almost beyond recognition. In time, even the Buddha himself was 'converted' to Hinduism. Legends and myths were devised to demonstrate that he had not really been a human being, whose life and example could inspire others, but an incarnation of the old god, Vishnu.

Gaining favour at court again, the Brahmins stirred up rumours, instigated rivalries, and generally did all they could to discredit Buddhism and its followers. Soon, Buddhist monks and nuns who had not already fled to other lands were being persecuted and killed.

All in all, the Brahmins performed their task so efficiently that even today many Hindus regard Buddhism as nothing more than an archaic branch of Hinduism.

The decline of Indian Buddhism came about in just a few centuries. By the time the Muslim invaders swept down, there was very little left. All the same, such death-blows as were necessary were quickly administered. Surviving Buddhists were forcibly converted to Islam, or killed; temples and monasteries were reduced to rubble; statues of the Buddha defaced—on the mistaken supposition that they were meant to represent the face of 'God'; and the vast libraries, which housed unique originals of written scriptures and commentaries, were set to the torch. The destruction was so complete that it has only been in the past century that some important centres of Buddhism, such as the 'Deer Park' at Sarnath, where the Buddha began his years of teaching, were rediscovered and unearthed.

As a Buddhist travelling in India, picking my way through the minimal, defaced ruins of the Buddhist past, I sometimes found it hard not to feel uncharitable towards those ancient monks. Their lack of dynamism had allowed all this to happen. It didn't seem unreasonable to hope that Buddhism, which had subsequently flourished in any number of political and cultural contexts, and which had even attracted me, a modern Westerner, could have withstood those hostile forces, had there been a few more people around taking its message seriously, and putting it into practice.

By the middle of this century there were no more than 50,000 Buddhists in the whole of India. Most of these were immigrants from neighbouring lands.

As I said, there are other theories to explain the collapse of Buddhism in India. Perhaps the full truth will never really be known. Meanwhile, a more terse way of putting things—which goes right to the heart of the matter—might be to say, as did one prominent commentator, 'Buddhism is very difficult to practise.'

Mind you, if that commentator had thought it impossible to practise Buddhism, rather than just 'very difficult', the eventual fate of Buddhism in modern India would have been quite different. I for one would have no story to tell, and my new friend Sanjay Kamblay would not be a Buddhist at all. He would still be an 'ex-Untouchable Hindu', a member of one of the largest 'depressed' communities in western India.

The commentator's name was Bhimrao Ramji Ambedkar, and in

Jai Bhim!

October 1956, he recited the words, *'Buddham Saranam Gacchami;
Dhammam Saranam Gacchami; Sangham Saranam Gacchami,'* and became
a Buddhist himself. Because of him, there are now more than six million
Buddhists in India. The Buddha-Dhamma is coming back home.

three

Sanjay Kamblay was a soft-spoken, sensitive young man, a little shy but
instantly likeable. It turned out we were neighbours, for he lived almost
opposite Parthay Sadan. As we set off for our walk, he pointed out his
home. I was surprised by the grandeur of the place, an extensive, solid
bungalow, at the end of a rough, sloping track. It was in a completely
different league to most other Buddhist homes I had seen in
Maharashtra.

'My father works at the Anjuman-i-Islam School, a little way up the
road. We live with some of the teachers.'

I was taken aback. 'Is your father a teacher, too?'

Sanjay gave a wry laugh. 'Oh no. He serves in the school canteen, and
cares for the teachers in their home.'

'Still,' I said, 'that looks like a nice place to live. Things could be
worse.'

Sanjay seemed confused. I peered down the shadowy driveway
again, and then noticed the crude wattle and daub huts a few yards to
the left of the main bungalow. I felt awkward, realizing that this must be
where he lived. In the West a cow barn would be more substantial.

His father's job did however offer one major perk: his sons received
a free education at the school—an expensive 'English medium'
establishment for the sons of wealthy Moslems. So even if the father
had nothing much to hope for but a life of menial work and a pittance in
reward, his sons had a chance of escaping to something better. Sanjay's
older brother was now an electronics technician, and Sanjay himself
hoped to go to agricultural college in Poona, taking up one of the places
reserved for members of the 'Scheduled Castes'—formerly known as
'Untouchables'.

It all added up to something of a paradox. Smartly dressed—to the
extent that cheap clothes and hand-me-downs allowed—well
educated, and obviously highly intelligent, Sanjay lived with his family,

and (I was to discover) a small herd of goats, in a dung-floored hovel, supported by a father who worked punitive hours, seven days a week if required, for a wage of about $25 a month. Now he was coming to the end of his stay in a good public school, his English was better than his Marathi, and he held high hopes for a bright career.

'There are many young men like me in Panchgani,' he said. 'With all these schools in the area there are plenty of menial positions to be filled. These are reserved for our people by law; so if they don't have jobs in the tourist hotels, most of our fathers work in the schools.'

There were two sizeable Buddhist localities in Panchgani, both on the edge of town: 'Bhim Nagar' and 'Ambedkar Colony'. Many more Buddhists lived in the surrounding villages where they worked as farm labourers, or commuted—each day climbing the steep paths which criss-crossed the ghats, to schools and hotels in town. Just a few enterprising Buddhists had managed to fix themselves up as taxi-drivers, or donkey-ride vendors.

The population of Panchgani was around five thousand, one thousand of whom were Buddhists. This exceptionally high proportion allowed them a strong voice on the local council, and gave them the right to hold their own noisy processions on festival days. Sanjay told me that they had even started to build their own *vihara*, a real Buddhist meeting place, somewhere where visiting monks could stay and give talks. But money was short, and the building—started a couple of years ago—was still not finished.

* * *

A couple of days later Sanjay came to see me again, this time with a friend, Ashok Kamblay.

Sanjay laughed when I asked whether they were related. 'Oh no! Well, perhaps we are in some way; our community is not so very big. We are probably all related somehow or other.'

'—And I suppose you're all called Kamblay too?' Kamblay is a very common Buddhist name in Maharashtra, perhaps the most common, though Kharat, Shinday, Moray, and Kadam must be close contenders.

Ashok had attended the same school as Sanjay, but because of money problems at home he had had to leave when he was fifteen. He was a few years older than Sanjay, now married with two daughters, and working as a servant in the school where he had once been a pupil. He felt wearily dispirited by his prospects.

Now, sitting with them both, I could sense an atmosphere—a presence almost—that I had noticed many times before when meeting 'new Buddhists' for the first time. It was a sort of congenital diffidence: not an ordinary social shyness so much as an ingrained, deep-rooted tendency to self-effacement, as if any notion of self-respect or personal worth clung to them like a thin, easily chipped veneer.

As we talked about the local Buddhist community, it soon became obvious that Sanjay and Ashok were very unhappy about things. They quickly admitted that they knew next to nothing about Buddhism themselves, and added that nobody else seemed to know very much either. Ashok's uncle had tried to do something about this; he had gone on a course with some Thai monks in Poona. When he came back he had trekked around the Buddhist localities in town and in the nearby villages, giving talks and teaching a few Buddhist chants and ceremonies. He had also tried to arrange some 'Dhamma programmes'—meetings where people could hear talks on Buddhism from visiting speakers. But nothing much had come of his efforts, and now he was getting too old and sick to do any more.

'So what does it mean to you to be Buddhists?' I asked.

'What difference can our Buddhism make?' said Sanjay. 'The old people are not educated. They do not know any Buddha-Dhamma. Many of them are going back to the old ways; they are performing Hindu *pujas*; they keep calendars with pictures of Hindu gods and celebrate Hindu festivals.'

Ashok simmered: 'There is one old lady in my village. She will not give us water. She will not come near us. She treats us in the old way, as if we are Untouchable.'

'But if your people act in the old way, then people will treat you in the old way. Didn't Dr Ambedkar ask his followers to accept Buddhism, and have absolutely nothing to do with the old Hindu customs? Don't your people respect his advice? Aren't they really followers of Dr Ambedkar?'

'Oh yes!' said Sanjay. 'They are followers of Dr Ambedkar. But that is all they are. They talk about him all the time, and have all kinds of slogans. But all they ever do is worship his name. That's all everyone ever does. Ambedkar this, Ambedkar that. We've been hearing it all our lives: "Ambedkar . . . Ambedkar . . . Ambedkar." '

* * *

Ambedkar? Doctor Babasaheb Ambedkar? Dr Bhimrao Ramji Ambedkar? Unless you're familiar with modern Indian history, a constitutional lawyer, or a sociologist, it may well be that you've never heard of the man. And yet it is impossible to overstate the passionate reverence felt for him by millions of people who share our world.

Like my host Balasaheb's hero, Shivaji, you can meet him at traffic intersections or in little parks all over Maharashtra, and in a few more states besides. Clad in the uniform grey of the sculptor's medium, he cuts a statesmanlike figure in this municipal incarnation. His is no humble statue, nor is it consigned to the remote side-streets. In Poona, at the spot where Mahatma Gandhi Road collides with Dr Ambedkar Road, it is not the *khadi*-clad Mahatma but the besuited Doctor who stands with one arm held forth and one finger raised to address the frenzied traffic from his plinth. And as India's first Law Minister, prime architect of her Constitution, who would begrudge him his place in the sun?

But if you leave behind the wide streets and manicured gardens, make your way to the fringes of town where the road stumbles through seething hutments and lines of crumbling tenements, you'll meet him again, in the centre of a muddy clearing, or parked on the pavement between a tea stall and a cigarette kiosk. Here, he will probably manifest as a simple plaster bust mounted on a white pedestal, intriguingly housed in a cage of chicken wire. If you are lucky, though, you may find a complete, life-sized statue, crudely finished but richly painted and accessoried. Here, he is portrayed as a rather fat man in a blue, Western suit. The skin of his face has been painted bright pink, and a pair of wire spectacles balances on his nose. Note the rows of gleaming gold and silver pens in his breast pocket, the bulging tie-knot, the cherry-red lips, the beaming, benevolent face.

If you ask someone the name of this locality, like as not they'll reply, *'Bhim Nagar'*—'Bhim's place', or 'Ambedkar Colony'. If you keep them talking for very long, they may invite you to their home for a cup of tea. Be very careful as you step through the narrow lanes that separate the hovels. Stay close to your guide, and mind where you put your feet. The ground is covered with refuse and excrement, scored with open sewers. Gangs of thigh-high children will scramble around your legs, chasing rats and dogs.

Your destination will probably be a small, rectangular hut, built of corrugated iron, where you'll be offered a big iron bed to sit on (since there are no chairs in the place) and served a glass of water by a shy, giggling daughter. Then you'll be left alone while your hosts go off to make the tea. As you wait for what will seem like an eternity, you'll have a chance to look around; but there is very little to see. The walls are of rough brick and corrugated iron, the floor coated with old, flaking dung. The bed fills most of the room, but there are probably a few water pots somewhere around, and perhaps a rack crammed with metal plates and glasses. It is all very simple, very minimal, entirely functional—except for one detail. Up on the wall, strung with an old garland, there he is again.

This time it's a photograph, a full-face portrait in black and white. Benign, avuncular, those fleshy, intelligent features loom down on you with subdued concern. Circular glasses magnify eyes that are kindly now, but which could turn sharp at any moment. The lips are slightly pursed, the mouth almost lost in a soft, round face.

Or perhaps the photograph shows him sitting at his desk in the Law Ministry, resting the weight of his massive head on his fist. The apparently oversized desk (it juts awkwardly into his chest) is neatly crowded with documents, flowers, and a monumental pen-and-ink-stand. He looks, for all his substance, as if he could pounce on you at any moment; but for the time being he seems content to take you in with alert, if preoccupied, eyes.

Or, again, maybe he is sitting sideways on, framed by a dreamy, cloud-softened sky: a proud, visionary young man wearing a mortar board. The dark folds of an academic gown flow richly over his pin-stripe suit, the uniform of a newly-qualified barrister.

But what is a man like him doing in a place like this? If you ask your hosts, they will smile with pride, and explain that he is their *Babasaheb*: their 'father', leader, and champion.

If you are ever in Bombay on 6 December, go along to Dadar Chowpatty, a vast odiferous beach not far from the station. You will not feel lonely since you'll be surrounded by a million of Bombay's poorest inhabitants. They go there every year to mark the anniversary of Ambedkar's death, in 1956. For one day, in every direction, loudspeakers broadcast pop-songs about his life and deeds. There are entire arcades of book stalls, each crammed with books about him, or by him: *Who Were the Untouchables?*, *The Annihilation of Caste*, *Thoughts on Pakistan*, *What Congress and Gandhi Have Done to the Untouchables*, *The Buddha and His Dhamma*, . . .

Near the bookstalls you will find poster stands. There are the photographs you've already seen, as well as a few new ones. But most of the posters will be the exuberant creations of artists. Here, for example, is a 'Mahabodhisattva Babasaheb Ambedkar' standing stiffly to attention in full military dress, his chest glittering with medals, and a golden dress-sword hanging from his belt. Through the open window behind him we catch a glimpse of the Maha Bodhi Temple at Bodh Gaya, the place where the Buddha gained Enlightenment. In another we see the fierce, uncompromising delegate to a 'Round Table Conference' on India's independence. Standing in the capacious committee room, he holds up that finger to emphasize his words while massed ranks of fellow delegates turn their heads in unison to gaze admiringly upon him.

In another poster, he is an older, thinner man, staring down at the ground, as if to look up would cost too much effort. Dressed in a collarless white jacket he steadies himself with a massive bamboo staff, which rises far above the dome of his sparsely covered head. Beside him stands the Buddha, laying an encouraging hand on his shoulder. Around the fringes of this main image the artist has arranged a series of vignettes. In one, a small boy pores over a pile of books by the light of an oil lamp. Then comes that graduation picture again, only here the visionary expression has defeated the artist, and in its place is a certain hint of smugness. Then there's a wrathful Ambedkar, hurling a richly ornamented book into the flames of a bonfire. Next, set against a background of imposing government buildings, he hands a thick tome to a delighted Nehru. Finally he stands at a microphone, his hands folded in salutation, surrounded by hosts of orange-robed monks.

There is no time now to look at the rows of shiny medallions hanging from a pole next to the poster stand. As you might have guessed, they each bear a crude likeness of him. It is now time to go and pay your respects to the man himself.

The queue stretches for hundreds of yards: along the back of the beach, through some ornamental gardens, past the swooping corrugated iron roof of the municipal crematorium, up and down a few back-streets, and finally out onto the road to Dadar station. Policemen and stewards in blue Gandhi-caps direct you to the end of the line.

After an hour or so you will come to the 'stupa' itself, a white dome that rises out of the sand at the back of the beach. This is where his ashes have been laid to rest.

Perched on balustrades and flimsy stools, a gang of elderly women line the chamber's circumference, beating the walls with sticks and hands, hollering: *'Tsala! Tsala!'*—'Come on! Keep moving!' Their job is to see that the queue keeps flowing. Here you'll be allowed a brief moment to make your salutation. But no more.

'Come on! Come on!' Sticks and palms clatter and slap in insistent rhythm; you toss a few blooms onto a mound of marigolds that looks set to fill the entire room, take a last look—for now anyway—at the face of a man who hated hero worship, and leave.

Just one last point. Even if you don't speak a word of Marathi, you may well notice the way these people greet each other. *'Jai Bhim!'*—'Victory to Bhim!' 'May Bhim prevail!'

* * *

In the course of two visits to India I had now spent more than six months living among Dr Ambedkar's followers. I knew very well what

Sanjay meant when he accused his people of worshipping Ambedkar's name and doing little else. But I had also seen that there could be more to the movement he had founded than that.

'All right,' I said, 'But if people do respect him, surely they ought to try to find out about the Dhamma. Don't they owe him that? Don't they realize he had some reason for asking his followers to convert to Buddhism?'

Ashok spoke fast, and angrily. Perhaps I had gone too far, rubbed their noses in a common failure for which they could hardly be blamed. Sanjay translated.

'He says he can hear your words, and he feels stupid because he just wants to say "Yes" to everything. He can only agree with you. But where does that get him? He doesn't know how to find out about the Dhamma, even though he knows he ought to, and wants to.'

'But don't you ever have people coming here to give talks?'

'No. Never. Nobody ever comes here.' Ashok was bitter.

'I don't believe that,' I said. 'Are you sure that nobody's ever been here, say, in the last couple of years or so?'

Sanjay was thrown by my persistence. Then he remembered.

'Ah yes. Just once. About three years ago, one English monk came and gave a talk.'

'I know,' I said. 'As a matter of fact I was here too that day.' I turned to Ashok. 'Actually, I've met your uncle.'

Now *that* was quite a day.

f o u r

It was four o'clock in the morning, Christmas Eve, 1981. To my amazement I was awake, alert, and ready for the day to begin.

I lay in the dubious security of my mosquito-net, observing the many forms of wildlife that sported in its folds; by that stage of the night it resembled something half-way between an aviary and a game reserve. Noises surrounded me, the assorted snores, grunts, and wheezes of a yogi and three assorted monks. Savouring the venerable racket, I wondered how I had managed to sleep at all.

Anyway, I was happy to be awake, still at that stage in my relationship with India when each new day brought the promise of adventure and discovery. And today I was about to get my first real taste of life on the road. We were off on a two-day trip to Panchgani and Mahad, a curtain-raiser for the much grander tour to come.

I had been in the country for just two weeks, staying in one of two box-like buildings that served as a centre of operations for 'Trailokya Bauddha Mahasangha Sahayak Gana', a new Indian Buddhist movement, known to its friends as 'TBMSG'.

Although one of these houses contained a small office and one slightly larger room, used for community meditation sessions and public classes, neither of them housed more than a skeletal permanent community: they were facilities, fully used, twenty-four hours a day, for eating, sleeping, chatting, entertaining, organizing, and teaching, by the bewildering procession of people I was beginning to call my friends.

It was a chaotic way to live. One night there could be as few as six of us spread out on the floors to sleep; the next there would be twelve or thirteen. On Monday, ten of us had squeezed onto the floor to eat our lunch in the front room at number fifty; on Tuesday there had been just the three of us, and Jyotipala, the uneven complexioned 'robe' from Barnsley, had fussed and clucked about left-over food. At all times, day and night, people called by, usually looking for Lokamitra, sometimes just hoping for a glass of tea and a chat.

'You're going to have to give up your Western notions of space and privacy here,' chirped Purna, a powerfully built *anagarika*—a sort of freelance monk—from Auckland. 'It's not that they don't respect your right to peace; they just don't understand it. Most people here come from extended families; they grew up in crowded homes; they've got no experience of privacy.' From the sometimes rigid set of his jaw, it was obvious that Purna didn't always find this life easy either, but after two years in India he was more or less accustomed to it.

For my part, I had been getting tetchy. Used to having a room of my own, I was beginning to suspect that I would go insane if I didn't get at least a little time to myself, alone, every day. This place seemed like a madhouse. Just when you were locking up, thinking about bed, a gang of fiery-eyed lads from Chikhalwadi would come hammering on the door, wanting to book someone for a *vihara* dedication. Or, at the precise moment when lunch was being served, a monk or two from Nagpur would glide in—for no clearly discernible reason—and portions would be reduced to accommodate them. It was actually fascinating and rather enjoyable, but the old demon 'culture shock' was taking its toll.

For most Westerners, India comes as nothing less than a massive, uninterrupted assault on the senses. For two weeks, my eyes had been pulled from their sockets by sights wonderous, bizarre, and disgusting, my ears under constant attack from clanging pots, screaming dogs, tinny radios, temple bells, and two-stroke traffic, my taste-buds stormed three times a day by volcanic victuals, my skin dried out and charred by the the sun—then whipped into ecstasies of irritation by insects; and my nose . . . well, the less said the better. With one's awareness being goaded so persistently to the sensory surface, was it so wrong to feel the need for a quiet, cool hole somewhere or other, where one might stop the world and sink deep into oneself? But this, my friends were telling me, was a decadent, Western attitude: not the desire to sink-in, so much as the idea that one needed a quiet place in which to do it.

The two houses faced each other across a small square, at the extreme southern end of 'Doctor Ambedkar Housing Society', in Yerawada, on the outskirts of Poona. In the realm of cliché, Poona is that archetypal place whence come 'disgusted' colonels. In reality, it is a busy centre of commerce, administration, industry, and the military, a hill station with a climate infinitely preferable to that of Bombay. Two famous contemporary 'gurus' have lived there. The world-renowned Hatha Yoga master, B. K. S. Iyengar, runs his Institute over in Deccan Gymkhana, and the shrewd, millionaire superstar of psycho-spiritual ambiguity, Bhagwan Shri Rajneesh, had just fluttered from his roost down the road in Koregaon Park.

Yerawada's own claim to fame was that it was the place where the British incarcerated Mahatma Gandhi in the thirties. Locally it was known for its sizeable lunatic asylum.

The Housing Society was established in the sixties, by some of Dr Ambedkar's Buddhist followers, to provide themselves with cheap but decent homes. It was one of three identically constructed estates lining the road between the golf-course and the military cantonment, where many Society residents worked as clerks and peons in the munitions factory. The houses were unremarkable: two- or three-roomed dwellings, all yellow-brown, all box-like, but each was equipped with a bathroom (a bare, concrete-floored chamber with a tap and a few buckets), a toilet, and running water for a couple of hours each day.

Between the houses ran a grid of dirt lanes, alive with cricket-playing children, wandering goats and pigs, and serving as extensions to the houses. From six to ten each morning the women would be out, scrubbing ziggurats of dull metal pots, lighting fires in bucket stoves, covering the ground with formations of fuel cakes made from mud and coal dust. A caravanserai of street vendors haunted the place with monotonous cries, selling everything and anything: vegetables, ice-lollies, blankets, newspapers, balloons, . . .

For all that, it was a relatively quiet and civilized spot, at least on the few days of the year when no-one was getting married. If they were, then a brightly coloured *pandal*—a stage and awning combination—would be set up on an open space, and the din of film music would pour over the neighbourhood for hours on end, broken at last by the deafening explosions of fire-crackers as the party continued into the night.

It was here that Lokamitra had established his beach-head for a new Buddhist movement in India.

I had known Lokamitra for ten years, having first encountered him when he offered me a lift back to London from a Buddhist retreat in Surrey. Garbed in flared trousers and a decorative Afghan waistcoat, he drove his mini-van at terrifying speed. He had a wild bush of gingery-brown hair, and an equally wild energy about him. It was hard to believe that he was the son of a Cambridge professor, and harder still to believe that he had just enjoyed two days of rural peace and meditation.

Later, I was to find out a little about his past. I will not dwell it on here. Suffice it to say that, in a sixties sort of way, it was rather disturbing.

Although we were both getting involved with Buddhism at around the same time, and associating with the same teacher, I saw little of him in those early days. He had a demanding job, teaching history in a London comprehensive, and, that apart, never felt drawn to crowded meditation classes, or to the semi-social scene that was growing up around our little Buddhist centre in north London. In the years that followed, however, his unwavering dedication to our fledgling movement was to become something of legend.

The change took place around the time when his doctor told him he had colitis and needed an operation. He didn't want an operation, and looked for alternatives. An acupuncturist suggested he might be able to cure himself with an exclusive regimen of 'slippery elm food' and a strictly regular lifestyle.

For months on end he subsisted on that bland liquid diet, organized his time to ensure early nights, took up Hatha Yoga, and threw himself into his meditation practice. After a year he had not only cured himself—and developed an enviable physique into the bargain—but had also become an expert yogi. Soon he was giving classes and was on course to becoming a leading instructor.

He gave up his job to become the Buddhist centre's treasurer, and collaborated with friends to take over a house nearby, where they undertook the first serious attempt yet made by any of us to establish a residential 'spiritual community'.

The idea of a house where everyone is working to evolve a Buddhist lifestyle may sound idyllically tame. 'Number Five Balmore Street' was anything but that. Rumours began to circulate, of people being dragged physically from their beds to the shrine-room for morning meditations, of a pile of dirty dishes that had found its way into the bed of the man who had forgotten his cleaning job; of an overloaded kitchen table that had been capsized in the heat of a debate on 'responsibility'. . . . Perhaps a few of the stories were apocryphal, but there was no doubt that something a bit more gutsy than usual was going on. Lokamitra and his companions were trying to break away from the vague and sentimental fusion of new-age psychology and Eastern mysticism which so often passed for Buddhism in those days. For hours on end they talked and argued, about themselves, about the centre, about the community, about Buddhism, groping—sometimes in the dark, and sometimes with the raw fervour of visionaries—for a kind of Buddhism that would acknowledge and refine whatever was most real and most vital in them. They wanted something challenging, something dynamic.

In those days, Lokamitra was a bull and a whirlwind of a man, combining an incendiary disposition with a total dedication to the cause he had espoused. With his relentless insistence on the virtues of efficiency, commitment, and self-sacrifice, he could give people a hard time, and was occasionally accused of being a bully. And yet his anger, though formidable at times, was never malicious; he could overflow human warmth in greater measure than almost anyone else around. All in all, he probably attracted more people along to the centre than the rest of us put together.

Able to know, more or less instantly, how he felt about any issue under debate, whether in 'one-to-one' communication, or in the centre's council meetings, where he wielded his fat, black Filofax like a sledge-hammer, he would seize the initiative in a discussion before most of us had grasped the bare outlines of the issue. He could be stopped, he could be convinced, he could be swayed, but only by an argument that held a weight and conviction equal to his own.

More people would admit to having a love-hate relationship with Lokamitra than with anyone I have ever known. He and I were ordained on the same day, in January 1974, by the English Buddhist monk, Sangharakshita.

Before coming to London to establish a new Buddhist movement, Sangharakshita had spent twenty years in India. He had met Dr Ambedkar a few times; and during the late fifties and early sixties he had been one of the few Buddhist monks to work closely with

Ambedkar's followers. When, in 1977, Lokamitra was about to leave for Poona to attend an advanced Yoga course with B. K. S. Iyengar, he naturally asked Sangharakshita whether there were any of his old friends he would like him to visit.

He left for Maharashtra armed with a list of names and addresses, and on 14 October paid his first call, on a man in Nagpur. By an extraordinary coincidence—of which Lokamitra was entirely ignorant—14 October happened to be the very day on which Ambedkar converted to Buddhism—at a mass rally in Nagpur.

For the purpose of his trip to India, Lokamitra had taken a vow of celibacy, and wore the yellow robe of an *anagarika*, or 'homeless one'. So it was that, when he looked in on the spectacular celebratory meeting being held on the site of the original rally, he was immediately spotted and offered the respect due to a monk. Coaxing, pulling, and pushing him through a crowd almost half a mile deep, the organizers gave him a chair on stage, alongside a phalanx of monks and dignitaries. Recovering his breath he looked up to see half a million pairs of eyes taking him in.

At midnight he was asked to give a talk. By now, he had been travelling, without sleep, for two days. Although confused by the situation he managed to put together a few words of greeting and encouragement. When he mentioned Sangharakshita's name he was astonished by the response. People remembered him, and were happy to welcome Lokamitra as his emissary.

He established himself on his Yoga course, and then set about contacting more of Sangharakshita's old friends; there were a lot of them. Inevitably, his social visits led to more formal engagements. He gave talks, taught meditation, led some study groups, and concluded his stay with a meditation retreat.

It was a marriage made in heaven. On one side was Lokamitra with his fierce determination and drive—combined with several years at the heart of a modern Buddhist movement; on the other side were six million people, at least nominally Buddhist, keen to know how Buddhism could make their lives better.

Within five months of returning to England, Lokamitra had tidied up his affairs and was back in Poona, this time to work with Sangharakshita's old friends in establishing a new Buddhist movement in India.

Although he had managed to tempt a few of his Western friends into joining him—even persuading some of them to take the robe as well— by the time I made my visit, three years later, there were already eleven Indian Order members, or 'Dhammacharis' as they were called. The movement was beginning to spread, with a couple of tentative branches in Aurangabad and Ahmedabad; a host of publications had been printed in English and Marathi, and the quarterly magazine, *Buddhayana*, was being read by ten thousand people. Lokamitra had not only established himself, but could already claim to be in touch with more people than all the movement's Western centres put together.

The first Indian Dhammachari I met when I arrived in Yerawada was Dhammaditya, a retired sergeant from the Bombay CID. Now a specialist in weddings, funerals, and in being known everywhere by everyone, he was only mildly surprised when I recognized his twinkling, pudgy features from slides I had seen in England. Holding my hands in his, he gazed on me with paternal tenderness, wheezy laughter jingling in the pendulous sack of his throat, like a purse of dancing coins.

One by one I had now been introduced to most of the Poona Order members, and to a host of the movement's non-ordained friends— known as *Sahayaks*. Among them, I felt myself bathed in a continual glow of ready warmth, and what I could only describe as a sort of 'spiritual excitement'. They seemed to be in love with Buddhism, in love with TBMSG, and wanted nothing more out of life than to see their movement grow and thrive.

Now, that mood of excitement was gathering intensity, for Sangharakshita had just arrived in India for his second visit since Lokamitra had established himself. There would be more ordinations, more contacts, and, above all, a hectic schedule of public meetings throughout central Maharashtra.

By four-thirty the community was stirring. Jyotipala, looking like a discarded bendy-doll in robes, stooped over the kerosene stove, choking on fumes as he pumped it to life. Khemadhammo, a dapper young monk from Aurangabad, shambled around in a groggy daze. Two bleary eyes cavorted in the gleaming roundness of his shaven head, like tropical fish in a brown bowl. He looked as if he had just tripped upon a startling insight into the nature of existence, without being quite old enough or experienced enough to handle it. He would look like this until he had completed the blood-curdling process of washing his teeth, mouth and throat.

Purna came across from number 32 where he slept on the shrine room floor. Exuding an untimely bonhommie, he bristled about the place, checking that we were awake, piling up the books we'd be taking, sorting out loose change, . . .

By now most of us were up, even Dhammavir, the seventy-three-year-old *Shramanera*, or novice monk, from Ahmednagar. He was not coming with us, but crept noiselessly around the place all the same, peering inquisitively into whatever we were doing, cackling quietly through an almost toothless mouth. Only Glynn the yogi slept on, probably dreaming of the very few Punjabi delicacies he had yet to sample between visits to the Iyengar Institute. The rest of us ate the standard breakfast of plain white bread, a boiled egg, a banana, and a substantial glass of Jyotipala's tea, before setting off.

It was dark outside. Above, the thin bowl of an old moon floated in a star-studded sky. As we staggered away, heavily laden with personal baggage and—literally—thousands of books, Dhammavir stood in the doorway, still cackling, waving angular waves.

It was a fair way from Ambedkar Society to the nearest busy road, and we had steeled ourselves for a long, arduous march. But, to our amazement, we suddenly heard the staccato whine of an approaching rickshaw. The driver, as delighted to see a fare at this time and in this place as were we to see a ride, quickly helped us aboard. Purna and I squeezed into the back with the luggage, while Khemadhammo, his robes billowing in the slipstream, hung on to the meter column and rode shotgun beside the driver.

The rickshaw, bucking and bouncing on the pot-holed road, snaked down the hutment-strewn hill, through the bazaar, and emerged beside the river in Yerawada proper. We were swerving wildly as we headed towards the bridge, avoiding the herds of fat black pigs that wandered about the place rooting for morsels of unmentionable nourishment. Here and there we flashed past tiny encampments where men, huddled in sackcloth, warmed themselves beside fires. A couple of juice-bars, empty but alight, remained open from the night before: 'Orange Heaven', 'The Joint'. Sooner or later they would adjust to the fact that Rajneesh had gone.

Sickly green light was beginning to infect the sky by the time we arrived at the bus station, which was an obstacle course of beggars and bodies. The entire floor area of the reception hall seeming to serve as a dormitory. Fresh-eyed children blinked up at me, peering out from beneath heavy blankets. I asked Khemadhammo whether these people were waiting for buses, or whether they lived here all the time. He didn't know. In all likelihood nobody knew.

The previous day I had tried to book some reserved seats on the bus, but the official I approached began by denying the existence of any such bus and then, after a fierce row with his superior, insisted that every seat was already booked.

So we waited at our bay, watching the crowd grow, until there were fifty or sixty of us. The minutes ticked by, the tension grew. People looked around, openly assessing the competition. . . .'

Eventually the bus appeared, nosing its way across the yard, a filthy, unwashed brute. There was immediate uproar. It was already half full.

Some unscrupulous passengers had obviously found a way of slipping aboard before it even reached the loading bay.

The bus backed into its niche to the accompaniment of terrifying noises: people were hammering on its dull red sides, arguments broke out in the crowd, insults were hurled through the windows. The conductor added his own volley of curses, aimed as yet at no one in particular, and stood filling the door like a colossus. Even so, desperate contestants were trying to squeeze a way in, through his legs and under his armpits, while others yelled appeals to his sense of justice.

He was a reasonable man. Slamming and locking the door, he stomped up and down the gangway demanding to see 'reservation dockets', sparing no one his insults and invective. Those who could not satisfy him were pulled from their seats, pushed to the door and cast out. Thence, within moments, they found themselves at the back of the press, thrust by the peristaltic action of the mob. Once the bus was almost empty, the conductor retook his place at the door and—clearly enjoying his moment of power—called out to the people below for reservation slips, inviting the chosen ones to take their places.

This left about fifty of us standing on the quay. Quite calmly, considering the circumstances, the conductor took one step backwards, gave his head a cursory shake to the side, and said, 'Okay.'

I was standing somewhere in the middle of the crowd when, without warning, the universe around me turned to iron. I was lifted clean off my feet, smothered and crushed by a surging wave of panting flesh. There was nothing to do but join in, no question whatsoever of 'going with the flow', for despite the fact that all that force was directed towards the door, anything that was not part of the force was treated as an obstacle, to be thrust aside, climbed over, and spat out at the back.

The one crucial fact about this contest that everybody understood was that there would be winners and there would be losers. The winners would get onto the bus, if only to stand jammed in a pack as they rattled along the road for hours on end, but at least heading for their destinations. The losers would watch the bus leave the station without them. They would have to try again for the next one, and the next, and the next. . . . Perhaps those people living in the entrance hall? Oh no! Surely not!

Inch by inch, inserting an arm here, a leg there, taking full advantage of my spindly form, I uncoiled and wound myself into any gaps that became available, willing my way towards that pulsating gap in the side of the bus. Eventually, grasping an arm that was in contact with the hand-rail, then clawing for the hand-rail itself, I somehow managed to get a foot onto the steps.

A transcendent moment arrives when, standing half-way into the door, one represents an obstruction more easily cleared by being pushed forward than by being pulled back. So it was that, after struggling for what had seemed like an eternity against a solid wall of resistance, I now felt myself rocketing into the Valhalla of the bus's interior, at a velocity approaching the speed of light.

* * *

'What is your good name, please?'

I looked up. My interrogator hung over me at a forty-five degree angle, held in place by a complex human cantilever system with roots somewhere to the rear of the gangway. From his shoulder dangled the battered cassette-recorder that had been deafening me for the past hour. At least I had a seat. Purna had saved one for me.

'England,' I replied.

'Then you are a cricketer, yes?'

He spent a while trying to draw me into a discussion about the test series currently being played between our two nations. Knowing little more about the current state of the game than that Ian Botham was good with a bat, I was not much use to him. Still, he did at least turn down the awful din from his music machine.

The aisle was so crowded that it was impossible to see anything over to the right of the bus, where the better views were to be had. But I was content to gaze out over fields of sorghum, sugar-cane, rice, and wheat-stubble as we droned across the plains. Each time we negotiated the hair-pin bends of a ghat, I had a terrifying close-up view of the rock walls as they flashed past—and occasionally almost through—my window.

We halted once beside a tiny wayside shrine, tucked into a little cave beside the road. Here the conductor, the driver, and a few passengers climbed down. Purna explained that the road ahead was so feared for its accident rate that a little divine help was being solicited. To be sure, a few offerings and salutations were made to the god, foreheads were smeared with red dust, and a flask of water piously splashed over the bonnet. I couldn't decide whether to feel more, or less, secure.

With or without divine help, we finally rumbled into Panchgani, and ground to a halt just past the first wave of hotels and boarding schools, and just before the busy main street.

According to Purna, we were to remain on the bus until the next stop, at the other end of town. I relaxed and peered idly through the window. There, amid all the chaos of the bus stop, was Dharmarakshita, one of Sangharakshita's oldest friends, and one of the first Indian Order members. He had a thick green scarf tied around his head, knotted under his chin, and was dancing up and down, laughing and waving energetically with his right hand. In his left hand was the right hand of a man who combined immensity of stature with all the frailty of age. This latter peered up mournfully through sad, unblinking eyes.

'No! No! We—Stay—Here!' called Purna.

'No! No! This is the place! Just come now! See! Yes!' Dharmarakshita giggled and trilled his insistence.

'Are you absolutely certain we shouldn't be getting off?' I asked. 'Dharmarakshita seems pretty sure down there.'

'No. He's got it wrong. We need to be at the other end of town. I don't fancy lugging all these books down the road. They'll catch us up.'

The bus shunted forward and began its slow crawl along main street. From one end to the other must have been two hundred yards, but our honking progress was so slow that by the time we arrived at the next stop, Dharmarakshita and his ward were waiting for us.

'Good! You are here, and so are we. Now we are all, all here. Shall we go?'

Purna was suspicious. 'Go? Where to?'

'Back there only. To the hotel. I was standing just exactly there when the bus was there. I was trying to tell you, but I don't think you could hear me. So "All right," I thought, "if they are happy on the bus, then I can meet them a little later." And see! Here I am! Shall we go? *Tsala!*'

Purna's capitulation was immediate. There was nothing more to discuss. Taking hold of the two heaviest sacks, in a gesture of contrition, he led us back down the street.

Despite the cooler climate of this high-altitude town, we were hot and sticky by the time we entered the grounds of 'Purohit's Rest Home'. Tall pine trees and palms stood sharp against a deep blue sky. Empty flower beds, rusty swings, and a dried-up lawn bordered the driveway. Inside the old wooden bungalow it was deliciously cool, each dusty room reposing in a dull green light that filtered through tinted window-panes. I threw myself onto a hard iron bed while Purna and Khemadhammo were guided directly to a pair of stately wicker armchairs. Peace at last.

So far as I could tell they came from nowhere. Hardly had we caught our breath when we realized that six wrinkled old men, clad in clean, white homespun garments, were among us. Wordlessly, they formed a queue and took turns to prostrate at the feet of Purna and Khemadhammo.

Neither of the two 'robes' seemed quite at ease with this, mainly because they suspected that Purna was being mistaken for Sangharakshita, whose taxi had yet to arrive. All the same, his voice a little strained, Purna intoned the stock response, 'Ahem. *Sukhi-ho!* Yes, *Sukhi-ho!'*—'Be happy! Be happy!'

Robeless, I was superfluous, and decided to take a quick look at the town.

There was not a lot to see: one main street and a few winding lanes leading off to a series of distinct localities. But it was a lively place all the same, a carnival of hotels, cafés, and juice bars, interspersed with the inevitable general stores, tailors' parlours, and *pan* kiosks. A hundred signs jostled for attention. 'Wel-Come!', 'Chikkin Sand-Witches', and 'Frank Furters'. Soon I had acquired a contrail of vendors proffering strawberries, raspberries, freshly roasted sweet-corn, and taxi drivers offering to drive me to the local 'view-points'. I fled back to the sombre peace of the hotel.

Sangharakshita had just arrived, and a tidy line of men now waited by the door to his room. For all their fresh, clean clothes, they were obviously poor, and a little unsure of themselves as they waited to take his 'darshan'.

Nobody seemed yet to know when our meeting would begin. But they did know that there was going to be a procession to the site, complete with a band. This last detail, however, was still under debate in the inner room. Sangharakshita was suffering from some kind of stomach bug and was reluctant to take part in too many preliminaries.

The issue was still unresolved when we were led off to take lunch in a nearby restaurant: 'Purohit's Lunch Home', presumably a subsidiary of the hotel. By now our party had increased to ten, some of our number having arrived on a later bus. None of our hosts had the facilities to cater for so many people, and a deal had been struck with the restaurant's supercilious proprietor to provide us with 'rice-plates' at a reduced rate.

As we ate, the big man from the bus stop (who was in fact Mr Kamblay, Ashok's uncle) paced round the tables, checking that everything was to our liking, just as he would have done had we been eating in his home. The restaurateur, obviously irritated by his shambling presence, launched impatient glares his way from his perch beside the cash-till, causing him considerable embarrassment and discomfort. Unable to relinquish his responsibilities as host, however, Mr Kamblay withstood the attack.

According to Khemadhammo, he lived in awful poverty, in a shack full of holes, with polythene strips for window-panes. He added that there were some Buddhists here who earned as little as seventy-five rupees a month. I worked that out in sterling. Five pounds! I couldn't believe it, even though Khemadhammo swore he was telling the truth. I looked at the old man. There were seven of us eating here, which meant a bill of at least thirty-five rupees in this particular establishment, even if he had got a good discount. I felt numb. It was hard to go on eating.

Full, however, we trooped out. The proprietor's head quivered from side to side as he bestowed a generalized smirk of a smile. I was about to offer fulsome thanks to Mr Kamblay when Purna took me by the arm.

'Don't go overboard: it's often the done thing not to thank people at all. If you thank someone too much it's as if you're taking away their sense of having given. They may even feel you're depriving them of the "merit" they've gained from their action. That's an attitude the Burmese and Thai monks have imported here.'

Obviously I had a lot to learn. Not all of it was going to make sense.

Back at the hotel I lazed on the terrace, soaking up the midday heat. From somewhere inside came rumbling fragments of a conversation: Sangharakshita and Lokamitra were discussing the tour ahead. Lokamitra flowed on, the high-pitched descant of his voice lapping softly against Sangharakshita's resonant 'Ah's and 'Hoom's.

Just once, I caught an entire sentence, 'You know, Lokamitra, I'm afraid I'm reluctantly coming to the conclusion that I must face up to the fact that I'm not as young as I used to be.'

five

The Venerable Maha Sthavira Sangharakshita came into my life at the end of 1970. At first sight I was not impressed.

I had recently left university to begin a career with the BBC. After just a few weeks in the cutting rooms, I met a Buddhist by the name of Steve Barnham.

I had already been developing an interest in Buddhism for a couple of years, since a mystical experience climaxed the trauma of my first college heart-break. Although hardly on the look-out for a religion to follow—considering myself an atheist—I felt attracted to Buddhism. It seemed to speak in terms which directly expressed the spirit of my own experience.

For a while, I kept a few Buddhist books by my bed, and even tried teaching myself to meditate. But for all that, my 'mystical' activities were little more than an incidental feature in a life otherwise dedicated to career ambitions, friends, drugs, and the pursuit of thoroughly mundane happiness. It wouldn't be fair to say that the experience had lost its importance; to the irritation of my friends I hugged it to myself as a kind of self-defining totem. I would even occasionally refer to myself as a Buddhist. But I was on no path: I was not trying to unfold the implications of the experience in any systematic way. I had had my moment of vision, but was not over-eager to transform my life as a result of it, and considered myself satisfied if, from time to time, I was able to 'touch base' and make an imaginative, intuitive link-up with the deeper side of myself that the experience had revealed. The very nature of that experience made me acutely distrustful of such outward impositions as teachers, teachings, rules, and religious groups. The 'Truth', or whatever one wanted to call it, which lay at the heart of me, simply *was*. It didn't seem to be making any special demands.

But when Steve found out about my interest in Buddhism, he embarked on an imaginative and single-minded campaign to make me take things further. This he did by befriending me—with a warmth and candour I had rarely experienced before—and above all by trying to get me to meet a friend of his, whose name sounded like 'Bunty'. For four months he cajoled, gushed, and nagged, assuring me that meeting Bunty would be 'like setting a match to dry tinder'. Out of desperation to silence him I finally agreed to go along, just once, to hear his friend give a talk.

By now I had formed an unflattering impression of 'Bunty'. To begin with, I was slightly embarrassed by Steve's unashamed reverence for the man. Then there was that name. Anyone who could allow his friends to dub him with such a flaccid nick-name had either to be naïve or careless. By failing to listen carefully when Steve talked about Bunty's time in India, I had come to envisage him as a kind of super-hippy, someone who had done the India-thing a little more thoroughly than most, and who now hung around the pads of Notting Hill Gate and Portobello, lording it over less experienced, independent friends with his travel tales and scraps of wisdom.

When we arrived at the hired room where the talk was to take place I was therefore surprised only by the man's age. He was older than I had expected, perhaps in his mid-forties. In all other respects he fitted the bill. Thrown in a haphazard way over a chassis of urbane, seemingly diffident, middle-aged Englishness, was a random superstructure of crumpled orange robes, a thick, stained, fawn pullover, some Turkish puzzle rings, a pair of dull, black walking shoes, and a tangled mane of

43

greasy hair that fell from his crown, past enormous lamb-chop side-burns, to rest—or rather riot—about his shoulders.

'Bunty, this is Terry, a friend of mine from the BBC.'

'Ah,' said Bunty in a fulsome, paternal way, accepting my offer of a handshake. Behind heavy glasses his eyes gleamed with alertness in a face that combined strength with sensitivity. Unable to fathom the man—who was making no attempt of his own to take our conversation any further—I withdrew quickly, and sat down to wait for the talk.

Other elements in the scene were as unsettling as Bunty himself. A perfectly preserved relic of the beatnik era, complete with black polo-neck sweater and a closely trimmed beard, fumbled with the controls of a bulky tape-recorder. The evening's chairman, a glazed, corpulent apparition, rigidly clamped in the iron grip of his buttoned and belted raincoat, sat bolt-upright at the table, staring straight ahead with unseeing eyes.

He did at least throw some light on a few points when he rose to make his nervous introductory speech. He referred to Bunty as 'Bhante', aspirating the *B*, and making the *U* into more of an *A*. He also referred to him by another name: 'Sangharakshita'. 'Bhante', as I later learned, was not a name at all, but a term used by Buddhists when addressing or referring to a monk.

Eventually the talk began. It almost literally knocked me out.

Sangharakshita's title was 'The Jewel in the Lotus', and his theme was the mantra *Om mani padme hum*, which is associated in the Mahayana Buddhist tradition with Avalokiteshvara, the *Bodhisattva* of Transcendental Compassion. He spoke about the 'jewel' of integrity and authenticity which resides at the core of individual human existence, buried within the 'lotus' of mundane life. His treatment was at once an extravagant display of scholarship, and an enchantment. And as he tried to communicate something of the symbolism and insight compressed into those few Sanskrit syllables, I began to feel faint.

There was nothing mystical happening. Sangharakshita was not aiming any bolts of magical power my way. This was no guru claiming his disciple, as the books have it; it was just that as he spoke, in his slightly stilted, even archaic, way, I felt threatened by his substance. He was so completely *himself*. Despite the bizarre accoutrements, he was perfectly at ease, supremely confident. There was nothing crude or obvious about it, but beneath his outward appearance there was, indeed, a jewel, a power born of experience—and the genuine desire to communicate that experience. He not only knew what he was talking about: in his own, unique way he *was* what he was talking about. By contrast—and quite instinctively—I felt so hollow in his presence that my consciousness reeled in shock.

It took Steve six months to get me along to another meeting, a festival celebrating the anniversary of the Buddha's Enlightenment.

There he was again: the same taterdermalion bundle, the same urbanity. He stood at the hall's entrance, greeting people as they arrived—observing me as I stubbed out a half-smoked cigarette.

'That's not really necessary,' he said, 'but it's a nice thought.'

His smile was encouraging. Some minutes later I decided I ought to say something, introduce myself a little more fully. I also wanted to impress him.

'Bhante,' I began, a little self-consciously, 'I'm at that stage in my development when I can't tell whether the spiritual life is something organic, or something one has to impose on oneself.'

Feeling satisfied, I awaited his reply; he would have to come up with something pretty decent to follow that.

His eyes roamed the hall, where flowers were being arranged, streamers draped, candles lit.

'Well,' he said at last, 'it's both.'

That was it. I waited, but nothing else was forthcoming. I couldn't be sure, but his darting eyes seemed to be noting my discomfort with some amusement.

Had I asked him to explain himself, rather than saying 'Yes. Yes. Of course.'—which was what I did say, then I feel sure he would have offered me more. Perhaps he would have explained that in the Buddhist conception of spiritual life, the individual develops towards Enlightenment—or 'evolves'—quite naturally, but only in dependence on conditions brought about by consciously applied effort.

But I was not ready. I was not receptive. My question had really been nothing more than a statement about my own cleverness and imagined depths. Sensing this, he had given me my chance, but had felt no need to do any more. The strange thing is, he did exactly what was necessary at the time. The subtle sense of humiliation I felt in the face of his non-co-operation actually drew me closer to him, at first as a brooding, passive competitor, and finally as a disciple.

* * *

Born and raised in South London, Sangharakshita—or Dennis Lingwood as he was christened—had an exceptional childhood. When he was eight, doctors told his parents that he was suffering from a serious heart condition and confined him to bed for several years. He would discover, much later on in life, that this diagnosis, which effectively torpedoed his formal education, was probably based on a mistake.

Alone in his room, yet as lively and curious as any normal child, he became a voracious reader. Shrugging off the comics his father brought home, he turned his attention to books, devouring the classics of Western literature, and poring over tomes on history and philosophy. These precocious literary investigations led in time to an encounter with the riches of Islam, and then with the literature and philosophy of the East.

At the age of fourteen, he discovered Madam Blavatsky's *Isis Unveiled*, and came to the abrupt conclusion that he was not a Christian, and—despite years of happy church-going—had never really been one at all. When, just a short while later, he came upon two Buddhist works: the *Vajracchedikkha*, or 'Diamond Sutra', and the *Platform Teaching of Hui Neng*, he realized that he was actually a Buddhist.

How and why such a revelation should have dawned at such an early age—and in an England where Buddhism was hardly known—he was never able to say. But from that moment on, he had no doubts about his kinship with Buddhism, nor about his fundamental understanding of it. Forty years later, he was to tell me that none of his subsequent scholarship or practice, no time spent with teachers, and none of his maturing insight into the Path, had necessitated any radical modification of that initial grasp of its fundamental spiritual principles. 'And that', he acknowledged with a laugh, 'is quite a claim to make!'

Conscripted into the army at the tail end of the Second World War, he was sent East, to India, Ceylon, Singapore, and finally back to India. He passed the duration monitoring meaningless Japanese radio transmissions and, once the war was over, performing the even less comprehensible rituals of army life.

Slipping out of camp as often as possible, he located Buddhist and Hindu institutions where he could continue with his studies, and even give lectures himself. He contributed articles to Buddhist journals. He also learned to meditate, and must have startled his friends back at the barracks by sitting on his bunk late into the night practising *anapana sati*, an exercise involving prolonged periods of intense concentration on the breath.

Tired of waiting for the army to take him home—and now realizing that he no longer wanted to go home anyway—he 'demobilized' himself, slipping quietly out of the camp one day, never to return.

He spent several years travelling around India, wandering the South on foot, begging his food as he went. Not once did his devotion to Buddhism waver, but in those days it was hard to find other Buddhists in India. He therefore took inspiration, and occasionally guidance, wherever he could find it, spending periods of time with Ramana

Maharshi, Anandamayi Ma, and Ramdas.

He tried to get himself ordained as a Buddhist monk in Sri Lanka. Because he kept no money or identification papers, he was not allowed to enter the country.

He was ordained instead at Sarnath, in 1950. In a photograph I've seen of the occasion, he stands behind the officiating monks, holding his lacquered begging bowl. Above the clean, new robe hovers a thin, bony, bespectacled face, his head freshly shaved and shining brightly. His features seem a little taut, the eyes half-closed, fixed, presumably, on some profound mystical goal.

He once told me that, during those years, the Buddha, or some aspect of his teaching, was *always* in his mind. He made the point so categorically that I felt bound to ask whether I was really to take that literally. He paused and gazed at the ceiling for a moment, before admitting, 'Well, perhaps there were just a few lapses, for two or three minutes, but only very occasionally.'

He spent a while at the Hindu University in Benares, studying Pali, Buddhist logic, and *Abhidhamma*, with the renowned Jagdish Kashyap. After a year, however, his teacher took him to Kalimpong, a town just a few miles from the Tibetan border, and left him there, suggesting that he should stay and 'work for the good of Buddhism'.

He remained in Kalimpong for fourteen years, giving talks, writing articles, editing magazines, and producing a substantial amount of poetry. He also met and befriended a number of Tibetan refugees, and established a centre dedicated to the study and practice of the three *yanas*, or 'schools', of Buddhism. This was a pioneering, even revolutionary, step, which attracted interest throughout the Buddhist world. To many scholars, and even to many Buddhists, these schools were so different in approach and ambience that they were effectively regarded as separate, even contradictory, religions in their own right.

In an authoritative work, *A Survey of Buddhism*, which he wrote when he was just twenty-nine, Sangharakshita voiced his belief in their fundamental unity. He believed that the major schools, along with their many subsects, not only subscribed to a common body of fundamental doctrines, but were crucially united in intention. Their unique and overriding purpose was to help people perceive 'Reality' as the Buddha had perceived it. The admittedly bewildering diversity was to be taken not so much as a sign of corruption, but as a clear indication that the Buddha-Dhamma, as a method of development, had the vitality and flexibility to pass from one culture to another, and address itself to people with vastly different temperaments and at different stages of development.

It was in 1949 that he first came to hear about Dr Ambedkar. The Doctor's doomed struggle to pilot a number of radical social reforms through Parliament was well documented in the press, and Ambedkar was now making it increasingly clear that he was considering conversion to Buddhism. A correspondence developed, and in time the two men came together. Ambedkar must have been impressed by the young British monk, for at their second meeting he asked whether he would conduct his conversion ceremony.

This was an extraordinary honour, for that ceremony would mark the beginning of a massive conversion programme extending, Ambedkar hoped, to include millions—even tens of millions—of 'ex-Untouchables'. It would also mark the beginning of the Buddhist revival in India. But Sangharakshita declined, suggesting that the ceremony should instead be conducted by U Chandramani Mahathera, the man who had conducted his own 'lower' ordination, at Kusinara. U Chandramani was the seniormost bhikkhu on Indian soil at the time; were he to perform the ceremony for Ambedkar, the new Buddhists would receive far more attention and help from the wider Buddhist world. Ambedkar took this advice.

Sangharakshita served the new movement as well as he could, taking monks to meet Ambedkar in Delhi, conducting a few of the subsequent conversion rallies, and giving talks. It was a speaking engagement that took him to Nagpur, the 'heart-city' of the conversion movement, on the very day Ambedkar died, just six weeks after his conversion. In the four days that followed, Sangharakshita gave thirty-five talks, averting despair, rekindling confidence. He spent the winter months of the next seven years down in Maharashtra, working among the newly converted Buddhists.

By now Sangharakshita was quite at home in India, and assumed that he would spend the rest of his life there. Something happened in 1964, however, which was to change everything. Back in England, factional tensions had developed in the fledgling Buddhist world, and it was hoped that Sangharakshita, being now the seniormost monk of British origin, might provide a moderating influence. He was invited for a short visit.

The visit lasted longer than anyone expected, two years in all, which he spent trying to forge a spirit of harmony in the strange, drawing room world of British Buddhism. Although his willingness to stay on good terms with all the opposing groups, and even to speak from their various platforms, made him a number of friends, he was soon branded by extremists from both camps as a controversial, problematic figure. Many of them were pleased to see the back of him when he returned to India—though he had now decided that this would be nothing more than a farewell tour.

Despite all the difficulties, he was convinced that the West was ripe for Buddhism. His only concern was that it might be very hard to participate in the existing scene without adding to the conflicts and tensions. So, when a letter arrived from representatives of the British Buddhist 'establishment' informing him that they were no longer prepared to act as his sponsors, he felt acute relief. He was morally free to start something of his own.

In so doing, his long-term intention was to make Buddhism as relevant and accessible in the West as it had once been in the East. For, although Buddhism was gaining favour in England and America, it was still thought of, and approached, as something of an exotic eccentricity. What Sangharakshita envisaged was a radically 'Western Buddhist' movement, rooted in practice rather than scholarship or cultural interest, and run by people whose Buddhism was a matter of personal commitment, rather than detached interest or intellectual sympathy.

He returned to London in 1967, and his little group, consisting of loyal friends from his previous visit, held its first meetings in the cramped basement of an orientalist's shop in central London. Being himself the only full-timer, he dealt with much of the publicity and organizational work, and made sandwiches for the evening sessions, where he taught meditation and gave lectures.

While in India, he had observed the monks' rules and obligations to the traditional letter, wearing his robes in the correct manner, keeping his head shaved, refraining from meals after noon, and so on. But such a code was hardly suited to this new line of work. He therefore made a number of outward changes: he was prepared to handle money, ride in wheeled conveyances, spend time alone in rooms with women, in fact do any number of things which contravened the accepted letter of the *Vinaya* or 'Book of Discipline'. His robes made him the object of unquestioning respect and candyfloss smiles, but they prevented people from recognizing him as a person, and therefore undermined the process which would turn formal respect into creative appreciation, or devotion into direct communication. Retaining the robes just for ceremonial occasions, he took to wearing 'civilian' dress, and let his hair grow.

The new movement was to be focussed on a *sangha*, or 'order', a community of people clearly committed to an active, full-time, Buddhist life. These, however, would not be monks and nuns, living on permanent retreat in secluded monasteries, but individuals who were prepared to go out and meet the world head-on, to teach the Dhamma, and to create suitable conditions for its practice in the West. Twelve 'ordinations' took place just one year after the first meeting. The glow of publicity was faint, but the movement had a nucleus.

All this was quite new, and without any clear precedent. Sangharakshita could give lectures, write books, and talk about the Buddhist approach to life, but he could not, at will, conjure a genuinely Buddhist climate and ethos out of thin air. Nor could he hope for sympathy or understanding from the wider Buddhist world. Plenty of people outside his movement looked on with scorn. Was Sangharakshita still a monk, or had he really disrobed? This new *sangha* of his, was it a lay order? Was it a 'real' order at all? Was Sangharakshita even teaching *Buddhism* in that movement of his? For their own part, the early recruits, both to the movement in general and to the Order in particular, had little idea what they were letting themselves in for. There would be difficulties.

That particular phase of the sixties was a time of ferment and experimentation. If only for a brief while, thousands of young people were at least superficially open to the notion that life held other options than those offered by the 'straight' world. It was the era of hippies, LSD, university occupations, radical politics, and the drop-out mentality. Doubting whether his own 'radical alternative' would make much impact on the comfortable, church-going British establishment, Sangharakshita made himself accessible to this 'alternative' fringe. His hair grew ever longer, his fingers sprouted rings, his reading extended to include Leary and Laing, Marcuse and Maslow, Perls and Janov.

He believed he had a real alternative to offer. To those sincere enough about change to listen and do the necessary work, he would show that their drug- and dress-conscious flirtation with alternative ideas was a pale shadow, if that, of the vision he had to retail. Dressing as he did, he was not so much showing the hippies that he was 'one of them' as calling their bluff. Like Tolkein's creation, Tom Bombadil (to use an analogy that would have gone down well at the time), he was able to toy with the 'ring', and could do so—as I had discovered— without himself disappearing from view. Sooner or later he would toss it back into the air, and laugh as it disappeared.

For a while, his movement comprised an uneasy mixture of 'straights', culled from the old Buddhist world, and 'hippies'. Although Sangharakshita would one day claim that there were never any *real* hippies around, tensions began to develop. Around the time when Lokamitra and I became involved, the movement was still small, temporarily without a permanent base, and seemingly in the grip of the 'hippy front'—itself fast turning into what Tom Woolf was to call the 'me-generation'. The two annual retreats—which we so eagerly anticipated—were hybrid affairs, combining meditation, talks, Yoga, karate, and devotional practices with a variety of fringe activities such as Gestalt, encounter groups, dream therapy, rolfing sessions, and, of course, love-ins.

Sangharakshita appeared tolerant. There was at least some energy and warmth in us. He still retained disturbing memories of the retreats he had visited on his first trip to England. Grappling wilfully, and one-sidedly cerebrally, with notions of mindfulness, 'insight', and 'no-self', most of the participants seemed to spend their days in a catatonic daze. To his horror, he had even had to visit some of them in mental homes afterwards.

Delicately, however, with polite suggestions or words of warning, and with an occasional display of contempt for some of the 'far-out' things that were happening, he managed to communicate the impression that there were deeper, wider oceans to chart.

'It's a matter of context,' he would say, if asked for an opinion on our latest therapeutic or psychedelic adventures, and made increasingly clear his view that the voyage of self-discovery and self-realization could be more thoroughly, safely, and effectively made with Buddhism than with drugs or psycho-therapeutic techniques. He stressed the value of age-old meditation practices as tools in the process of psychological growth and integration. But he also made it clear that what mattered above all was the pursuit of a goal which went far beyond the psychological, far beyond learning how to cope with one's own 'leisure-time' complexities. He talked earnestly about the necessity of 'true humanity', even of the need to cultivate one's 'pagan roots', but added that these were just starting points, the healthy context for something he sometimes called the 'higher evolution': a life of creative effort, of continuous growth and expansion in all dimensions, towards Buddhahood itself.

Working like a patient gardener: encouraging healthy tendencies here, pruning back distracting elements there, airing his views in talks and study seminars, and supporting the efforts of those most alive to his vision, he gave the movement clearer shape, and a more inspiring direction. He urged us to build something more substantial than a haven of repose and regeneration for the few. We had to become more outward-going, more able to deal with the world, able to meet it on its own terms if necessary, and thus more able to reach out with increasing effect towards the world.

He encouraged us to form more communities like the one in Balmore Street, and work together in 'Right-Livelihood' co-operatives. 'Work', he once said, 'is the Tantric guru.' And the Tantric path, he had also said, was a short and easy path—if you were prepared to put yourself into it hard enough, and for long enough! In short, he wanted us to turn the whole of our lives into a spiritual practice, and, in the process, create a 'new society', a world within the world, materially self-sufficient, emotionally positive enough to attract new people all the time, clear and confident enough to exert a benign influence on the wider world around us. He wanted us to grow up, and to keep on growing.

By the time we were in India together, that 'new society' was beginning to emerge. There were now nearly two hundred Order members, and a large number of communities, in the orbit of eleven public centres around the world. Several co-operatives had been formed, and some of them were already earning enough money to support the activities of their parent centres. Two well-appointed retreat centres had been built, in one of which, with his library, his files of minutes from meetings all over the movement, and his ever-busy typewriter, lived the Venerable Maha Sthavira Sangharakshita.

six

Over the years I had come to hear a fair amount about Sangharakshita's Indian past. He loved to talk about it and frequently referred to it in his lectures. He had even written a book, *The Thousand-Petalled Lotus*, about his early years as a wanderer.

But in 1978, when Lokamitra was about to leave for Poona, he referred more than ever to his connection with Ambedkar and the Buddhist revival in India. And as he did so, it gradually became clear that Lokamitra's project meant far more to him than many of us had realized. Through Lokamitra he was recontacting a major current in his life.

Even so, it had still come as quite a shock to see him arrive at Poona station, just a week before our trip to Panchgani.

Three hundred men stood on the blacked-out platform holding banners and waving petromax lanterns as the 'Deccan Queen'—the evening train from Bombay—squealed to a halt. Cheers erupted the moment Sangharakshita appeared in the doorway and, as he stepped down into a mass of garlands, a cheerleader led the throng through a series of slogans:

'Doctor Babasaheb Ambedkar—ki!'

'JAI SO!'

'Bhagwan Gautam Buddha—ki!'
'JAI SO!'
'Maha Sthavir Sangharakshita—ki!'
'JAI SO!'
The chanting continued as we processed along the platform and entered the station foyer, where fifty women, ashimmer in their white and blue saris, stood in line to wave trays of flowers, candles, and incense before him. He stood for a while with cheerful dignity while one person after another prostrated at his feet.

An upright man with the uniform and bearing of an army officer beckoned me across and pointed towards the scene with his baton. 'Who is this man?'

I shrugged and laughed: 'Sangharakshita. An English bhikkhu. A friend of mine.' But I was already wondering whether I knew him at all.

Beyond the station entrance, two chauffeurs quarrelled beside their gleaming Ambassador limousines over who would get to drive him away.

In the event, he went with one of them and—by what may or may not have been an accident—his luggage went with the other. In a comfortable flat on the smart side of town, made available by a wealthy Buddhist friend, he was reunited with his baggage, and we with him.

Then, despite the long flight, the train journey, the rapturous welcome, and despite the fact that he was now back in his beloved India, he sat down to eat a quiet meal, outwardly calm, quite unmoved by anything. He asked questions about business matters and retailed a few scraps of news from England while he ate, then slipped off to bed. Next morning he followed his normal routine, remaining in his room to prepare talks, read minutes, and check the proofs of a magazine article. It was as if he had never left England.

He remained cloistered in that room for the next few days. There were a few visitors: some of them old friends, anxious to bring him up to date, and others who came to look at him for a few minutes, taking his *darshan*. Occasionally, he would step out onto the balcony and take in the palm-lined avenues, or gaze pensively towards the Parvati temple which dominated the landscape from its hill-top site.

He left the flat just twice, stepping into taxis which bore him to dusty compounds where thousands of people greeted his arrival with more cheers, more slogans, garlands, and prostrations. Mounting the stage, he gave talks such as I had never heard before, sparkling with local jokes and anecdotes, so perfectly tailored to this different world that they went directly to the hearts of his listeners. Now it was as if he had never left India.

His popularity was obvious and spectacular. How many times had I watched TV reports of massive receptions for giggling jet-age gurus, newly landed in Britain! This was a dream-like reversal of the syndrome. Here was Sangharakshita, so English, still employing that classical rhetorical style, effortlessly delighting multitudes of Indian devotees.

It was hard to believe, and, in a way, it was disquieting. After all, I knew the *English* Sangharakshita. True, he had changed in many ways during the time I had known him: that flood of hair had gradually receded to a respectable length; the rings had disappeared; the jeans and sloppy pullovers had given way to sports jackets and slacks, even to an occasional suit and tie; we had managed to shift him from his draughty flat in Muswell Hill, first to a tiny country cottage with an outdoor Elsan, and finally to a comfortable room at the retreat centre. His apparent flirtation with the language and ideology of the 'alternative' world had diminished by degrees, through mild questioning, to serious criticism, to eventual derision. If one thought about it, all those little changes—viewed in retrospect—added up to a substantial transformation.

But as I watched him now, transformed yet again into an 'Ambedkarite', explaining the principles of Buddhism almost entirely in social, rather than psychological, terms, speaking so fluently the language of the 'Dhamma Revolution', and creating an instant rapport with his audience, who laughed, clapped, and burst into cheers and spontaneous chants, I wondered whether I had ever caught a glimpse of the real Sangharakshita at all. Suddenly I realized that all those 'changes' had been little more than shifts of tactic; he had never been taken in by anything or anyone. He—whoever or whatever he was— was someone and something else altogether. The realization was at once disturbing and exhilarating.

* * *

Soon after we had returned from lunch he came out into the garden, a loud pink shawl draped over his robes; he looked rather frail. Even though he had recently arrived from snow-bound Britain, he seemed to feel the chill of the Indian winter in this high place. As I lounged on the terrace in a T-shirt and pyjama trousers, enjoying a warmth rarely known in the English summer, I registered again that he had spent twenty years of his life in this country. It was as if his sense-perceptions had reverted to those of his old self: just as he took no particular interest in sights and happenings that had my eyes perpetually out on stalks, so too did he now feel the cold.

Mr Kamblay sat beside him and lamented the decline of the local Buddhist community: men were taking to drink, families going into debt because of dowry weddings, people were worshipping the old gods; there was even a rumour that some of them had been participating in animal sacrifices. He feared that in time the entire community would forget Ambedkar's message and revert to Hinduism. As I watched from across the garden, Sangharakshita's sympathetic growls drifted over like the moans of a fog-horn on a wintry sea.

But then the reception committee arrived, about twenty of them, all dressed in their best dhotis, shirts, and turbans. Lokamitra must have prevailed in his negotiations for there was no sight nor sound of a band. As I lined everyone up for a photograph, Sangharakshita gave a sudden playful smile from their midst. Whatever it was he could do to put aside feelings of sickness, he had done. The show would go on.

As our party set off, Sangharakshita took the lead, walking with unsmiling, almost funereal dignity. We passed the entrance to a side-road, and a goatherd appeared—along with thirty of his charges—nearly bringing chaos to the scene—until he disappeared down another lane. But nobody laughed. I knew there wasn't going to be a band, but I couldn't understand why everything had to be so solemn.

Later, Sangharakshita explained. Laughing informality might be a popular, even charismatic, virtue in the West—where religion has given sobriety a bad name—but here it could surprise and dismay people. Here, an important person was expected to look serious and cool. He therefore adopted the mien of a VIP in our procession not to win extra respect from his hosts—something that would have been impossible—but because he knew how much it meant to them to be organizing a meeting like this. They were parading him through town as much as anything to assert their own value and dignity. His contribution was to *be* the big man, to make himself and his presence fully and demonstrably worthy of the importance they were bestowing on him. Not long ago, he added, his hosts had been forbidden to wear clean clothes, or enter temples. Even now there were some people in town who could not bring themselves to offer one of them a glass of water.

At length, we took a right hand turning off the main road, passed a few hotels, and entered 'Bhim Nagar'.

Because of its situation on the narrow crest of a high ridge, Panchgani can hardly have changed its shape over the years. No new roads, and certainly no railway lines, have dared the steep ghat which rises up to it.

And apart from the hotels and schools, no new industries have been established here. So, because there has been no urban sprawl to blur the edges of distinction between the town's localities and their relationships with each other, it is clear that Bhim Nagar is not so much a part of the town as just outside it. To my untrained eye on that first visit, those few hotels, with their lush gardens and red-dirt driveways, provided a link between Bhim Nagar and the packed lanes and streets of the town proper. But the link was an illusory one, for here, slightly cut off from everything else, was where the locality had always been, in the days before it was known as Bhim Nagar, and when its population of Kamblays, Kharats, and Kadams were not Buddhists but 'Mahars'.

In pre-Independence India, the Mahars were the largest sub-caste of 'Untouchables' in what is now the state of Maharashtra. They were quite exceptional among Untouchable communities, renowned for their robustness, adaptability, and pride. For this, the British accorded them a special privilege, allowing them to bear arms in the Bombay Company of the East Indian Army. Such a right was no small matter, since by custom, tradition, and holy writ, a Mahar was not permitted to carry weapons of any kind. But then, a Mahar was not allowed to eat certain kinds of food, wear certain kinds of dress, drink water from public wells, enter the temples, read holy books, receive an education, . . . The list goes on, for the restrictions and prohibitions were legion, and intruded into every aspect of the Mahar's public and private life.

As 'Untouchables', the Mahars were members of the lowest stratum of Hindu society, considered to be less than human, and innately 'polluting'. Their touch, sometimes their appearance, and in some places even the sounds they made, were believed to have an intrinsic spiritual impurity. A high-caste Hindu accidentally tainted by such a touch, sight, or sound, would undergo lengthy ritual ablutions to shake off the stigma. In some villages the Mahars were required to wear spitoons around their necks to protect the ground from their saliva, and to tie brushes to their wastes which trailed behind them, erasing all trace of their polluting footprints. They had to cry out, or tinkle a bell, as they passed along the roads, warning Caste-Hindus of their approach so that they could keep clear. For, on their side, the Mahars believed that to pollute a Caste-Hindu, even accidentally, would bring evil consequences, and a harsh punishment from God.

Each Untouchable community had its strictly ordained occupation. The Bhangis were sweepers and collectors of night-soil; the Vankars were weavers; other communities were variously washermen, leather-workers, rope-makers, and so on; the Mahars were village servants.

One might be tempted to assume a link between the dirty or menial nature of such occupations and the supposed impurity of the people performing them. But that would be to miss the point. Not only were many 'Untouchable' occupations—such as bearing messages— physically clean by any standards, but the ample use of agents like cow's dung and urine in the Hindus' caste purification rites betrayed the complete absence of reason in the system. An Untouchable was impure because he or she was an Untouchable; and an Untouchable was Untouchable for no other reason than that he or she had been born into an Untouchable family.

The system was inflexible. There was no notion of social mobility through the acquisition of wealth or by marriage. It would have been heresy to consider such a thing. As an Untouchable, one received in this lifetime one's just desserts for sins committed in previous incarnations. Similarly, the Brahmins, Kshatriyas, Vaishyas, and Shudras—that is, the priests and teachers, warriors and administrators, the merchants, and the servants—were enjoying the fruits of past virtues. Yours was not to reason why; yours was to live out your allotted span, performing your *dharma*, or caste duty, without resentment, question, or hope.

Like the people of Bhim Nagar, Vimalakirti—who was walking beside Sangharakshita, and who would be translating his talk into Marathi—had been born and brought up in this world. His parents, brothers, and sisters had been village servants in a hamlet near Poona. They had been 'on call' twenty-four hours a day, expected to perform a wide range of menial chores and duties, even at the whim of Caste-Hindu children. Disobedience resulted in an immediate beating. Forbidden the use of village wells, his family, along with the thirty other Untouchable families in the village, had to take their water from a brook which passed close to the village, but only from further downstream where it ran filthy from use. Although the Mahars owned a few patches of *watan* land—their traditional 'pay' for the work they did—there was never time to cultivate it, and they were forced instead to throw themselves on the mercy of the villagers, begging their food from door to door.

When he started school, at the age of eight, Vimalakirti could neither read nor write; he had never seen a pencil in his life and, to the amusement of his classmates, had no idea what to do with the one he was given.

In 1950 the Constitution of India had made 'Untouchability' illegal, thus formally outlawing a practice that had survived for at least one-and-a-half-thousand years. Even so, Vimalakirti was not allowed to enter the classroom, and instead had to sit outside, close to a window, straining his ears to catch whatever words of wisdom passed through. It would take a long time for social attitudes to catch up with the law.

Ambedkar had been an architect of that Constitution, and was also responsible for an important set of safeguards designed to protect the now 'ex-Untouchables'. Even so, he had gone ahead with his long-standing promise to have done with Hinduism altogether. Thus it was that our little procession ended its march in the heart of a locality that was no longer Mahar, but Buddhist.

A red and blue awning flapped in the breeze above the stage. A few slight trees threw shade onto some sections of the audience. The well-trodden grassy meadow on which the meeting was to take place reached across to some agricultural buildings and haystacks, before redefining itself into a field. Above loomed the sheer black walls of 'Table-Land', a massive plug of black volcanic rock that dominated the entire town.

At first sight it was all idyllically rustic. One hut even had a quaint wooden sign-board above its door: 'Kamblay Cottage'. But a second look at the homes revealed that they were cramped, draughty, semi-dilapidated hovels, one-roomed dwellings of brick and corrugated iron. Outside their doors ran streams of sewage. The bustle of activity around the latrines and water taps disclosed that none of the houses had running water or toilets. And these were the good houses. Just behind them were the shoddy encampments of shacks and shelters, fashioned from scrap wood, raffia, and flattened biscuit tins.

Hutments, filth, and poverty can be seen on the fringes, or even in the heart, of any town in India. Not all of these are the homes of ex-Untouchables. Muslims, Christians, Sikhs, and Caste-Hindus—even Brahmins—can be found living in abject poverty. It is not that poverty equals Untouchability. The point is, however, that Untouchability—and even ex-Untouchability—almost invariably does mean poverty. In the past this was because poverty was the Untouchable's 'natural', 'God-given' lot. Now, despite compulsory education for all, and quotas of reserved places for the 'Scheduled Castes' (as they are technically called) in higher education and government service, the lack of any cultural basis for notions of self-improvement, education, and striving after material success, condemns most ex-Untouchables to lives of continued degradation.

Like many others, the bus that brought us to Panchgani had borne one of Gandhi's maxims on its side-panel: 'Untouchability is a crime against God and man'. In the cities, perhaps, caste practice is on the wane, Untouchability becoming a thing of the past. Although there are still very few inter-caste marriages, there can be no doubt that the circumstances of modern living are changing people's attitudes. The ideals of social mobility and conspicuous consumption have arrived; the motor scooter and the colour TV set compete with the sacred thread in the status stakes. And when buses and trains jam people together into an indistinguishable biriani of flesh and 'suitings', nobody who wants to get to work in the morning can afford to be fussy about who he rubs shoulders with.

But almost eighty percent of Indians still live in the villages, where traditional customs go largely unchallenged. Many of the people in our audience that day had laboured up the steep terraces to Panchgani from their little clusters of huts on the edges of villages down on the plain. They still knew what it meant to be treated like dirt. That was why they had come dressed in their newest and cleanest dhotis and saris. This was their day.

It was not a big audience. By Indian standards it was tiny for an outdoor meeting. But it was moving to know that here was the entire Buddhist population of Panchgani and its environs. I found myself wondering how much we would have had to spend on publicity to attract a thousand people to a talk on Buddhism back in London!

The key could still be turned to effect. And the key was Dr 'Babasaheb' Ambedkar.

seven

In a frank acknowledgement of that fact, the proceedings up on stage began with a simple ritual. Sangharakshita was asked to place a garland of marigolds first over a picture of Dr Ambedkar, and then over one of the Buddha. This little procedure was to be repeated again and again, at every talk, and sometimes even when we were invited into peoples' homes for lunch: first Dr Ambedkar, and then the Buddha.

When I had first arrived in India, Lokamitra took me on a tour of the centre at Ambedkar Society. I was surprised, even distressed, to see that kindly, bookish face peering down from a niche over the shrine-room door.

'Don't tell me he's here as well!' I blurted. 'I would have thought that once people were actually coming along, he wouldn't be necessary any more.'

I liked my Buddhism undiluted. To maintain the 'Ambedkar profile' in the centre itself seemed to be pandering to the purely cultural, groupish aspect of the Buddhist movement here. Certainly, Ambedkar was good advertising, a helpful gift from history, but that apart, I had dismissed him as a feature of the nursery slopes.

The strength of Lokamitra's retort surprised me.

'Of course we have his picture here. And we have it on the shrine at our retreats, too. Ambedkar is the reason all these people are open to Buddhism; he advised them to convert to Buddhism in the first place. You wouldn't question our having a Buddha-image on the shrine, would you? This is similar. Ambedkar's as much a symbol of self-development here as the Buddha is. He inspires people.'

I was still suspicious. 'But what do *you* think? Do you see Ambedkar as a great man? Do you see him as an *ideal* man?'

There was an instant's hesitation, then, 'Yes I do. Well, he was definitely a great man. And his life certainly points the way to important ideals. 'Look, I think you should find out more about him. If you're going to be travelling with us, you've got to do some homework.'

As was often the case, Lokamitra's intuition was on to something. He had sensed a patronizing note in my voice. There *was* something about Ambedkar that made me want to keep my distance. I had never really bothered to analyse my reaction, but I knew it had been sparked off by some of the biographical material I'd seen: pages of awesomely researched but fawning, hyperbolic hero-worship. Then there were all those posters and pictures. Ambedkarite culture, with its crude plaster busts, garish paintings, and raucous slogans, seemed rough and limited. Then, finally, somewhere behind those more 'sophisticated' reactions, lurked a deep abhorrence of the awful, shabby world from which he had emerged.

But I did my homework. More to the point, I met hundreds, even thousands, of his followers. There really was no denying it. He was a great man.

* * *

Ambedkar was born in 1891, the fourteenth child of a comparatively prosperous Mahar family, in the village of Mhow, in south-west Maharashtra.

His family's material comfort—though of a sort which would strike most Westerners as hopelessly squalid—was due to the fact that his father, taking full advantage of opportunities provided by the Bombay army, had risen to the rank of 'Subedar Major', and worked as headmaster in an army school. Just a year after 'Bhim''s birth, the British stopped recruiting and employing Mahars in the army, and he was forced to look for work elsewhere. All the same, Ambedkar was reared in an environment where the virtues of self-discipline and education, and a belief in the possibility of self-improvement, were strongly upheld. Such a home was rare, if not unique, in the wider Mahar and Untouchable context.

Since 1858, primary education, and a certain level of secondary education, had been made available by law to children from all castes. Bhim was consequently sent to school as soon he was old enough. Once there, however, he was lazy, argumentative, and truant—in fact, quite unremarkable among his low-caste fellows. This was hardly surprising. The Mahar children were old enough to know what it meant to be 'Untouchable'. Prosperous or not, they could get no water from the villages they passed on their way to school; fearing pollution, no barber would cut their hair, no bullock-cart driver would give them a lift. And the Caste-Hindu children, themselves developing a rudimentary grasp of their own 'superiority', teased them. With the army option closed, caste occupations and caste degradations were all they had to look forward to. Why should they bother to try?

By the time he was nine, Ambedkar was disillusioned with the whole farce, and conceived a scheme to run away to Bombay to find a little money and a little freedom working in the cotton mills.

His entire plan depended on one thing. To pay his fare he would have to steal a tiny amount of cash from his step-mother's purse while she slept. He failed, defeated by the woman's habit of sleeping with the purse tied to her body, beneath several layers of sari cloth.

His response to this set-back was quite extraordinary and, given the circumstances, wildly idealistic. He resolved to achieve such a resounding success at school that some kind of breakthrough would absolutely have to come, something with the power to lever him from his otherwise hopeless prospects.

He studied all day, and most of the night, rising at three in the morning to pore over books by the light of a smokey, chimneyless oil lamp. His delighted father gave support and encouragement, but everything was loaded against him at school. Teachers ignored, or actively derided, his upstart ambitions. Caste-Hindu children scurried to retrieve their lunch-boxes if he passed close to them on his way to the blackboard. He was also forbidden access to the classes on Sanskrit. Sanskrit, being the language of the holy scriptures, was forbidden fruit for the Untouchables. He retaliated by learning it secretly, from books.

By the time he was attending high-school, his family had moved to Bombay, and it was there that he passed his matriculation exams.

Despite average marks, such an achievement was almost without precedent in the Mahar community. The event was celebrated with a large meeting, and a number of dignitaries turned up to offer their congratulations.

His education, which actually equipped him to be little more than an office clerk, could have come to a halt right there. Instead, a philanthropical prince, the Maharaja of Baroda, stepped in with the offer of a scholarship. He moved on to college and, in 1912, became the first Mahar ever to win a BA degree, in English and Persian languages.

The Maharaja too was an ambitious, idealistic man. He wanted to help bring into being a kind of intellectual elite among the Depressed Classes, and made further scholarships available so that the most promising students could attend universities in Europe and America, thus gaining a taste of the highest levels of education available. Ambedkar was singled out and offered the chance to study economics at the University of Columbia in New York. He jumped at the chance.

He obtained his MA in 1915, and was awarded a Ph.D in 1916, for a thesis on 'The Evolution of Finance in British India'. Yet, even now, he was not satisfied. He asked for the Maharaja's blessing to proceed directly to London where he enrolled at Grays Inn to study Law, and at the London School of Economics to study Political Science. In 1917, however, the period of his scholarship came to an end. It was time to go home.

According to the terms of his award, he was committed to serving a ten-year period with the Baroda State Government, where the Maharaja had him earmarked for the post of Finance Minister. He arrived in Baroda fresh from London, equipped with knowledge and qualifications, and incidentally infused with the liberal, humanistic ideas he'd imbibed along with his lectures and reading in the West. The shock he was to receive was terrible and decisive.

Nobody came to meet him at the station, and no accommodation had been arranged. Only by lying about his caste did he manage to find somewhere to live. Starting work as Military Secretary to the Maharaja, he was forbidden use of the office water supply, and discovered that no messenger or clerk would go near him. As they threw him the books and documents he wanted from across the room, he realized that in their eyes, and in the eyes of the Hindu world, none of his achievements meant a thing.

After a while, his deception at the boarding house was discovered, and he was put out on the street. When he appealed to the Maharaja for help, no one could see any way of intervening without stirring up a hornet's nest of protest sufficient to bring the State apparatus to a halt. Dejected and defeated, Ambedkar left Baroda.

He took up the post of Professor of Economics at Sydenham College in Bombay. Although he had to steel himself against the abusive taunts and petty ostracization of his colleagues, he was at least able to house himself and his family, in a shabby tenement block in the mill-workers' district.

But something had snapped. Despite the prestige of his post, he knew for sure that he would not be living out his days as a college teacher. The indignities he had experienced as a child, and the knocks received in Baroda and Bombay, fermented painfully alongside his knowledge that casteless, egalitarian societies really did exist. The driving personal ambition that had brought him so far now turned into a social, political commitment. His mind became set on doing whatever he could for 'his people', the Untouchables.

His subsequent career must stand as one of the most dramatic examples of single-minded dedication to a social cause in history. A major biography of the man, by Dhananjay Keer, is entitled *Dr Ambedkar: Life and Mission*. It could equally be called *Dr Ambedkar: Life* as *Mission*.

His first task was to complete his education. Skimping, saving, and borrowing, he scrambled together enough funds to return to London where he lived the life of a virtual ascetic, rarely leaving his eyrie in the British Museum's reading room. When he did emerge, it was as a barrister, with an MA and Doctorate in Political Science. He moved immediately to Germany, and enrolled himself at the University of Bonn. Had his money not finally run out, he would doubtless have left that establishment with more initials to add to the list that now trailed after his name.

His formal education was over. But an informal process of self-education was to continue. For the rest of his life he spent every spare moment in the company of books: eating with them, taking them to bed at night, waking up to them. Wherever he went he combed the second-hand bookstores, looking for anything that might push his knowledge and understanding ever wider, ever further. His hunger for learning was imperialistic; it meant power. With knowledge he would be able to argue on equal intellectual terms with anyone. And with knowledge he would be able to break the prison bars of superstition.

During the interlude that separated his years in England, he had founded his first newspaper: *Mook Nayak*—'Leader of the Dumb'. Now, through this, and through the *Bahiskrit Hitkarini Sabha* ('The Society for the Benefit of the Excluded Classes')—the first of many organizations he was to found—he set out to promote education and the spread of culture among the Untouchables. Hoping to stir them from their age-old resignation and entrenched defeatism, he also composed his first slogan: 'Educate, Agitate, Organize!'

Education had given him the chance to get a decent job; it was education that had freed him from superstitious fear and mute acceptance of the status quo; and it was education that had made him see the need to help others. If more educated people could emerge from the Depressed Classes they would stir up—agitate—the others into a new mood of self-respect, and foster a healthy disillusionment with existing norms and forms. Then, of course, the ferment engendered would have to be organized into a powerful, coherent force for change.

He initiated a string of 'hostels': cheap, even free, boarding houses for Untouchable students who were intellectually equipped to take advantage of government-funded opportunities in higher education, but too poor to support themselves while they studied. Giving evidence before the Southborough Committee on Franchise Reforms, Ambedkar admitted that he was the only Mahar educated to university level in the entire Bombay presidency. And besides himself there were no more than six or seven Matriculates!

Although some of his organizations directed their message towards the Caste-Hindus, seeking to introduce the ideals of social equality among people for whom such notions were alien, another of his more popular slogans was 'Self help is best help!' In the end, the Untouchables would have to take responsibility for their own uplift. It should be said that, in those early years, Ambedkar was offered a great deal of support and encouragement by liberal Caste-Hindus, but he was always cautious about accepting it. That sort of help was too often shallow and limited, patronizing, or, like the formal 'inter-caste dinners' these reformers liked to attend, it confused the fundamental issue. Hindu society was corrupt. It needed a complete overhaul.

A radical change was necessary, not just for the sake of the Untouchables themselves, but to upgrade the moral life of India as a whole. Again and again he stressed that he did not hate the Hindus, nor did he hate Hinduism, but he detested the way Hinduism had been warped and twisted to rationalize a corrupt society—and to provide a sanction for slavery.

By now, Ambedkar's career was taking off on all fronts. To support his family and much of his activism, he ran a legal practice at the Bombay High Court. Soon he would become a professor at the Bombay Law College, and, more significantly, a member of the Bombay Legislative Assembly. His various newspapers and journals were increasingly widely read, the hostels programme well under way, and his societies and political unions were spreading his message.

On the wider Indian scene, the inexorable approach of Independence was creating a climate in which his voice could gain a hearing. *Swaraj* loomed on the horizon, not as a hope but as an inevitability; the entire nation was in a state of creative political ferment. As the British began to loosen their hold, and threw increasingly significant morsels of self-determination into the bubbling pot, Ambedkar, with his outstanding intellectual abilities and an ever-growing following, was securing valuable platforms.

As a matter of policy, the British had always tried to avoid interfering in the social patterns of their subject territories. Even so, the Untouchables had enjoyed certain advantages, and a quantum of basic 'human rights' under the Raj. Now, unless people were prepared to change, Ambedkar feared that in an independent, Hindu-dominated India, the Untouchables would fall back into the mire.

The party most likely to seize the reins of power after Independence was the Indian National Congress. In Ambedkar's view, its key figures shared an important characteristic. Despite being English-educated, they were culturally traditional.

'Everybody in India, apart from the Hindus,' he said, 'knows that whatever may be its title, it is beyond question that the Congress is a body of middle class Hindus supported by the Hindu capitalists. Their object is not to make Indians free, but to be independent of British control, and to occupy places of power now occupied by the British. If the kind of freedom which the Congress wants was achieved, there is no doubt that the Hindus would do to the Untouchables exactly what they have been doing in the past.'

Certainly, the Congress people were making a lot of sympathetic noises about the uplift of Untouchables but, so far as Ambedkar could see, they were showing no real or effective concern. For all his talk about the evils of Untouchability, even the great Mahatma Gandhi betrayed an underlying faith in the traditional gradations of Hindu society. He honestly believed that the caste system was based on a natural and desirable social ideal. That people should follow a caste-occupation struck him as an admirable way to ensure harmony and fulfilment. The 'progressive' rider he attached to this view was that no particular task or occupation should enjoy any higher status than another. Before God, he said, all tasks and people are equal. Symptomatic of this approach was his euphemistic redubbing of the Untouchables as *Harijans*—or 'Children of God.' It is a term that has never been used by the Untouchables themselves.

Ambedkar's scepticism deepened, soon taking the form of open contempt. In a series of dramatic statements, he asserted that he and his people could hardly be expected to support the struggle for Independence with any enthusiasm while it offered such enormous perils. It alarmed him to see the Congress wooing the British with its pious but empty platitudes. Believing that the Hindus' teeth had to be drawn—and displayed for all the world to see—he embarked upon what was, perhaps ironically, a rather Gandhian form of 'non-violent direct action'.

In March 1927, in the course of a conference in Mahad, he led several thousand delegates to a tank—an artificial lake—in the heart of town, and, stepping down into it, sipped a little of its water.

This may not sound like an outrageous act, but it caused a furore. There were broken bodies, death-threats, court injunctions, and a long legal battle—even though the tank was legally open to all.

The tank was situated in a Brahmin locality, and the locals, in blatant disregard of the law, had been refusing to allow any Untouchables near it. Moslems and Christians could use it, clothes could be washed in it, buffaloes and oxen could descend into it, but an Untouchable, they held, would pollute it.

Ambedkar knew that his demonstration would do little to change the hearts of people in Mahad. But he did hope that the frenzy of protest unleashed by his act might serve as an alarm bell, alerting thinking people to the fact that traditional attitudes still reigned supreme, and were never going to be dissipated by gestures, vague promises, or platitudes about 'Hindu repentance'.

'According to Gandhi,' he said, 'Hindus should do repentance, and themselves voluntarily endeavour to eradicate Untouchability. Untouchables themselves need not do anything for the removal of Untouchability and their own upliftment. The Untouchables should simply sit with folded hands and pray "Oh Lord, grant the Hindus wisdom and courage and light, so that they may be forgiven for their evil deeds. Let their sins be forgiven, and grant them the knowledge and strength to reform their society." This is the pious advice of Gandhi to the Untouchables. These pious platitudes can do no good to anybody, nor can they solve any problems. No sane person can ever agree to such a proposal. This sounds more like advice tendered by an idiot to the people of an area affected by a plague epidemic: "Brothers, halt and listen to me! Do not be afraid of the disease. The Municipal Committee members will have to repent one day for the dereliction of duty on their part; some plan will surely be chalked out for the eradication of the plague. Meanwhile you must wait and see." '

At Mahad, a court injunction was sought, and granted, preventing any such protest from taking place again. Ambedkar took the local Hindus to court after court in a process which ended in victory—ten years later. Meanwhile the Hindus continued to use their tank quite happily, for they had 'purified' it. To the accompaniment of sacred mantras, one hundred and eight pitchers filled with a mixture of cow's dung and urine, curds, and water, were tipped into the lake, and its waters declared free of taint.

This was an insult Ambedkar would never forgive. Some years later, he would confess his utter disillusionment with Hinduism, and declare his intention to quit its fold altogether.

But in Mahad, just a few months after the tank episode, he publically burned a copy of the *Manusmriti*.

The *Manusmriti* was an anthology of divinely inspired pronouncements on Hindu social life, the text which gave sanction to the horrors associated with Untouchability. Ambedkar's new inflammatory act provoked another storm of abuse and threats, and violent fights. Now he lost the support of most of his Caste-Hindu associates and sympathizers. But the message was clear. India was so deeply immersed in her superstitious past that a gesture of this sort could repel even the most sympathetic, reform-minded Hindus Ambedkar could find.

As these and similar campaigns unfolded, Ambedkar's fame—and notoriety—continued to spread. This was part of the plan. He wanted his name and his message to carry as widely as possible; he wanted to be acknowledged as the clear leader of the Untouchables. In the run-up to Independence, all kinds of meetings and conferences were taking place, all manner of committees being formed. If anyone was going to represent the Untouchables on these bodies then it would have to be him, rather than some Congress 'puppet', or even Gandhi himself.

At the 'Round Table Conferences' on Independence, in London, he voiced his concerns at every opportunity: nobody would do a thing about social reform unless the Untouchables achieved some effective political power. To offset their enormous handicaps, the Constitution would have to positively discriminate in favour of the Untouchables. Unless these conditions were met, the ignorant, unsophisticated, disorganized Untouchable masses would be quietly and firmly pressed back into the ground, perhaps never to re-emerge. This would be tragic for the Untouchables, and it would spell disaster for India. The price of whatever 'harmony'—and cheap labour—the caste system bestowed, would be chronic communal instability, continued ignorance, and national impotence in the face of whatever shocks the modern world had to offer.

He also made clear his belief that the Untouchable population was not to be regarded as part of the Hindu majority at all, but was, more properly, a kind of separate minority within the state. He demanded that they should be allowed to present their own candidates at elections and, further, that they should be able to vote for them in discrete, separate electorates.

Now the other 'champion' of the Untouchables drew his sword. Gandhi passionately opposed the concept of separate electorates, sensing in them the very threat to India's unity and stability that Ambedkar hoped to avert. India had enough communal problems already, said Gandhi. What good could be done by introducing yet another clearly defined minority into the situation? The Untouchables were Hindus; it was dangerously eccentric of Ambedkar to portray them otherwise.

When the British accepted Ambedkar's proposals, Gandhi—then in his Yerawada gaol cell, protested with a 'fast unto death'. There followed a series of urgent meetings, and under the stress of mounting pressure Ambedkar withdrew his demand for separate electorates, while managing all the same to win a bigger allocation of reserved seats for Untouchable representatives.

To this day nobody really knows whether Ambedkar withdrew his insistence on separate electorates because he had changed his mind on the issue, or because he knew he was pursuing a hopeless dream, or because he wanted to save Gandhi's life. And if he did choose to save Gandhi, was he acting out of human compassion, or because he knew that, if Gandhi died 'at his hands', the result could have been at best the end of his political career, and at worst a communal bloodbath between Caste-Hindus and Untouchables?

Meanwhile, he made full use of the political arena, founding political parties to unify the Untouchables, and fighting for hand-holds on the political machine as soon as they became available. In 1941, he achieved a position of considerable importance, being appointed 'Labour Member' on the Governor-General's Executive Council. He was now effectively a cabinet minister, with a portfolio that recognized and gave scope for his life-long dedication to the 'working masses' of the sub-continent. It was an extraordinary achievement for a man from an Untouchable background, and gave renewed strength and inspiration to the entire Untouchable population. Could anything have argued so firmly against the notion that an Untouchable was 'sub-human'?

With Independence came a Congress government. Despite his constant sniping, brooding criticism, and chronic distrust of the Congress, he was invited to join the Cabinet, as Law Minister. It says a great deal about Nehru that he extended this invitation; it also reveals something about Ambedkar that he accepted. His career had not been without its sudden changes of pace, mood, and even direction; he liked to quote Emerson's aphorism: 'A foolish consistency is the hobgoblin of little minds.' He had never been averse to dropping a line of attack if it proved impracticable or politically inexpedient. For all his scholarship and bookishness, he was a political pragmatist, his eyes always open for the main chance.

He was also offered a position on the Bombay High Court Bench, but this he refused. His reformist activities required him to take stands and make statements incompatible with the dignity and sobriety of the post. But, as he told a meeting of his followers, he had now achieved any personal goals he had ever set himself, and more. He had shown what was possible.

Being an expert on constitutional law, he was asked to chair the committee responsible for drafting the new Republic's Constitution. Although that Constitution would express the political will of many of the Republic's founders, Ambedkar's position gave him an opportunity to incorporate at least something of his own vision. From various points of retrospect he would speak of his involvement in the project firstly with pride, then with qualification, and finally with deep regret that he had not taken things further. But the new Constitution did enshrine his beloved principles of Liberty, Equality, and Fraternity; it outlawed Untouchability; it made the individual human being—rather than the village—its basic political 'unit'; and it went some way towards determining a socialistically inclined state, whose citizens enjoyed democratic rights and freedoms.

Nehru now invited him to take responsibility for an important set of legal reforms, dealing with the Hindu code of social organization, collectively entitled 'The Hindu Code Bill'. The Bill had been in preparation for a decade or more, and was considered long overdue by many Hindus. Although it sought mainly to unify and codify Hindu law, making it consistent throughout India; and although its proposed modifications were themselves carefully rooted in scriptural authority, the Bill was doomed from the moment Ambedkar stepped forward as its champion. He was simply not the man for the job: a man who had made a blasphemous bonfire of the *Manusmriti*, and who had consistently presented himself as a vociferous enemy of Hindu society. He was blocked, filibusterd, and opposed at every turn.

Nehru wavered. Initially, he helped Ambedkar to introduce the Bill, proclaiming it the most important set of reforms on the country's agenda. But, as opposition gathered strength, he permitted delays, postponed debates in favour of other business, and finally shelved the Bill for a decade. Ambedkar was crestfallen. Personally frustrated after so much painstaking research, more sceptical that ever about the prospects for change in Hindu society, he resigned from the Cabinet, crossed the floor, and joined the Opposition. At the following general election he lost his place in the House, and then failed to make a comeback at a by-election.

He had his seat on the Council of States, which gave him a platform of considerable importance; he still spoke out whenever and wherever he had the opportunity; he also founded the Republican Party of India. But the political phase of his mission was effectively over. He was extremely sick with diabetes and a host of other painful disabilities; he could walk and stand only with difficulty, and found public meetings— and the travel they entailed—almost intolerably wearing. His entire life's struggle was drawing to an end.

But he still had one major step to take. He had a promise to redeem. And, in redeeming it, he would move his mission onto an entirely new level.

eight

'Unfortunately for me I was born a Hindu Untouchable. It was beyond my power to prevent that. But I solemnly assure you that I will not die a Hindu.'

Ambedkar made this pledge in 1935, in a nondescript sugar town called Yeola. Yet he would give no sign that Buddhism was to be his refuge until the early fifties. His formal conversion came at the end of 1956. Why did he wait so long?

His Hindu detractors have always maintained that the Yeola declaration was nothing more than a shock tactic characteristic of his approach at the time, his conversion no more than a stunt, the last frantic gesture of a failed politician still looking for the lime-light.

His own followers naturally see things differently. Some explained to me that his political, social, and educational work left him no time to devote to the question of conversion. Others pointed to his posthumously published work, *The Buddha and His Dhamma*, suggesting that he was reluctant to launch a mass conversion movement among poor, uneducated folk until he had produced at least one simple book with which to guide them. Yet others declared that the question of conversion was so important to him that he spent those fifteen to twenty years making a conscientious study of the options before him.

This, to be fair, was the reason he gave himself.

The main contenders were Islam, Christianity, and Sikkhism. Each had sizeable communities in India; they were relatively wealthy and had spawned well-developed sub-cultures. In the past, they had drawn many of their recruits from the Untouchable castes; now they had their own schools, colleges, religious teachers, and temples, and substantial political power-bases. When a few Untouchable communities, inspired by Ambedkar's pronouncement, took the initiative and converted to one or another of these faiths, he was sympathetic. But he held back, and held back the majority of Untouchables with him.

In so doing, he had to contend with some enormous positive pressure. Fabulous sums of money were offered to his followers, and to him; universities, housing deals, all manner of inducements were dangled as bait. After all, any religious community that could suddenly increase its numerical strength by a factor of something like forty million souls—ten percent of the total population—at the precise historical moment when all the possibilities of Independence were in the offing, would be placed in a position of enviable power.

But Ambedkar was not a man to be bought. The more persistently the emissaries sought him out, the more firmly he closed his doors. He wanted to escape from Hinduism all right, but he wanted much more than a cosmetic change—no matter how materially beneficial it turned out to be. He wanted to move *towards* something.

To Ambedkar, religion was something of all-transcending importance. Properly understood and honestly practised, religion was the indispensable foundation of society, the leaven which made it truly human. The virtues of 'Liberty, Equality, and Fraternity', he insisted, were not merely social or political slogans, but spiritual imperatives, taking their sanction from the innate potential of human consciousness and human life.

He knew—better than most—that religion could serve as an opiate for the masses; worse, its name could be invoked to justify the vilest forms of oppression. For all that, he still believed that religion alone, and not politics, held the key to the reserves of compassion, wisdom, and imagination which lay buried in the human heart, without which human society could be human in name alone.

But what sort of religion did he have in mind? His criteria were stringent. The ideal religion would be free from any taint of caste and Untouchability. It would place man, rather than an authoritarian god, at its centre, and would work *for* man rather than requiring him to live in unquestioning obedience to a god. He had no respect for religions which shrouded themselves in superstitious mystery, and insisted that there was no reason why religious teachings shouldn't accord with the principles of reason and science. Finally, no true religion could sanction or ennoble poverty; instead it should promote the principles of Liberty, Equality, and Fraternity.

One by one, the world's religions failed his test. Islam and Christianity were not only god-based and essentially authoritarian, but they were also foreign. Still a patriot at heart, Ambedkar feared that mass conversion to an 'alien' faith could have a destabilizing effect on the country's cultural integrity. Sikkhism appealed for a while; many of his lieutenants favoured it, if only because it allowed, even encouraged, its adherents to bear arms. But he finally rejected that on the grounds that it was too closely allied to Hinduism, and even infected with the canker of caste.

There are those who claim that Ambedkar never really had anything else in mind but Buddhism. We shall never know; the truth is already too tangled up with legend. But we do know he had some interest in Buddhism even in his youth. At the meeting convened to celebrate his matriculation, one of his teachers presented him with a book about the Buddha's life. It is said to have affected him deeply. There are even those who assert that this early encounter with the principles of Buddhism played as important a role in shaping his humanistic, humanitarian ideals as did his sojourn in the West.

Throughout his career he dropped a number hints about his attraction to Buddhism. When his 'People's Education Society' established two colleges, in Bombay and Aurangabad, they were respectively named 'Siddharth College' and 'Milind College', names with obviously Buddhist associations. He even dubbed his Bombay home 'Rajagriha', after the hill in Bihar where the Buddha gave many of his teachings.

So what were the Buddhists doing to secure his 'vote'? Shortly after Ambedkar's Yeola statement, the Honourable Secretary of the Maha Bodhi Society—the most established Buddhist organization in India—sent a telegram: 'Shocked very much to read your decision to renounce Hinduism. . . . Please reconsider your decision. . . . But if still you persist in embracing another religion, you with your community are most cordially welcome to embrace Buddhism. . . .'

Most cordial! On the other hand, there was an Italian monk who wrote to him a couple of times, seeking with wonderful bombast and hyperbole to bolster his enthusiasm for Buddhism, reminding him that a substantial mass conversion would inevitably herald the revival of the religion in its native land.

And there was Sangharakshita, the English monk from Kalimpong, who now, thirty years later, began his talk to the Buddhists of Panchgani with an account of his own meetings with Dr Ambedkar. . . .

Although they had been exchanging letters since 1950, he said, the two men did not meet until the end of 1952. By then Ambedkar had effectively made it clear that he was thinking of converting to Buddhism. However, his few experiences of 'living Buddhism', in Sri Lanka and Burma, had come as a terrible disappointment. He had seen monks acting like minor despots towards the laity, accepting veneration and food, but giving nothing in return except a few mumbled chants and empty rituals. Even worse, however, was the fact that the Maha Bodhi Society was now more or less overrun by Hindus. Its president was a Brahmin!

As usual, the ante-room at Ambedkar's residence was filled to capacity when Sangharakshita paid his first call. So he waited his turn along with a throng of lieutenants and well-wishers, each bearing a garland for their leader. When he appeared, the great man spurned their offerings, berated them for wasting money on such things. The more he lashed them, however, the happier everyone seemed to be. At length Sangharakshita was ushered into the inner sanctum.

The old warrior's attack was sharp and immediate: 'What can your Maha Bodhi Society do for us with a Brahmin for a President?'

But Sangharakshita was not there as a representative of the Maha Bodhi Society. Indeed, he was as eager to see things changed at the Society as was the Doctor.

Mollified, Ambedkar moved the conversation onto friendlier ground. He wanted to be absolutely clear what conversion to Buddhism would involve, and wondered what form the conversion ceremony should take. Encouraged by Sangharakshita's replies, he asked—next time they met—whether he would be willing to say some of these things to a larger gathering. He had planned a rally for that very night, in a slum area of Bombay, and wanted Sangharakshita to go along and explain exactly what it meant to become a Buddhist. . . .

In Panchgani, just as they would have done in Bombay so many years before, old men squinted in concentration, and cupped hands to their ears to catch the words as they spluttered from dented loudspeaker horns. Over to one side, women stroked or threatened babies into silence. Some of the younger men bent over exercise books, taking notes—though few of the rest could read or write. Today, as before, everyone had come along hoping to find out why their 'Babasaheb' had asked them to become Buddhists.

In traditional Buddhist language, Sangharakshita explained, a Buddhist is someone who 'Goes for Refuge to the Three Jewels'. These 'Three Jewels' are the Buddha himself, the *Dhamma*—which is his teaching, and the *Sangha*, which is the community of his followers.

The first thing that must be said about the Buddha is that he was neither a God nor an incarnation of God. He was not even a messenger of God. He was a human being like any of us. Through his own efforts he arrived at a state of moral and spiritual perfection. His mind became bright with wisdom; his heart was filled with unbounded love for all beings. He was someone who had liberated himself from all illusions. He enjoyed perfect happiness, complete freedom.

Most religions place a god at the centre of the universe. In relation to him we humans are nothing. We must only serve him, obey him, and try to please him. But in Buddhism there is no God. The highest being in the universe is a Buddha, someone who is radiantly wise and utterly free, a being without any limits at all.

But even though a Buddha is such a special kind of being, he is still someone who has achieved that state through self-development. We too can become Buddhas. We can gain Enlightenment just as he did. There is therefore nothing at all pathetic about our human state; on the contrary, it is the best possible starting point. As human beings we can work on ourselves until we are like the Buddha. To 'Go for Refuge' to the Buddha means that we too are prepared to do that work.

Sangharakshita moved on to the second 'Jewel', first explaining that the Pali word, *Dhamma*, was not to be confused with its Sanskrit equivalent, *Dharma*. A Hindu's 'Dharma' is his way of living in accordance with the will of God, obeying to the letter all the rules and obligations of the caste into which he has been born. The Buddha-Dhamma, on the other hand, is the Path to Buddhahood.

There are many teachings and many formulations of that Path, but none of them are of any use unless we are prepared to practise them. You can't be a Buddhist and not practise the Dhamma: it's a contradiction in terms. If you do that then you are only calling yourself a Buddhist; you are not a Buddhist in any real sense.

There is no place for blind faith in Buddhism, either. Faith in the Buddha and the Dhamma arises as we practise, and as we experience the delight and happiness of changing. When we know for ourselves that it is possible to make progress on the Path, then we feel a tremendous gratitude for the Three Jewels, and a wonderful joy. That is the real meaning of faith for us.

If we want to practise the Buddha's teachings then, naturally, we will have to learn about a few of them. But our learning should never be just book learning. It is not enough to fill our heads with ideas. We must back up our study with thought and reflection, and balance it with a determination to put it into practice. If we work with the Dhamma in this way, we will find that it helps us overcome our old attitudes and old habits.

The Dhamma is effective. If we practise just a few of the teachings, watching our progress and taking the necessary steps when we encounter difficulties, then, without doubt, we will find ourselves changing for the better. Then, as we change, and as the people around us change—assuming that they are practising too—we will gradually find that our whole locality is becoming a different place. People will have more self-respect, more energy, and more resolve to make a better life for themselves. People will be able to work together, able to show more courage in the face of opposition. And there will be more vision as to how things could be better.

The *Sangha* is the community of all the Buddha's followers. It does not just mean the *bhikkhus*, or 'monks'. The Sangha consists of all those who are trying to follow the Buddha's Path. They help each other, encourage each other, give each other advice, and work together to make a better world. They try to act as if they are brothers and sisters, because, in a way, that is what they really are: they have the Buddha as a father and the Dhamma as a mother. Those who know more about the Dhamma, who have already gone a little way along the path, are like elder brothers and sisters. They should not forget the younger ones; it is their job to try and help them in any way they can.

These are the Three Jewels. Anyone who accepts them as guiding principles in their life, and who then tries to practise them, is a Buddhist. It doesn't matter whether you are old or young, male or female, educated or uneducated. It doesn't matter if you can't read or write. The Buddha and his main disciples were all 'illiterate'; none of them could read or write. But if you really Go for Refuge to the Three Jewels, and do whatever you can to make them part of your life, then you will be Buddhists, and in time you will experience the benefits of the Buddha's teaching. . . .

It was now the hottest time of day, and the tiny canopy that reached out from the stage offered no shade at all to most of the audience. Luckily, the trees provided at least a few dark pools of shadow. What with our early start, the journey, and the big lunch, I was beginning to feel drowsy.

I took a look around. No one else seemed to be at all worried by the heat. After all, for these people, this was a very special occasion. On some of their faces I could see a glow of deep contentment—of fulfilment. Connections were being made. Words and phrases that I had heard so many times before were bearing these people into the heart of a myth that had accompanied them throughout their lives, a myth that linked each of their personal worlds with that of their fabled leader. Sangharakshita continued. . . .

It is 'Going for Refuge' that makes one a Buddhist, so it is the recitation of the Three Refuges which provides the core to the *Diksha*, or conversion ceremony. But that ceremony has another important section: the recitation of the *Pancha-sila*, when we undertake to observe five moral precepts.

Nobody becomes a Buddhist to please a god. In becoming Buddhists, we have decided to live truly human lives, and to reach towards the highest possibilities of human existence. Our lives must therefore *become* truly human lives. This is the real starting point. This is why Doctor Ambedkar attached so much importance to morality, and why morality has such an important place in Buddhism. A human being, in the fullest sense of the word, is someone who is aware of his or her actions, aware of their effects—on themselves and on others—and who is prepared to take responsibility for those actions.

The five precepts can help us with this. If we can learn to look at ourselves and at our actions in the light of these precepts, we will be able to see whether we are living in a way which makes further development possible.

With the first precept, we undertake not to harm any living beings. We try to recognize that all living beings have feelings just as we do; they do not want to be hurt any more than we do. Nobody wants to suffer. If we have any imagination or awareness at all we will know this in our hearts. Of course, the precept goes further than this: to really practise it, we must also try to develop feelings of love and friendliness, so that kind thoughts and deeds will flow from us naturally.

Next, we undertake not to take anything that has not been freely given to us. This means that we do not cheat, we do not give false weight, we do not try to force or manipulate people into parting with things they don't want to part with. Instead, we try to develop a spirit of generosity, and try to practise giving whenever we can. We may not be able to give money or material goods, but there are all kinds of other things we can give. We can give our time, our advice, our skills, and we can give our friendship. The important thing is to try, to do whatever we can, when we can.

Then we undertake to avoid 'sexual misconduct'. In traditional terms this is taken to mean avoiding adultery, rape, and abduction. But what the precept is really saying is that we should practise contentment. If you are single, then you should aim to be content with the single state, and if you are married then you should work to be content in your marriage. It is no good running off to someone else when your husband or wife starts to get a bit old or ugly. You must try to build up a strong, friendly relationship, one that goes beyond habit and instinct.

Then we undertake to abstain from false speech. Maybe we very rarely harm others with our actions. We may never steal, or commit adultery, but our speech so often lets us down. We probably speak more than we do anything else, and it is very easy to slip. Our speech should therefore express what is best in us, what is most real, what is most loving, what is most conscious.

Finally, we undertake to avoid all drugs and intoxicants. Our higher development consists very largely in the development of our minds. It's about seeing things more clearly, becoming more awake, more alert. So if we keep clouding our minds with liquor, then no Buddhist life—no real human life—will be possible.

When a man gets drunk he loses his mindfulness. He may start beating his wife, throwing his food about, or falling down in the road. He might start fighting with another man. He may even stab him! How can one practise the Dhamma if one behaves like that?

Ripples of laughter ran around the field. Leather-skinned field workers nudged each other, winked and shook their heads. A few looked down at the grass while their friends slapped them on the back. In rural India there was no such thing as social drinking. If a man drank, then he invariably got drunk—often with the help of coarse, occasionally lethal, distillations of sugar-cane juice. Everyone there was used to seeing drunkenness, and its often disastrous effects.

They continued to nod vigorously and to murmur among themselves as Sangharakshita reminded them of Ambedkar's attacks on old Hindu habits: dowry marriage, the worship of Hindu gods, and animal sacrifice. Even if none of these practices were completely dead here, the audience seemed happy to hear his words, and even appreciated his reminders. From his place on the stage, Mr Kamblay looked fierce.

Bringing his talk to an end, Sangharakshita reminded his audience that they were free to practise the Refuges and Precepts or not, just as they chose. But if they did practise them, he said, they would become 'one hundred percent Buddhists'. They would become happier because they would have more energy and more clarity; they would gain dignity, for themselves and for their community; and they would take charge of their own destiny. 'This is what Dr Babasaheb Ambedkar wanted for you. If you work together you will be able to build the kind of society that he dreamed of.'

* * *

Ambedkar took the *Dhamma Diksha* at a huge rally in Nagpur, on 14 October 1956. About half a million people were there to watch him as he stood on the stage, beneath a mighty replica of the great stupa at Sanchi, taking the Refuges and Precepts from U Chandramani. Then, turning to face his followers, he himself led them through the same recitation.

'This conversion has given me enormous satisfaction and pleasure unimaginable. I feel as if I have been liberated from Hell,' he said immediately afterwards, adding that his one regret was that he had not taken the step earlier. He really believed that his day's work marked the dawn of a new age for his people: 'We shall go ahead undauntedly on the path we have chosen. We have found a new way to life and we shall follow it. This path leads to progress.'

The former Mahars were reclaiming their freedom and self-respect. From now on they would live as human beings, and expect to be treated as such. If they could only hold fast to this new strength and purpose, Ambedkar was convinced that, even without his help, they would make progress on the social, economic, and political fronts. They would be able to look after themselves.

As Ambedkar well knew, the mass conversion marked the revival of Buddhism in India. The 'Wheel of the Dhamma' was turning again. The stage was set for a cultural and spiritual renaissance of tremendous scope. Perhaps out of this renaissance would come all the vision, idealism, and understanding needed to launch India into a new age.

Despite the political set-backs, Ambedkar's career had reached its climax. He had started out as a social reformer, shifted when necessary into the political arena, and now—without rejecting his social or political goals—he was making a 'transcendental leap' into the dimension of spiritual reform, setting in motion a process which would deal with the evils of oppression, exploitation, and persecution at their root: in the human mind and spirit. His conversion to Buddhism was a cry from the heart—to the heart, a communication from one human being to his fellows, in which he was asking them to become better people, live on better terms with one another, and provide an example that no one could ignore.

It was never Ambedkar's intention to restrict the conversion movement to his own Mahar sub-caste. He had always hoped that the other Untouchable castes would come forward and take this step. Then, perhaps, the Caste-Hindus, shamed by the Untouchables' flight, would redouble their efforts to reform society, not just with laws and words, but with deeds as well. He even hoped that some of them would embrace Buddhism too. He envisaged a kind of 'Dhamma Revolution', a radical transformation of Indian society, based upon individual effort and collective understanding.

It was an awesomely ambitious programme. Quite apart from the logistics involved in convincing the other sub-castes and organizing their mass conversion rallies, how could so many individuals be persuaded and helped to put the Dhamma into practice? There were hardly any Buddhist teachers at work on Indian soil; he had not even seen much evidence of them elsewhere!

The leaders of other Scheduled Castes were hesitant, even sceptical. There had been a considerable improvement in their lot, largely due to Ambedkar's political efforts; the conversions would be unpopular with the Caste-Hindus. . . . Perhaps it would be better not to rock the boat. The Government, as if to fan the flames of doubt, announced that anyone converting to Buddhism would sacrifice their right to the reserved places in colleges and government service that Ambedkar had won as Labour Minister. . . . And yet, as Ambedkar understood it, Buddhism offered the precise path to the revolution he so desired. He was determined to see his task through.

But then, just six weeks after his conversion, he died. He died before he had managed to persuade more than a handful of non-Mahar communities to convert, and before he had been able to win any Government sympathy for the new Buddhists. He had not even finished work on *The Buddha and His Dhamma*. Suddenly, his followers were left leaderless, rudderless, and with little understanding of the step they had so recently taken.

Sangharakshita had just arrived in Nagpur when the news of Ambedkar's death came through. A meeting was hastily arranged for that night.

Thousands of people had dropped everything and crammed themselves into trains bound for Bombay to witness the cremation. But even so, several hundred thousand more gathered at the park where the meeting was to take place. They came from all over Nagpur and from nearby towns and villages; they came bearing flaming torches, and they came in complete silence.

Dharmarakshita—our friend at the bus stop—was in that crowd. Like everyone else, he was hoping to be told that there had been a mistake; nobody could believe that Ambedkar was really dead. It was a scene of unmitigated despair and utter dejection. One by one, the speakers climbed up onto the seat of a rickshaw—there had been no time to build a stage—and took the microphone. But none of them managed to say a word before bursting into tears. Twenty, thirty speakers passed by in this way. It was terrible; the atmosphere was growing more despondent by the minute.

Then Dharmarakshita saw an English monk mount the platform. It was Sangharakshita. He didn't say much; but he could at least speak, and he offered some much-needed encouragement. He talked mainly about Buddhism, telling his stunned listeners that their duty to Ambedkar was now to try to understand and practise Buddhism.

'Doctor Ambedkar is not dead,' he said, 'He lives on and will live on in the hearts of his followers. His work will not come to an end. It will be carried on by each one of you.'

Our own meeting in Panchgani was now almost over. Lokamitra had given his short talk about the books we'd brought along, and asked people to think about coming on a Buddhist 'retreat' where they would get a real taste of Dhamma practice. The *Dhammapalam Gatha*, a string of verses from the *Dhammapada*, had been chanted. Now, a small crowd had formed around the bookshop, while another pressed in on Sangharakshita who was chatting and signing autographs. Pop-songs split the air again; the lanes around the huts and hovels started to fill as people returned home; a few bucket-stoves exhaled plumes of blue wood smoke.

I wondered what we had achieved. How many of these people would remember Sangharakshita's talk in twenty years time—as some of today's audience remembered his last visit to Panchgani, twenty years before? Perhaps a spark had been ignited in a few minds; perhaps that was all we could hope for. And perhaps that was enough. In a small locality like this, even a couple of determined people could have a significant effect.

But surely, just by being there we had added something to the community's stock of self-respect. The men had been clean, smart, and proud for a day; the women had worn colour and even jewels. Not long ago they had been forbidden these things. Such statements still needed to be made.

Above all, we had reminded them of Dr Ambedkar. A few children would be scolded back to their studies now, with exhortations to be like him, and try to improve themselves as he had. A lot of people would remember, for just a little longer, that his last gift to them, the one in which he had invested so much hope, had been the gift of the Dhamma. Who was to say what would come of that?

For a few hours we had been taking part in history. Whether it was history-past or the beginnings of history-future I couldn't tell. That would be up to our audience. It would depend on how many of them could preserve and cultivate the seed that Doctor Bhimrao Ramji Ambedkar—MA, Ph.D, Bar-at-Law, social reformer, cabinet minister, and tireless fighter for freedom—had planted in their hearts.

nine

It's a funny thing, but I've no idea how we got from Panchgani to Mahad. Perhaps some form of benign amnesia has erased all trace of a journey so frightful that it were best forgotten. Suffice it to say that by late morning on 25 December we had arrived in Mahad, and were now peering over the calm expanse of the Chowdar Tank, wilting slightly in the awful, humid heat of a town four-and-a-half-thousand feet lower than Panchgani.

We had come to celebrate an anniversary, not of a birth but of a cremation. For it was in Mahad, on 25 December 1927, that Ambedkar burned a copy of the *Manusmriti*. Our first port of call, however, was the tank into whose forbidden waters he had led his followers just nine months earlier.

It was a far larger stretch of water than I had expected, almost big enough to be mistaken for a lake, except that its sheer stone walls and steps indicated it was man-made. Sited in an attractive spot, there were good views of the distant ghats from its banks. Some trees provided shade, and a few pleasant dwellings graced the far shore. Where we stood, however, just beside a broad sweep of steps leading down into the water, we were surrounded by the squalid huts of a poor Brahmin community.

To my untrained eye, the people who lived here looked no different from hutment dwellers anywhere else. But whatever their present misfortune, they, and their ancestors through the centuries, had been able to regard themselves as 'twice-born', engendered from the head of God. They had never been slaves; they had always been free at least to try to improve their fortunes. And they had always enjoyed the use of the tank.

A sign marked the spot where Ambedkar and his followers took their symbolic bath. But there was no sign to indicate where the conference stage a little way off had been smashed to pieces, nor where several of Ambedkar's followers were attacked by outraged locals with sticks. Even when some of the delegates ran in terror from the storm, they were assaulted, beaten, and raped by Caste-Hindus when they got home to their villages. A few cows lumbered about, grazing on the sparse scrub beside the tank, bearing some kind of testimony to the rites of purification that had been used to purge the tank of pollution.

I should admit that I was still finding it hard to come to terms with the whole business of caste. As an Englishman, I was familiar with the dynamics of class, class oppression, and class conflict. But this was something else altogether, something far more mysterious and dark. It took some imagination to register that Caste-Hindus had literally refused to acknowledge the Untouchables as human beings. In the old days, a Caste-Hindu could kill an Untouchable without shame and without having to pay more than a nominal sum in 'compensation' to the victim's family.

My friends were at pains to insist that, in those old days, no one had seen the system as wrong or unjust. On the contrary, a Caste-Hindu, coming upon an Untouchable dying of thirst, would be acting more in line with his 'Dharma' by keeping a wide berth and avoiding the risk of pollution, than he would by approaching him with a glass of water. Inter-caste sexual intercourse, however—particularly under the aspects of rape and prostitution—was awarded a sort of moral neutrality; it was quite common for the wealthy to demand the services of their menials' wives, or to keep low-caste prostitutes at their beck and call.

For all its mystery and absurdity, the system survived, and survived quite simply because everyone believed in it. Superstition and superstitious dread kept the scheme intact and smoothly functioning. Caste-Hindus and Untouchables alike believed that God had ordered the world in this way. It was in the holy books, and the holy books were not open to criticism or question.

Ambedkar was different. He was free because he had no dread. He had a healthy respect for sticks, knives, and fists—though he could occasionally display an admirable degree of physical courage—but if he really feared anything it was ignorance and the fruits of ignorance. He had no fear of the scriptures, no dread of the gods represented in their pages, and certainly no sense of inferiority with regard to the Caste-Hindus. Far from being divinely appointed authority figures, they were in his view as ignorant and misguided as everyone else.

He had been brought up in a devout Hindu home with its gods and daily prayer recitations. But his studies had revealed that the concept of caste duty was an abominable aberration grafted onto the original body of Hinduism, above all by the 'daredevil' who wrote the *Manusmriti*. Working from earlier, 'purer' sources, he could find no evidence to suggest that the iniquities of the caste system had anything to do with original Hindu belief. The caste system was not the work of God, but of man—and man in his most cynical, heartless aspect at that.

A number of theories have been developed to explain the origins of the caste system. There is the mythic theory which I had learned at school, which says that God gave birth to the four castes from different parts of his body. The Brahmins issued from his head, the Kshatriyas from his shoulders, the Vaishyas from his stomach, and the Shudras from his feet. The Untouchables, or *Ati-Shudras*, have no place in this system at all. They are outside caste altogether or, perhaps, had still to be 'invented' when this account was devised.

A more scientific theory suggests that some kind of class system, which came into being along with the development of specialization and division of labour, became entangled with notions of status and respectability more firmly than elsewhere, ultimately becoming completely rigid and deterministic. Yet another theory suggests that the Aryan invaders from the north pressed the conquered aboriginals into defined occupational slots and thus into a form of self-perpetuating slavery. A similar hypothesis suggests that the Untouchables were 'broken men', the scattered remnants of tribes that had been fragmented by wars. With no home territories of their own, they were forced to live on the fringes of other tribal communities, earning their keep by doing whatever was asked of them. Another, related, theory, and one which Ambedkar championed, is that the Untouchables are the remnants of India's former Buddhist communities.

As a religious doctrine, the caste system was initially proclaimed as an ideal principle, a divine model for human society, according to which people perform the tasks for which they are best suited, and through which they can find fulfilment. Later scriptures were to bring this ideal principle down to earth.

In the *Bhagavad Gita* the practice of caste duty is given a position of supreme moral pre-eminence. There, the warrior Arjuna, depressed by the prospect of a bloody battle which will bring suffering to so many people—including his friends and relatives on the opposing side—finds himself talking to the Lord Krishna. Krishna tells him in no uncertain terms that he will be closer to God by performing his Dharma, and fighting well, than by holding back out of compassion. The *Bhagavad Gita* is a metaphysical, allegorical work. Even so, Ambedkar believed that it prepared the ground for the more worldly vision of caste duty that was to come.

It was the *Manusmriti* which finally gave institutional religious sanction to the caste system. Through the medium of this work—or collection of works—the caste system became a part of the psyche, shrouded by an aura of protective divinity. Once Manu had done his work it was no longer possible to read the scriptures simply as myths and allegories. Now the ideal patterns of social organization, hinted at in earlier works, became a fixed, rigid system. Marriage between members of different castes and sub-castes was outlawed, the remarriage of widows was forbidden while child marriage was condoned, even encouraged, since it offered a guarantee against promiscuity and, therefore, the problematic social consequences of accidental inter-caste pregnancy. And in the *Manusmriti* the practice of Untouchability was fully proclaimed.

An Untouchable was to be a pariah with minimal rights and plenty of duties. His status was beyond question and beyond redemption; he was to be denied any access to the means of material betterment through education, or spiritual self-improvement through religion. An Untouchable caught in the act of chanting the sacred texts could have his tongue cut in two, and one caught overhearing such chants could have molten tin poured into his ears. It was with the *Manusmriti* that the real enslavement began. Through its edicts, free-will was removed even from the simplest affairs of daily life.

This is why Ambedkar burned the book. The authority had to be challenged, even humbled, the confidence trick exposed. Unless the sickness could be treated at its source, no number of 'inter-caste dinners', no amount of liberalism or even legislation, would have any effect. The disease was in people's minds, in their unquestioning allegiance to divine will as represented in the pages of a book. Ambedkar hoped to shock people—Caste-Hindus and Untouchables alike—into a shift of vision, away from the cramped, life-denying security of caste, to the life-affirming challenges of Liberty, Equality, and Fraternity. His book-burning was much more than stage-craft and propaganda: it was, in the deepest sense, a blow for freedom.

Soon after lunch our party arrived at the site of the burning, another semi-rural spot on the edge of town. The stage was not quite ready, and a team of *pandal-wallahs* scurried about fixing lengths of bright red cloth to its sides. They had erected it just beside a small ornamental garden, out of which rose an imposing, needle-like column and a bust of Dr Ambedkar, itself mounted on a tall plinth.

The day was hot and sultry, but there was work to be done. The moment we arrived, Purna rushed to the stage to set up his recording equipment, while I helped Bodhisen Jardow and Professor Kamblay, both *Sahayaks* from Poona, to arrange the bookstall.

Bodhisen was in charge. He was a strong, dark, curly haired man in his early thirties, an 'office boy' in a Bombay factory. I had never met anyone quite like him before, and wondered whether I ever would again, for he was not only prodigiously energetic and competent, but almost miraculously cheerful. He hardly spoke a word of English, but that was enough to express exactly how he seemed to feel about everything. 'Yes!' he would boom to anything anyone said or asked him to do. No matter how much effort was involved, no matter what time it was, Bodhisen would do whatever was needed, and would never rest until he had completed his assignment to the last detail.

He came from Worli, the same shabby tenement area where

Ambedkar had set up home after his disheartening spell in Baroda. Determined to devote his life to Buddhist activities, Bodhisen had recently moved to Poona and had joined the community at Ambedkar Society to spend a few months in close contact with TBMSG. When I first arrived he was still adjusting to the cooler Poona climate. While I lay gasping in the heat, he sat huddled in corners, shivering in a nest of blankets. After a few days he developed chapped lips.

Today, it was all I could do to stay upright in the afternoon sun, but he was now in his element in the lowland heat, and launched an all-out attack on the bookstall. There were so many books! How could so many books exist? How could anyone imagine that we were going to sell even a tenth of them? Yet Bodhisen rushed hither and thither, humping sacks of the things now here, now there, first establishing his stall under a tree near the entrance to the garden, then re-establishing it closer to the stage. Finally, he decided to split the books, and set up two separate stalls.

The bright red awning flopped lethargically in the breeze, offering pitifully little shade, hardly enough to cover half the audience, which was now beginning to thicken. There again were the smart, fresh whites, and the reds, greens, and golds of best saris. But today we had an impressive array of local organizers and minor VIPs as well. Resplendent in their freshly pressed 'suitings', they had arranged their chairs in two rows at the back of the stage.

When he arrived, Sangharakshita was escorted into the flower garden and asked to garland the bust of Dr Ambedkar. This posed something of a problem, however, since the bust stood twelve feet above the ground. After a hasty conference, a primitive ladder was procured, and a keen young man, taking the garland from Sangharakshita's hands, clambered up the flimsy steps to place it round the Doctor's neck. Then followed a pause while I took the obligatory group photographs, first with my own camera, then with a succession of pocket Instamatics and 'Agfa Clicks' passed across by my subjects.

The hot day, the bright awning, our little picture-taking party—all set in this pleasant green landscape—gave the event the air of a summer fête in a sleepy, country village. It was hard to believe we were there to commemorate an event that had rocked India.

Perhaps I would have found it hard to appreciate the significance of Ambedkar's act under any circumstances, had it not reminded me of some events which took place in England a few years earlier.

In 1978, a celebrated English moral crusader, Mary Whitehouse, brought a successful prosecution against the magazine *Gay News*. She alleged that a poem included in one issue contravened the blasphemy laws, and, to the surprise of a good many people who thought those laws a dead letter, her objection was sustained. The magazine's editor was given a suspended prison sentence; he and the publisher were fined.

Like many non-Christians in England, Sangharakshita deplored this turn of events, and wrote an essay expressive of his concern that such an archaic set of laws could still have effect in our secular, pluralistic times. The essay's deeper purpose, however, was to explore the links between theistic belief and the kind of authoritarianism which not only made an offence like 'blasphemy' possible, but which led to its being taken so seriously.

Trying to establish a Buddhist movement in England, Sangharakshita had naturally found himself working with people who no longer considered themselves to be Christians. Most of them had turned to Buddhism after coming to the conclusion that God and the Christian faith had no value or meaning in their lives. But there was a problem. For all their professed dedication, few of them seemed free to become Buddhists in more than an intellectual or sentimental sense. Somehow or other they seemed to remain enmeshed in a net of subtle, limiting attitudes and assumptions; they were not free to fly beyond the Christian, God-dominated outlook of their early religious conditioning into the very different realm of Buddhist spiritual vision. It was clearly not enough to reject Christianity with the intellect alone. The 'damage' went too deep; further steps were needed to loosen the hold that the authoritarian element in Christianity still exerted in their depths.

The negative effects of Christian conditioning seemed to include such syndromes as sexual guilt, a fear of one's own positive aggression, numerous varieties of neurotic self-denial and self-depreciation, and— underlying everything—a habitual intuition that some invisible, crushing force hovered over one, watching and judging. When that force was no longer being interpreted 'directly' as God, then it could still be experienced, indirectly, via psychological projections onto parents, teachers, employers, and even non-Christian gurus.

The pattern seemed to go very deep indeed, even among those who, so far as they could recall, had received little or no direct Christian indoctrination at any stage in their lives. To have been born in a Christian country and to have grown up in a Christian culture seemed enough. The lukewarm, institutional, and heirarchical nature of British Buddhism—as Sangharakshita had found it—provided ample evidence of this syndrome. He began to see that those who wished to break away from Christianity and God in order to pursue a new, God-less path of development, would have to deal with this backlog of conditioning; otherwise, their emotional and psychological lives would not be able to keep pace with their intellectual development—and Buddhism in the West would remain an exotic, but purely intellectual, pastime.

The antidote Sangharakshita proposed was what he called 'therapeutic blasphemy', the practice of humbling, and thus undermining, the object of one's irrational fears and illusions by subjecting them to ridicule.

Although he made it clear that this was an essentially private matter—he had no intention of giving offence to sincere Christians—he concluded his essay with some modest proposals regarding the further secularization of the British state. He called for the final disestablishment of the Church, the suspension of compulsory Christian worship in state-run schools, the dropping of all references to the deity in the national anthem, and the complete abolition of the blasphemy law.

When it was published, *Buddhism and Blasphemy* had an immediate effect on Sangharakshita's movement. There were those who already suspected that their Christian conditioning was confusing their efforts to practise Buddhism. Sangharakshita's straightforward remedy seemed worth a try.

The result was a general 'wave' of blasphemy. *Shabda*, a monthly newsletter circulating exclusively among Order members, erupted in a rash of blasphemous articles, poems, and cartoons. Rumours of bible-burnings on women's retreats started to circulate; people lulled themselves to sleep cursing the deity. . . .

It was all a bit of a craze at first, and some of the exploits seemed rather childish; there were even a few regrettable excesses. But then it began to have an effect.

The ex-Catholics were the first to report benefits, but soon all kinds of people, right down to the humdrum 'C of E by birth, never seen the inside of a church except for weddings and funerals' were discovering that, in a variety of ways, they could feel themselves reclaiming an initiative in their lives—one which they had perhaps never even been consciously aware of losing. They felt free, not just of God, but of an entire substructure of absolutes and inhibitions that had stultified and limited their lives hitherto.

Even some of those who found the whole business ridiculous, and felt no need to join in, if persuaded to 'give it a try', soon had their own stories to tell. Some discovered that their resistance to the practice was not as reasonable as they had imagined. Under the impact of a few casual gestures in the direction of blasphemy, they had watched their resistance define itself into the embarrassing spectre of superstitious dread. They had believed themselves to be quite beyond the reach of

Christian guilt or anxiety, confident that no God played any part in their lives. But there 'He' was, still powerful enough to put fear into their minds over a few mental incantations! The conditioning was far deeper and more all-pervading than many of us had suspected.

As the months went by, a tremendous amount of fresh energy and creativity was liberated. Suddenly we were walking—some of us for the first time—beneath an empty sky. Attitudes to the spiritual life itself changed as people purged themselves of the theistic assumptions and expectations they had brought to it. There was less hankering after special experiences, less grasping pursuit of elusive mystical states. We were moving closer to a distinctly 'Buddhistic' approach to the spiritual life, seeing that it was not so much a life which led up to a final, ecstatic, culminating experience, but was actually life itself, lived as consciously as possible and on as high a level as possible. The 'spiritual' was no longer something *outside* ourselves, to be courted, appeased, or simply awaited: it was something to be *lived*, something to be *done*.

In India, the consequences of the superstitious beliefs which encrusted Hinduism made our Western problems of anxiety, neurosis, and sexual guilt seem like luxuries. It would take more than a little profanity to dismantle those awful engines. Yet Ambedkar's act of blasphemy played its part, jolting the Untouchables from their unquestioning acceptance of divine decree, and giving them a taste of freedom. It also tested the commitment of his Caste-Hindu supporters. By recoiling from his act they showed their unreadiness—or unwillingness—to bring their emotional attitudes into line with their intellectual notions.

When Ambedkar was about to embrace Buddhism, he devised twenty-two vows—which he recited after taking the Refuges and Precepts. While most of these were concerned with communicating a positive vision of the Buddhist path, the first eight comprised a detailed rejection of the central Hindu gods and ritual practices. He knew how deep those old views went, and how insidiously they wove their spell. He devised this catechism in the hope that his followers would repeat it at all their meetings, just as they would repeat the Refuges and Precepts. Some Buddhist commentators have criticized this addition; but perhaps they failed to understand how much negative conditioning the new Buddhists had to overcome, and how difficult it would be to become 'one hundred percent Buddhists'. Buddhism proclaims that anyone who is prepared to make the effort can become a Buddha and outshine even the gods; but how could the converts accept that challenge in good faith unless they could eradicate a mental conditioning that made them see themselves as worthless and impure?

After the mass conversion rallies, many of the new Buddhists rushed home and threw their old god-images into fires and rivers. Professor Kamblay, the other man on our bookstall, was a child at the time. He could remember patrolling the houses, reporting to the elders about any gods still in residence. In those days too there was an element of groupish excitement about it all. There were doubtless a few excesses too. But every challenge to the dark forces that had restrained them for so long took the ex-Untouchables a step closer to freedom and self-respect. There was a wonderful exhilaration in the air, a genuine spirit of emancipation. Even if they were still dressed in rags and living in hovels on the fringes of the community, they were no longer doomed by fate, or by the gods, to remain there.

They knew they would be attacked for getting above themselves. Many were; such things were still happening thirty years later. But now, in their own hearts, they felt free. The other manifestations of freedom would follow—if only they could keep this new spirit alive.

* * *

At six o'clock the next morning we were at a bus station again, this time waiting for the bus back to Poona. It arrived half an hour late and, once again, half full—despite the fact that this was the route's starting point. It turned out that the conductor had fixed things so that he could pick up a large party of businessmen before appearing at the station.

There was the usual outcry, but the conductor was adamant: no one was going to tell him how to run his bus. Then Professor Kamblay got to work. A bright, cheerful, powerfully built man in his mid-thirties, he climbed aboard, forcing the conductor to retreat a little. At first he put questions and argued in a friendly, reasonable way. But when the conductor started shouting and insulting him, he met fire with fire. He took numbers, called for the inspector, stayed with the bus as it lurched across the yard, and rode with it as it thundered back in reverse. In the end he won his case, and the supernumeries were ordered to take their places at the back of the queue.

Professor Kamblay descended the bus's steps to a scene of general rejoicing. Strangers took him by the hand, slapped him on the back and no doubt told him that their homes were his. It had been an impressive display by any standards. It was particularly impressive for a man who had grown up in a village where the Caste-Hindus defecated on the steps of the Untouchables' well and threw the carcasses of dead buffaloes down it to keep the low-born in their place. But, then again, it was impressive that he had managed to get himself a post as a teacher of

physics at a government college. Things need not have turned out that way, and probably never would have done had Dr Ambedkar not set an example, and given him the self-respect and faith to follow it.

A few days later we were in Worli, where Sangharakshita was to address several thousand tenement-dwellers. This was Bodhisen's home patch, and he and his friends put everything they had into the organization. Their most spectacular feat was to get every one of the four-storey tenement blocks surrounding the *maidan* quite literally coated with fairy lights. As darkness fell on that bleak, grim world, the lights came on, transporting us to paradise; and for the rest of the evening we stayed there.

Sangharakshita's theme was a parable from the *White Lotus Sutra*. In a story reminiscent of the Christian parable of the good Samaritan, a rich man comes upon a poor man in need of food and help. The two of them spend an evening together, during which the rich man does all he can to assist his companion. At length, sated with food and drink, the pauper falls asleep. The time comes for the benefactor to move on, but before doing so he plants a fabulous jewel in the lining of the poor man's coat.

Some years later the two meet again. The rich man is surprised to find that the other is still poor, still in his old tattered clothes.

'But did you not find that jewel I placed in your coat?'

The pauper confesses that he has not, whereupon his benefactor removes it, and hands it to him, saying, 'Now go and redeem this jewel for money, food, and everything you desire. Live in comfort and happiness from now on.'

Any real progress in the spiritual life comes slowly, gradually, and often only after a lot of effort. It is hard to envisage what we can truly become, and it can be harder still to sustain that vision. But there are those priceless moments when we wake up to the fact that we have inestimable riches buried within us. Such moments do not just make all the exertion worthwhile: they make it possible. Sometimes the intimations arise spontaneously from our own depths; at other times we may need to be reminded of them by a friend or guide.

We still have to grasp our visions, and learn to take their message seriously. We also have to find a way of reaching into ourselves to recover the treasure. Finally, we have to devise the alchemy whereby that treasure will become the stuff of a better, richer life. None of this is easy; it is a unique challenge. But what better purpose can life hold?

In Mahad, Ambedkar held aloft the jewel of fearlessness and self-respect that he had discovered in himself. As he did so, he reached into the coats of his followers and revealed millions more. The sparkling lights which illuminated a slum district in Bombay that night proved that, even if the jewels had still to be redeemed, at least they had not been forgotten.

t e n

The *chai* stall was rather like a cave made of stone, corrugated iron, and sack-cloth. Just inside, shrouded in darkness, the proprietor tended a vat of smoking oil where balls of onion bhaji foamed themselves brown. Behind, almost buried in the gloom, farmers and goatherds sipped tea from saucers. Outside, the day was brilliantly sunny and pleasantly hot. Purna and I sat with Buddhapriya on a low wall, throwing chunks of bhaji to a threadbare local dog. It was a blissful way to recover from our journey on the crowded 'local' from Poona.

The crowd had been a happy one at least; our carriage had been full of people bound for the retreat, 'our boys', as Bodhisen called them. As the carriage had filled, and filled—until we were squeezed into an immovable huddle—the air had crackled with 'Jai Bhims' as 'our boys' came aboard.

Now the train had gone, leaving us in the middle of a wide valley, bounded on both sides by lines of ghats. Some way off, the yellow-grey masses of rock hovered insubstantially in the haze; between them lay dry, cracked fields of rice and wheat-stubble, dotted here and there with the black shapes of wandering buffaloes, and the smaller white blobs which were their herdsmen. A narrow road led away from the café, heading straight through the fields to meet the Bombay-Poona highway at the extreme edge of the valley floor. High up on the ghats' summits stood the hard, black walls of Shivaji's ruined forts. Beneath them, about half-way up, could just be seen a few dark, horizontal gashes. These were natural caves, some of which had been fashioned into temples, complete with ornamented entrance-ways, delicately carved columns, and polished stupas: the Buddhist caves of Karla and Bhaja.

Most of our contingent had set off, and were now negotiating the rough pathways across the fields to the retreat site. Purna and I lingered, savouring our tea, waiting to see whether Buddhapriya really was going to find a bullock cart to take the heavier pieces of equipment—and us—to our destination. I watched as the last stragglers disappeared into the scrub.

'Do they know where they're going?'

Purna chuckled. 'No. I don't think it's that way at all. We have to follow this road; it's somewhere way down there. Don't worry, though, they'll find the place sooner or later. We may have to start late, but that's normal.'

Buddhapriya laughed him good-naturedly to scorn, and assured me that of course they were on the right track. Discreetly, not wanting to offend him, Purna indicated that, when the time came, we would leave Buddhapriya to it, and go the right way ourselves.

I should have had more faith in Buddhapriya. He had lived around here for much of his life. He knew every man, woman, child, chicken, and goat within a ten-mile radius. Until recently, he had been headmaster of a local school, but had taken early retirement—at the age of fifty-three—in order to work full-time for TBMSG. Everyone seemed to fall in love with him at their first sight of his warm, vulnerable features—invariably softened by a mist of grey stubble. Strange as it always seemed to me, I was the only person around to notice how remarkably he resembled Frank Sinatra—though I could not vouch for his voice.

I knew very little about his life, except that he had burst into tears when trying to give an account of it at a meeting of Order members in Poona. I did know that he had had five mothers—his father having been an enthusiastic marrier—and had himself been wed at the age of nine.

Knowing that I wanted to get some pictures of Indian schoolchildren, he had brought me here just a couple of days before, and led me into a village school as if he owned the place. Tiny little things in rags and less had shuddered in an ecstasy of excitement as the shutter clicked. He guided me through the narrow, dirt lanes of quiet, private villages, and brought me first to an exquisite lake, carpeted with pink lotuses, and then to the booming main *Chaitya* Hall of the Bhaja caves. After scrambling down the sides of the ghat, we had arrived in time for lunch at a wattle-and-daub hut on the plain. The lady of the house, Mrs Pawar, fed us rice and dal, and showed me a gilt-framed photograph of her recently departed husband. We sat on her flaking dung floor for an hour or so, eating and talking, while goats chewed at their tether ropes beside us.

'This lady is going to sell us her land', announced Buddhapriya, 'so that we can build a retreat centre. Today I must see a man—one inspector fellow—to give him certain documents.'

'How long will the negotiations take?' I asked.

'Already done! This is very last thing!'

'I'll believe that when I see it,' I jeered.

Buddhapriya found that hugely amusing, and held out a hand for me to slap.

Today he seemed to be having trouble locating a bullock cart. Since Purna was to lead the retreat, he suggested we leave Buddhapriya to his researches, and set off on foot.

I had not yet been to a retreat in India, and suspected that it would be rather different to anything I was familiar with. I had been warned that the food would be awful, the facilities crowded, and the participants active at alarmingly early hours of the morning. All the same, I was looking forward to it. By now we had held the programmes in Panchgani and Mahad, as well as five in Poona and three in Bombay. Very soon, we would be setting out on our tour of Marathwada: a 'Dhamma Revolution Roadshow', with non-stop travel and one-night-stands all the way. A few days of peace, quiet, and meditation, all in one place, would be a boon.

Over the years I had been on more retreats than I could remember: long ones, short ones, mixed retreats—for men and women, and retreats for men only; easy-going beginners' retreats, and intense meditation retreats, big retreats with eighty people or more, and solitary retreats entirely on my own.

In England, it was now possible to choose from a wide range of possibilities. Since the early days, retreats had been upgraded continuously, but the basic ingredients were always the same: a quiet, preferably rural, setting, a simple daily routine, the complete absence of newspapers, radios, and televisions, and a programme of meditation, Yoga, study groups, 'communication exercises', and devotional practices, mixed in a ratio according the specific aim of each retreat. Their purpose was to give people a chance to experience themselves more fully, and to work at their spiritual practice more deeply than normal circumstances allowed. The 'collective' experience of a retreat, however, was often quite remarkable, and participants would sometimes blink in wonder as, between them, they brought a kind of heaven into existence. Had the pleasures and lessons of these retreats had no reference to the world beyond, they would perhaps have been effete, escapist affairs. But people who signed up, thinking they were in for a tranquil rest-cure, usually found themselves plunging back into their lives refreshed, invigorated, brimming with insights—sometimes painfully won—into how their lives could be made better.

Realizing that they were not looking forward to the routines that awaited them 'outside', a few people had tried to incorporate some features of these retreats into their everyday lives. The result had been the communities and co-operatives which were now such an essential feature of the movement.

If, in the West, retreats turned armchair Buddhists into practising ones, here in India they helped people discover, at first hand, why Dr Ambedkar had guided them to Buddhism. In Maharashtra there was a small industry serving the purely cultural aspect of the Buddhist movement, but it did nothing for those who wanted to get to grips with Ambedkar's vision. Many of them knew that there must have been something significant about his conversion to Buddhism, but had no idea what that something was. So they picked up books on Buddhism and talked with the Burmese and Thai monks who were dotted around the place. But nothing seemed to make sense. One by one, a few had begun to realize that the only way to find out what their Babasaheb had had in mind would be to *practise* Buddhism for themselves. But how were they to do that? Until Lokamitra set up TBMSG there was almost nowhere to turn.

Some of the more adventurous had got themselves ordained as *shramaneras*, or 'novice monks', on a kind of one- or two-week 'package deal'. Buddhapriya, Vimalakirti, in fact several of the Order members, had been through that little routine. Buddhapriya almost laughed himself hoarse when I got him to talk about it:

'There was one bhikkhu. I would visit him to find out about the Dhamma. In the end he ordered me to become a *shramanera*. There was a special ceremony, and then, after that, he made me go to weddings and political meetings in my robes. I would sit up on the stage with him and chant a little, and then we got fed. So much food! I was in robes for just two weeks but I put on so much weight! All I learned about the Dhamma-life was eating!

'I was very angry with this bhikkhu. He did not even know any Dhamma himself; he had nothing to teach but eating.'

Some of the monks who conducted these token ordinations made a good living out of it, charging anything from twenty to thirty rupees a time for their services.

Then, out of the blue, Lokamitra had appeared on the scene, offering straightforward teachings, explaining the Refuges and Precepts—which had been little more than empty chants until then—teaching meditation, and explaining formulae like the 'Eightfold Path' and the 'Four Noble Truths' in plain, everyday language. He had organized retreats which offered a broad, balanced experience of spiritual practice, and had shown people how to take the benefits home with them. Suddenly, Buddhism was something that could be lived.

The retreat site was buried in trees just less than a mile from the tea shop. All in all, Purna and I must have walked about five, trekking down one achingly long road, then another, and then yet another. Undeterred, though discouraged by the failing light, Purna led on until, at last, we entered the congenial grounds of an out-of-season holiday camp where we were to spend the next three days. It was already bustling with all the life of a well-established retreat community. The others had been here an hour or more.

The camp consisted of a number of wooden bungalows and one main building which we would be using as a dining room-cum-meditation hall. It was surrounded on all sides by fields and trees; the land-bound waters of an evaporating river sparkled just a little way beyond the boundary. Snow-white cranes and buzzards circled and hovered gracefully in the sky above, silence reigned. For people who spent most of their lives in cramped one-room chawls and huts, the miracle had already begun.

Purna was to be our leader, and Lokamitra the organizer. Because Lokamitra was still on his way in Sangharakshita's taxi the others had been trying to sort things out as best they could, fitting themselves into bungalows that had been set aside for sleeping, getting fires going in the ovens, gathering flowers for the shrine, and unloading pots and pans from . . . Buddhapriya's bullock cart. In the kitchen, a giggling man in a torn khaki shirt and a heavily stained turban tended a colossal, clay-built range, eventually bringing forth a Brobdignagian pot of tea.

When he did arrive, Lokamitra hit the place like a tornado, checking the facilities and rearranging some of the arrangements made in his absence. Dormitories had still to be allocated, a good billet had to be established for Sangharakshita. From time to time this work would cease while he continued a running battle with the proprietors over the surcharge for 'mattress hire' they had just announced.

The rest of us dawdled in the dusk, drinking tea, chatting and arguing in happy groups. This was a real gathering of the clans with people from Poona, Bombay, and other areas of Maharashtra. There was also a small contingent from Ahmedabad, up in Gujerat. Its leader was Bakula, another friend of Sangharakshita's from the early days. He had been ordained along with Dharmarakshita on Sangharakshita's first return visit.

The Gujeratis stood in a huddle around Bippin Patel. Bippin's family came from Gujerat, but he had been born in Africa and educated in England. He had made contact with Buddhism at our movement's centre in Purley, Surrey, and, like me, was in India only for the duration of Sangharakshita's tour. He was tentatively thinking about working here as and when he became an Order member, and wanted to see how he would find things. I sidled up, intrigued to hear him using his long-forsaken mother tongue. To his obvious embarrassment he was floundering awfully, forming his sentences with painful deliberation, while his audience, touched by his efforts—if bewildered by the paradox he represented—fed him encouraging smiles and tense laughter.

Altogether, there were about sixty of us: a mixed bunch of Maharashtrans and Gujeratis, a handful of Englishmen, an Irishman, a Canadian, and a New Zealander; there were university lecturers, office clerks, and field labourers, old and young, men and—just a few—women.

Although this had been advertised as a 'mixed retreat', few men were willing to let their wives attend an event where there would be so many men—even if the vast majority of those men were married. Some husbands actually forbade their spouses from getting involved with TBMSG under any circumstances; they had no intention of giving them that kind of independence. Lokamitra told me that one woman came along to retreats quite regularly in the full knowledge that her husband would beat her when she returned home.

There were also the inevitable financial considerations. If a man disapproved of his wife's Buddhist activities he could simply cut off the money supply and put an end to her retreat outings. Many women, along with the poorer men, were therefore offered a considerable discount on retreat fees—which were already remarkably cheap: at the standard rate, one day on retreat cost just five rupees. Lokamitra was prepared to run these events at a loss, his only concern being that anyone wanting to come should be able to do so.

Eventually, everything was more or less ready. The retreat could begin. Purna now left his preparatory hideaway and appeared among us, tinkling a little brass bell, calling us to the first meditation session. From a hundred yards away came the sounds of a riotous dinner party; obviously we didn't have the camp quite to ourselves. But once we were inside the meditation hall, taking our places before the shrine, the outside world faded away, and almost immediately, almost effortlessly, we entered the retreat dimension.

Surrounded by candles and flowers, his right hand raised in a gesture of fearlessness, the Buddha gazed at us through a haze of incense smoke. To one side of the shrine sat Purna, with Vimalakirti beside him, translating his opening remarks.

This was to be a very special retreat, he said. Sangharakshita was here, and was going to conduct some ordinations. The programme would be balanced, but there would be an emphasis on meditation and silence. It was important that the ordinands should take this important step in the best possible conditions, and it would be up to all of us to help create those conditions.. . . . This retreat had been restricted to our more experienced friends, but all the same it was still a large one, and in a new setting; we would all have to be very mindful, very concentrated, to keep the retreat calm and clear. . . .

The retreatants followed his words attentively, though at the same time casting their eyes around the room, absorbing the scene, signalling their excitement to friends with smiles and gestures.

I had heard some remarkable tales about the lengths to which these people would go in order to maintain a daily meditation practice. Many were willing to rise at four in the morning to grab a brief hour of silence and stillness before the rest of their families were awake. One man I met, the elder in his house, had ordered every member of his eighteen-strong extended family—from the oldest granny to the tiniest tot—to learn meditation so that they could sit quietly with him in the mornings. Another had suggested to his son's fiancée's parents that they send the girl to a retreat, rather than pay a dowry. Now, having entered his household, she was his chief ally in the campaign for morning silence.

But most of them had simply learned to meditate under any conditions whatsoever.

Soon after arriving in India I spent a frustrating hour trying to meditate in a Bombay tenement, while the morning din of a neighbouring hutment colony battered the air around my head. It was a Hindu festival day, so the awful cacophony was overlaid with the coarse, monotonous drone of a *bhajan*. For me, the entire exercise was a farce; I spent most of the time trying to squeeze my earplugs more snugly into place. When an hour was up I opened my eyes to behold my companions utterly absorbed in their practice. I could even see the dark, glistening trails of ecstasy-born tears on a couple of cheeks. Not one of them rose from his cushion for another half-hour.

Now, watching the retreatants preparing for what would be, for some of them, their first experience of meditation in a quiet place, I wondered whether they would ever rise from their cushions again!

We recited some verses of dedication, written by Sangharakshita years ago in London:

. . . Though in the world outside there is strife,
Here may there be peace;
Though in the world outside there is hate,
Here may there be love;
Though in the world outside there is grief,
Here may there be joy. . . .

Jai Bhim!

> . . . Here seated, here practising,
> May our mind become Buddha,
> May our thought become Dhamma,
> May our communication with one another be Sangha. . .

And then Purna rang his bell to start a session of *maitri bhavana*, a meditation on universal loving-kindness.

No one coughed, nobody even shuffled on his cushion. A rich silence descended, more or less instantly, as people got to work on the practice. 'May I be happy; may I be well; may I be free from suffering. . . . May my friends be happy and well. . . . May my enemies be happy and well. . . . May all beings whatsoever be free from fear, free from sorrow. . . .' Mentally reciting such formulae, they were recollecting their friends, remembering good times, and waiting for these thoughts and ideas to give birth to a genuine feeling of warmth in their hearts, then nurturing and strengthening that feeling. . . .

For all the high spirits of our arrival, things settled down remarkably quickly. After that first meditation, by bedtime, it was as if we had always been here, always been on retreat.

The obvious signs of this were that people became quieter and more concentrated, able to pour themselves into the events and activities. But this was really just the superficial side of the shift. What really impressed me was an overpowering feeling that I was no longer in the company of a friendly group—or even network of groups—but instead surrounded by an assembly of distinct individuals, each one of whom was now working to bring something more of that individuality into being.

In the meditation sessions this feeling was palpable, but it was equally identifiable during the in-between times. The cooking and cleaning teams went about their business efficiently, without the outbursts and haggling sessions which seemed to accompany the simplest enterprises elsewhere. At mealtimes, as we sat in rows around the shrine room walls eating simple concoctions of rice and vegetables, those whose turn it was to serve seemed to take special delight in allowing the diners to decide for themselves whether they wanted second helpings or not. Having eaten in some of their homes, I knew—to my cost—with what difficulty this practice must have come to them!

Generally speaking, I had found that nobody in India ever seemed to go for a walk simply for the sake of it, and certainly never went alone. But now people were strolling around the pathways, idling time away, even stopping in fields to peer into the hearts of wild-flowers, or to watch the insects that flitted about among the leaves. It was almost bizarre to be among Indians, for whom the group seemed such a natural, fundamental part of life, and yet to feel the group dynamic dissolving. In its place there emerged, over the hours and days, a genuine spirit of *sangha*, of 'spiritual community', as we looked at each other and spoke with the growing awareness that we were each unique beings with a unique potential, no longer just group-members.

The chanting became gentler and more harmonious as we started listening to our own voices in relation to the others'. During the 'communication exercises' we could look at each other directly, for minutes on end, without dissolving into hoots and squawks of embarrassed laughter. Group-based familiarity gave way to appreciation, to real sensitivity, real friendship. The silent periods became relaxed and satisfying; there was a thrill in the air, a quiet excitement.

There was also, underlying everything, something that Dr Ambedkar might have recognized as the spirit of 'equality'. For as we began to reveal our more essential selves, contingent factors such as home background, educational achievements—or lack of them, our jobs and economic footings: all of those factors which so persistently defined Indian social organization, faded into the background. Here, for a few days at least, we were simply people, each doing what we could to get the most out of the retreat, each making our own, singular contribution to it. There was no social unease, no distance, no cliquishness.

I had witnessed—and experienced—these contrasts and transformations before. The 'emergence' of the individual from the group was as central a feature of a good retreat in the West as it was here; it had always been one of Sangharakshita's major themes. But here the difference was so blatant, such a startling departure from the normal run of things in a society where there was less of the 'pseudo-individualism' which tended to blur the process—and sometimes the issue—in the West. These people were coming alive: creating themselves. Even as I watched, they were redeeming those jewels.

With a leap of creative imagination, Ambedkar had grasped that the Buddha's community of followers, in which each individual worked on equal terms with others to create a kind of ideal 'world within the world'—could serve as a model for an ideal wider society. Here were some of his followers getting a taste of exactly that, if only for a few days, in rather special circumstances. They were discovering, at least, that such a society was achievable, and that they could derive enormous benefits from even a short excursion into it. Now there was no reason why they shouldn't try to incorporate a few of the retreat's features into their lives when they got home. They could meditate, study the Dhamma, try harder to observe the precepts; they could make their lives more regular and orderly, and they could work to develop a deeper level of communication with their fellows. Above all, they could try to carry on being themselves more fully and more completely, all the time bringing forth—and thus making available—their own special strengths and qualities.

Lokamitra told me that quite a few people started to give talks and teach meditation as soon as they got home from their first retreat. They would stir up the others, urging them to aim for higher standards, more honesty, more cleanliness, more generosity. . . . By the time the next retreat came round, there could be ten or more new people from such a locality ready to come along.

There was no reason why, in time, the workers' co-operatives shouldn't take off too, freeing thousands of them from low-paid, menial jobs. Come to think of it, there was no reason why all this should be restricted only to Ambedkar's immediate followers. Why shouldn't our 'retreat world' flow out in all directions, far beyond the present Buddhist world? It really was possible, at least then and there, to see a 'Dhamma Revolution' on the move, and to believe that it could all be accomplished in just a few years!

Sangharakshita spent much of the time in his room preparing talks for the coming tour, but seeing anyone who especially asked for a personal interview. Occasionally, when he ventured forth for a stroll along the river bank, people would stand motionless as he passed by, watching from a respectful distance, as if he were a king. Some of them had been to his talks in the fifties and sixties. They had perhaps put him up for the night in their village barn, or marched before the bullock cart that bore him into town yelling their slogans and waving the Buddhist flag. No one else had ever done what he had done for them. Few people even seemed to know what they needed. Sometimes, as he walked, people would rush up and present him with a flower, or prostrate at his feet; he would acknowledge such gestures with a welcoming laugh, or a few words, and carry on walking.

There was indeed something kingly about him. The mindfulness with which he walked gave him a striking air of nobility; he always seemed to know how to say the right thing to the right person at the right time, and was as at ease with the colourful, whole-hearted devotion of his Indian disciples as he was with the reserved respect and game-playing of his English followers. In either context he continued to unfold and disseminate his vision at whatever pace circumstances allowed. Objectively, he was ambitious, even impatient—perhaps more so than anyone I had ever known. Subjectively, he seemed able to accept things exactly as they were—again, more so than anyone else I knew.

I often wondered how it was that this man had come to exert such a formidable influence on my life. I had met a number of people who were intelligent, talented, rich, or famous; none of them had impressed me as he had done. Was it his extraordinary sensitivity to people, or his remarkable breadth of knowledge, or the awe-inspiring way he could bring difficult spiritual principles to life in a discussion? Was it his constant mindfulness, or his refusal to play games with people? Or was it simply that he was the only person of whom I could say with total confidence 'This man is happy'? Perhaps it was a combination of all of them. To be honest, there were still times when I felt the need to work it out. But whatever it was that made him so special, he *was* a king—though certainly not of England or India. And where his true realm lay, I longed to discover.

His one duty on this retreat was to conduct some ordination ceremonies. Professor Kamblay, Chandrakant Kamblay, and Dhammavir were about to join *Trailokya Bauddha Mahasangha*.

Although few of the people present had much idea of the real significance of ordination, everyone knew that something important was happening. As Purna had hoped, the approaching ceremonies gave focus to the entire retreat, and the three protagonists in the drama became the objects of many a furtive glance, as people tried to fathom what was going on in their minds, and what was so special about ordination.

Ambedkar's view of the Buddhist ordination tradition, as represented by the monks he had encountered, was jaded to say the least. So far as he could see, the traditional Eastern sangha was out of date, even 'useless'. Sequestered in monasteries, where they lived academic, or vacantly formal, lives, they were bound by lists of archaic rules and prohibitions. Lifestyle had become the pre-eminent factor, commitment to a spiritual ideal a secondary one, if that. So long as a monk looked and acted the part, people were content to revere him. Consequently, the bhikkhus had effectively ceased to act—and didn't seem even to have the institutional freedom to act—as transmitters of the Buddha's vision.

By contrast, the Jesuit missionaries working in India impressed him enormously. They knew their stuff, wore lay dress and adopted no 'airs'. They made themselves socially useful, and worked hard to spread their word. Why couldn't there be a branch of the Buddhist sangha like that? That was the kind of 'Dhamma worker' his people were going to need.

Sangharakshita shared many of Ambedkar's views on the shortcomings of the 'orthodox' sangha, and had felt prompted to found a 'new' (though he preferred to say 'radically authentic') kind of Order in the West. In so doing, his intention had been to establish a branch of the Order in which the 'Going for Refuge'—the act of *commitment* to Buddhist ideals and practice—would be restored to its proper position of centrality.

Obviously, the practical issue of lifestyle couldn't be ignored. A lifestyle, after all, is an inevitable reflex of one's views and ideals. At ordination, every new 'Dhammachari' or 'Dhammacharini' therefore undertook to observe ten ethical precepts, and worked consciously to upgrade the quality of his or her life in every way. Many of the co-operatives and the communities had something of a 'monastic' tone, being either for men or for women; and some people made use of vows. But for all that, it was the strength and depth of one's underlying commitment to the ideals and practices of Buddhism, rather than one's ability to conform to a specific lifestyle, that made one a Buddhist or not, and which therefore made one ready to join the Order.

To do that, one simply recited the three Refuges and the ten Precepts, firstly in a 'private' ceremony with Sangharakshita, and then in public, before a gathering of well-wishers. The new Order member might be married, single, or chaste, fully engaged in a professional career, or completely free to concentrate on Dhamma work, as he or she chose. The one thing that was expected of those who took this step was that they should understand the significance of what they were doing, recognize its implications in their lives, and be prepared to work out those implications to the full. This was no light matter. It could take anything from two to ten years for someone to take the step. Many people never took it at all.

Given the outward-going nature of Sangharakshita's movement, through which most Order members had discovered and immersed themselves in Buddhism, this commitment often found expression in some form of altruistic activity. But this was neither required nor firmly expected of an Order member; to go for Refuge was an entirely individual, ultimately spiritual, matter.

In a sense, because they were Buddhists, everyone on our retreat had 'gone for Refuge'; that had been the central element in their original conversion ceremony. But to have recited the old Pali formulae, without any experience or understanding of Buddhism, meant that their going for Refuge was at best provisional. With all the will in the world, none of the new converts could possibly have been 'one hundred percent Buddhists'. They were certainly not ready to join the Order.

Professor Kamblay had been involved with TBMSG ever since Lokamitra turned up in Poona three years before. He had now attended hundreds of classes and many retreats. For some while he had been devoting most of his spare time to helping out in the office and representing the movement's interests at innumerable bureaucratic hearings. But only now did he feel ready to make a commitment in this deeper sense.

A few weeks earlier, just after arriving in India, I had gone along to the weekly 'Order meeting' in Poona. That night, the assembled Dhammacharis were to hold their final discussion on Professor Kamblay's ordination request.

It was immediately obvious that everybody liked him a lot, and valued his contribution to the the work of TBMSG. Without doubt, if ordained, he would become a powerful force in the movement: he had an attractive personality, and a great deal of experience in student and union politics. He was a brilliant fixer; he could turn wheels. In India, such a man would be a fabulous asset to any organization.

But Lokamitra and Vimalakirti were adamant: these were secondary considerations. Talent and worldly wisdom were all very well, but what did they have to do with his readiness for ordination? A talented firebrand might get things going, but unless his understanding of the movement's principles went deep enough, then he could have a destructive effect on the integrity of the Order. It would be highly irresponsible to let Professor Kamblay go for Refuge if he was not completely ready—not only for the movement's sake, but for his own. If he were later to flounder, lose heart, feel he had made a mistake, they would all be responsible for letting him make such an undermining error of judgement.

But there were people there who had known him for years. They had seen him change, had seen him making changes in his life, not just to conform to any group expectation, they insisted, but because he had made the ideals of Buddhism his own. They were certain that he had developed a high degree of vision, and spoke enthusiastically of his determination to shape his life in the light of that vision.

Finally, a consensus was reached: Professor Kamblay was 'ready'.

There had been a similar discussion about Chandrakant, a mechanical draftsman from the north of Poona. I had met him just a few times, at the apartment where he was supervising some decoration work prior to Sangharakshita's arrival. When with him, I couldn't help sensing a sort of purity, that seemed to seep from deep within him into his surroundings. Oddly enough, for I had never encountered anything quite like it before, Professor Kamblay had something of the same quality. On occasion, when I was with either of them, I would feel as if I were being bathed in moonlight.

Dhammavir, the novice monk from Ambedkar society, was to have a slightly different ordination ceremony. When he came to recite the ten

Precepts—which were in a way an extension of the usual five—he would not be undertaking to 'abstain from sexual misconduct' but would instead be taking a vow of celibacy, thereby becoming an *anagarika*. Unlike the others, he would wear—or rather continue to wear—the robe.

Because the bhikkhus were an influential, if not spiritually effective, force in Maharashtra, Sangharakshita had felt that it would be helpful if a few Order members wore the robe, at least in the movement's early days. In robes, Lokamitra, Purna, and Jyotipala had gained an easy, almost automatic entrée into the local Buddhist world. As they went about establishing their credentials, getting themselves and their movement better known, it did no harm to meet conventional expectations half-way. In time they would be able to teach people that the robe was not an end in itself, and that 'lay' Buddhists could and should work just as hard—in fact much harder—than the monks, whom they held in such awe.

Once upon a time, Dhammavir had been a PE instructor with the police force in Ahmednagar district, a backward, drought-ridden region of Maharashtra. But it had always been his ambition to spend the last years of his life in robes. After retiring, he had therefore discussed things with his wife, his children, and his relatives, and had departed, at the age of seventy, to find a monk who would give him the 'lower ordination'.

After spending a frustrating time wandering around Maharashtra as a shramanera, attending the obligatory weddings and meetings, he concluded that he would be able to live a real Dhamma-life only by becoming a full monk. He was actively looking for an opportunity to receive the higher ordination when he met his old friend Dharmaditya, who told him something about Lokamitra's work in Poona, and the Order he had just joined. When he heard that Sangharakshita was connected with all this, Dhammavir's interest was stimulated. He had been to several of Sangharakshita's talks, twenty years before.

A little while later, Dhammavir made his way to Ambedkar Society to meet Lokamitra and book himself in for a retreat. It was late in the day when he and Lokamitra finished talking, so Dhammavir asked whether he could stay for the night. It was a night that was to change his life. He had never been anywhere before where people meditated, or observed strict vegetarianism, or where they even knew very much about Buddhism. When, at five-thirty next morning, he caught Lokamitra in the middle of his Hatha Yoga practice, he decided to stay around.

A few weeks later he went on retreat. On the last night, directly after the final meditation session, he solemnly rose from his cushion, approached Lokamitra, knelt before him and handed him a flower, saying, 'I have found real Dhamma.'

He stopped thinking about becoming a bhikkhu, and set himself the task of joining Sangharakshita's Order. Now, for a year or so, he had taken to wandering around the Buddhist localities of Maharashtra, retailing the story of his 'search for Dhamma', eulogizing the movement, and breathing fire and brimstone exhortations to *practise* over the heads of his listeners.

As our retreat progressed, the three ordinands seemed to sink ever more deeply into themselves as they made their final preparations. From time to time I would catch a glimpse of them, pacing the grounds alone, or absorbed in conversation with their friends. Occasionally the three came together in the shade of a bush, saying little, but allowing a bond to grow between them, each making sure that he would be completely present, able to take as much of himself as possible into the ceremony, when the time came.

Meanwhile, a special room was being prepared in one of the dormitory bungalows. An ad hoc team of craftsmen had built a shrine, and were now applying flowers, candles, and decorative designs to its surfaces and surrounds. This was where Sangharakshita would be conducting the 'private' ordination ceremonies.

At last, on the third night of the retreat, the private ordinations took place. At eight o'clock Purna's bell rang out, bidding us turn our backs on a gleaming full-moon and shuffle into the main shrine room. Our task would be to create the ideal context for the ceremonies by applying ourselves to an extended session of *maitri-bhavana* meditation practice. For almost two hours we would remain sitting while the ordinands slipped from the room, one by one, each to make his personal rendezvous with Sangharakshita. . .

Having joined him the ordinand would offer a freshly cut flower, a lighted candle, and a stick of incense to the shrine, before engaging in a traditional, ritualized 'dialogue' in which he would ask Sangharakshita to give him the Refuges and Precepts. Sangharakshita would respond by asking whether the request was complete and wholly authentic. The ordinand would reply, 'Yes.'

He would then follow as Sangharakshita led him through the recitation of the Three Refuges:

Buddham Saranam Gacchami;
Dhammam Saranam Gacchami;
Sangham Saranam Gacchami. . . .

Jai Bhim!

To the Buddha for Refuge I go;
To the Dhamma for Refuge I go;
To the Sangha for Refuge I go. . . .

Then, after the recitation of the Ten Precepts, would come more ritualized dialogue—and that would really be that. Although the ceremony was not quite over, this was its core and heart.

Outwardly, perhaps, it did not add up to much. With the exception of the extra precepts, the ordinand would have been reciting these formulae, at Buddhist gatherings and at TBMSG events, for years. But inwardly there was a world of added significance. This time he was not just reciting his *'vandanas'* as a member of a Buddhist group. Tonight he was declaring that he had reflected on the Buddha's teachings and contemplated the ideals the Buddha had presented; he had been practising the Dhamma and had thought deeply about the part it could play in his life. On that basis, he wanted to embrace the Three Jewels whole-heartedly. By making this statement solely in the presence of his teacher, he was indicating that this was something he would do even if no one else on earth wanted to join him.

There would follow an 'initiation' and a name-giving. At the time of ordination, each new *Dhammachari* was given a visualization meditation practice. On one level, this would serve as a link between the new Order member and Sangharakshita, and thus with the entire tradition that Sangharakshita represented. On another level, the visualization practice—of an 'archetypal' Buddha or Bodhisattva figure—would help him to form an imaginative, intuitive bond with the ideal to which he was now fully, and explicitly, committed.

Simple though it was, the ceremony marked the beginning of a new life. Consequently, the new Order member left the room with a new name, signifying that he was now 'reborn' into a life of consciously chosen purpose and direction. From now on, that name would act as a kind of blueprint for further development. Sometimes Sangharakshita chose a name which denoted strengths and qualities he intuited in the person concerned; at other times, the name hinted at qualities needing to be developed, or consolidated.

. . . The minutes flowed by, the rest of us sat on; the candles on the main shrine guttered, burned down, and were replaced. From time to time, those unused to prolonged periods of meditation rose from their places, drew blankets around their shoulders, and crept out to stroll in the calm moonlight. But most of us were content to remain sitting, strengthening the delicate filaments of friendship that reached out to Dhammavir, Chandrakant, and Professor Kamblay, sensing the crackle in the air as, in turn, each of them left us, and returned.

106

At last they were all back, each now re-absorbed in meditation; it was over. We went to bed in silence, casting secret glances towards the new *Dhammacharis*, wondering what their names might be, trying to imagine the exquisite turbulence of their minds.

Next morning, the retreat underwent a total transformation as the camp steadily filled with hosts of friends and relatives who had come to witness the public ordination ceremony.

Cameras popped and clicked as Sangharakshita spoke on the meaning of ordination, and then led the three men through the ceremony.

This public ceremony was in fact a recapitulation of the private ceremony; only the initiation was omitted. Sangharakshita reminded his listeners that one can only go for Refuge alone, since Going for Refuge was, perhaps, the *definitively* individual act. But all the same—as the public ceremony illustrated—there were others who had taken that step too.

Perhaps the chanting could have been a little more tuneful, but the sincerity with which the trio recited their Refuges and Precepts amply compensated for any lack of aesthetic refinement. Certainly, no one seemed to mind. Aside from drinking in Sangharakshita's words, most people were eager to hear the new names. What sort of job would he have made of those?

Dhammavir, he announced, would keep his old name. After all, 'Dhammavir' was already a perfectly good Buddhist one, meaning 'Hero of the Dhamma'. Chandrakant Kamblay would now take the name of 'Amritbodhi', 'the nectar of Enlightenment', and Professor Kamblay would be known as 'Bodhidharma'.

There was a gasp of delighted laughter. The historical Bodhidharma had taken Buddhism from India to China. He was one of the great heroes of Buddhist history, the legendary founder of the Cha'an—or Zen—tradition. It seemed a fitting name for—for Bodhidharma.

Soon we were back outside in the brilliant sunshine, lining up for the inevitable group photos, hugging or shaking hands with the new Order members. Already, a few people were leaving; the place was being cleared and swept. And, to some extent, we were already slipping back into the 'world'. Groups were forming again, the old familiar banter was returning; across the way I heard the tentative crescendos of a first squabble. But people were happily alive, full of confidence and energy.

Now they would return to their families, jobs, and their locality preoccupations. Without doubt most of our retreatants would find it impossible to hold on to the freshness and sparkle that the countryside, the numerous meditation sessions, and the retreat atmosphere had given them. But they would all retain much more than a memory. Something of the happier, clearer person each of them had met in themselves would survive and enrich their lives from now on. They would share that with their families, their friends, and with their colleagues. Soon, no doubt, they would come along to the Poona Centre, or book up for another retreat. They would keep on the trail.

It would be tempting to dismiss the Buddhist movement in Maharashtra as a purely ethnic, cultural phenomenon. The critics and the cynics have always done just that. Of course those millions of people did not become perfect Buddhists overnight. Most of them were still very much 'Buddhists in waiting'. But Ambedkar's stroke of genius was to transform a crude, uncultured, uncivilized community into a society that aspired to higher, more truly human values and which was receptive to a challenging vision.

Mahadhammavir, Amritbodhi, and Bodhidharma had grown up in that cultural group. What they had learned there had goaded them into making full use of a practising Buddhist movement. Now they were ready to leave groups altogether behind. From now on they would seek the sanction of no groups at all, taking their refuge, fully—and effectively—in their own highest ideals.

Some of 'our boys' were getting through.

eleven

No, you won't find them in the holiday brochures. You may even have a job finding some of them on the map: Daund, Kurdu Wadi, Ahmednagar, Sangamner, Nanded, Osmanabad . . . the towns we visited on our tour. Big commercial towns, small and shabby towns, one street towns, sugar cane towns, cotton towns: they all have their Buddhist localities, so we went.

They lie, squat and baking, beneath a dazzling sky; the whites, yellows, blues, and browns of their crumbling buildings pierce the eye with painful light. Flat-topped bungalows and temples, monumental banks and minarets, kiosks and shops, clamber around and over each other, wrestle, and learn to co-exist, only to dissolve back into light and dust before your eyes. Between the buildings, a few narrow lanes and a single main street enjoy lives of extravagant abandon, before petering out exhausted the moment no one is looking, blending back into the arid plains or the endless fields of sugar cane. A chaotic ferment of lorries, cycle-rickshaws, jeeps, bicycles, and bullock carts hammers and grinds their surfaces to white powder. Goats and cows weave purposeless courses between the vehicles while their harnessed brethren stare goggle-eyed at the path ahead and stagger beneath impossible burdens.

The roadsides support desultory archipelagos of garish kiosks. You can buy *pan* here, and cigarettes, cane juice, trousers, spices, plastic buckets, mirrors, in fact anything. A brigade of specialists crouch in the shade between, their tools spread on sacks before them: a shoe repair man, a watch repair man, a bicycle repair man. Here and there squat a few lonely traders with pathetic, improbable selections of goods: two papayas, three pairs of spectacles, one comb. . . . They fix you with resentful, accusing stares, as if you alone, by refusing to buy, are responsible for their ridiculous plight.

Down a side-street, ageless men attack heaps of mangled branches, hacking them into bundles of firewood. Just by looking, it's impossible to tell whether they are old, kept wiry by their heart-breaking work, or young—made prematurely old by it. A few urchins wipe down the dented hulk of a fifties Studebaker, which wallows like a beached whale in the shade of a bank. Tight huddles of card-players squat in the dirt, playing their eternal games, slapping cards down, one on top of the other, with a kind of savage impatience.

But look! Here comes a band! There are eight of them, all got up in outlandish, fairy-tale soldiers' uniforms, aglitter with gold braid, sequins, and tassles, carrying drums, trumpets, and clarinets. They're not playing but running. Clasping peaked caps to their heads, they stampede down the street, scanning the scene with wild eyes. They have lost their wedding!

Like everyone else, you walk in the road; the pavements are for sleeping and defecation. Even at the busiest time of day, the sleepers sprawl haphazardly in the middle of things like dumped corpses, enshrouded in sack-cloth and the stench of ammonia. Dogs do likewise, passing their days supine, motionless, as if dead, only to rise at night and fill the air with commotion. Mind you, to do even that they have to survive the hours of daylight. Those brutes have a hard time of it here, and the sound of a dog screaming in sudden, surprised agony would make a fitting anthem for small-town India. Sentimental though it may seem, I could never quite reconcile myself to the wanton cruelty that gets doled out to those quivering hounds. They get kicked, beaten with sticks and lengths of lead piping, showered with stones and bricks, even deliberately run over. For sure, the beggars and cripples, the homeless and sick, evoke a sturdier kind of compassion, but the plight of those dogs will give you a chance to catch a particularly ugly aspect of human nature red-handed: the faculty which turns categories into absolutes, which can't identify or empathize with anything but its own kind. It is deeply, dangerously amoral; it has made the caste system possible, just as it has made imperialistic exploitation possible, and religious persecution, and wars, and how many more features of 'human' life?

Life, human or otherwise, goes on, however. You work your way down the street, dodging through the crowds, transmitting shock-waves of wonder, curiosity, and suspicion. After all, when was a white face last seen here?

'Hey, Baba! What you want?'

'Yes, Baba?'

'Hey, Baba—You wanna nice shawl?'

'Baba! Baba! . . .'

Calls, cat-calls, and lip-squelching kissing sounds pursue you. A few lazily lobbed pebbles dance at your feet. You are not of their kind. The crazy thing is, you know that any one of these people would make a delightful friend, if only you could get to know each other somewhere else, away from the street-group, if only you could let each other in. . . .

There are the exceptions: the aged ragamuffin who appears from nowhere, announcing in impeccable English that he is at your entire disposal; the shopkeeper who beats the kids about the ears, telling them to 'Leave the Baba alone!'; the beggar who suddenly presents himself with a military salute and a warm smile—the only man around who seems to want nothing from you.

You can feel as if you've strayed into a mad-house, built on a farmyard with materials looted from a derelict fairground. But, then, the whole gaudy, colour-glutted scene is muted by a mist of fine dust that never leaves the air. With a bit of imagination you can kid yourself that you're not really there at all, but watching it in an old print of an early Technicolor film.

Sangharakshita had been to these places before, many times. He *had* been let in. He remembered the people, and they remembered him. For months before his arrival, Lokamitra had been planning this tour, riding around the region, meeting the local activists, finally deciding which towns we would visit.

Of course, to 'visit' meant to go there, and to get there meant travel; and that is never a straightforward matter in India.

I once tried to reserve myself a second-class seat on the train from

Bombay to Varanasi. A preliminary interview with the Tourist Officer at Bombay's Victoria Terminus offered grounds for hope:

'Yes, Mr Pilchick, no problem at all. I am now giving you this chit which you must take across the taxi park to the ACS office—second door on the right—and give to Mr Tharpar. He will immediately arrange your reservation.'

'Thank you!' I admired the docket as if it were the prize cheque from a lottery draw.

I had almost reached the door when he called me back. As I came within range of his desk he climbed to his feet, grasped my shoulder and looked hard into my eyes.

'Mr Pilchick! Be firm!'

'I beg your pardon?'

His eyes narrowed to conspiratorial slits, 'It All Depends On Your Approach!'

He enunciated the words like a death knell—which, in the circumstances, they were. Despite six more visits to the station's offices, over a period of three weeks, I succeeded in boarding the train without a reservation.

Now, on this tour, we would not even be travelling tourist class. We would be depending instead on a relay of arrangements made weeks before: sometimes making our own way by bus and train, and sometimes riding in cars, jeeps, taxis, and Matador vans supplied by regional organizers. Everything had been planned, agreed to, and prepared for; but those were to be hard miles.

Our troubles began at Poona Station, where the train that was due to take us on the first leg of our journey failed to arrive. We sat, stood, paced, chatted, and dozed on the hot, choked platform for two hours, basing ourselves around a little encampment dominated by a mountain of luggage and books. We were a sizeable party: Sangharakshita, Purna, Lokamitra, Vimalakirti, Kevala, Buddhapriya, Bodhisen, Mahadhammavir, Khemadhammo, Munindra, myself, and Mr Landgay—a tailor from Daund who would be helping Bodhisen with the books.

Trains came and went, but never ours. We sat on, enviously watching scrummages form around the carriage doors as people fought to get on and off; at least they were going somewhere. In the end we short-circuited the system altogether by jumping a slow train that took in, by a circuitous route, Daund, our first port of call. I spent the journey up on a luggage rack, reading Ambedkar's *Annihilation of Caste*, occasionally pausing to convince Buddhapriya that I was quite happy up there— particularly in view of the fact that there was actually nowhere else to go.

From time to time, a friendly Buddhist railway officer would be waiting to help us on our way. Because so much of the work involved in building and maintaining railways brought labourers into contact with the 'impure' earth, India's formidable railway network had always offered a considerable number of 'Untouchable' job opportunities. Then, since the introduction of reserved posts in Government employment for members of the Scheduled Castes, a fair number of Buddhists, in Maharashtra at least, had managed to infiltrate the middle echelons of the railway administration. Whenever we passed through a region where a Buddhist had attained a position of some rank, there he would be, bristling with an ungainly air of authority, directing subordinates to deal with our luggage, and moving passengers around to make room for us. He might even ride with us for a few stops, as far as the boundary of his domain.

This was valuable help, but Sangharakshita would tease the haughtier ones all the same. He had known some of them as students, and took a gently paternal delight in bringing them down to earth. Some of them—if not all—seemed to like it too; it made them feel young again. In India, even getting to the middle ranks could take its toll.

We jerked and bounced a good many miles away in 'ST' buses, squeezed, thigh to thigh, buttock to buttock against the tattered, canny people of these rural backwaters. Stops along the way were long, as farming couples struggled to get bulky sacks of grain, or bundles of freshly-cut sugar cane, through the doors. Impatient old men clambered into passenger compartments via the drivers' windows, nursing equally harassed hens within the folds of their jackets. Deeply-lined women dozed, frowning in the fumes, fanning themselves, and protecting their noses with folded layers of sari cloth.

Once on the move, it was never wise to look at the road. The driver's uninterrupted horn obligato would suffice to suggest the dangers ahead, the near-misses behind.

From time to time we struck lucky, and rode the plains in Ambassador saloons, lolling and luxuriating—so far as numbers allowed—in the dark green upholstery of those miraculous conveyances. Often they would come for us freshly washed and polished, their radiators festooned with marigold garlands. Buddhist flags fluttered from improvised masts as they bore us smoothly through the countryside, eating up the miles, leaving the buses behind in clouds of dust. . . .

. . . And then they stopped.

Sometimes they stopped because our organizers had arranged 'surprise' receptions. The first time this happened was slightly unnerving. Our chauffeur, who had been driving for a couple of hours in unassuming silence, abruptly came to life just on the edge of a small town, and steered us, without explanation or warning, onto the verge. The moment it came to a halt, the car was overwhelmed by a resplendent crowd and engulfed in a storm of chants, cheers, and slogans. Before we had time to gather our wits, they were passing flowers and coconuts through the windows, forming a queue beside the front passenger door, and thrusting themselves in to prostrate on the corrugated rubber mat at Sangharakshita's feet. Our driver, a study in innocence once again, was now gazing absently towards the distant cane fields, blind to the furore, deaf to our reminders that we were running late, until the last prostration had been performed, the final offering made.

Most of the delays were even less scheduled. We broke down. Often.

We rarely fitted into less than two vehicles, and sometimes it took three to get even the most essential members of our team from A to B. To expect three hastily procured cars to work in perfect synchronization over a distance of a hundred kilometers or more was to hope for too much.

'What's that terrible noise?' yelled Lokamitra to the driver of a Matador van one golden afternoon.

'What noise is that, Baba?' rejoined the driver.

'*That* noise!' Lokamitra had to shout to make himself heard above the abominable din of metal eating metal somewhere just beyond the dash-board.

'That? That is the engine, only!' The driver seemed offended, but that journey was to end just a few miles further down the road, in a cloud of black smoke and a stink of burning oil.

Our convoys hiccupped and leap-frogged along, as first one car then another drifted to a creaking halt, or slid and wobbled into the verge on burst tyres. The trick was to keep Sangharakshita moving, step by step, towards our final goal. If his car broke down, then he, Lokamitra, Vimalakirti, and the most indispensable baggage would be shifted into another—from which had to be emptied whatever people and luggage had been riding in it. The castaways were then left awaiting fresh mounts, or watching with growing trepidation while drivers fitted smooth, already-gashed spare tyres, or tinkered about with engines in a perplexed sort of way. From nowhere in particular, crowds of onlookers would soon descend on these reflective scenes, wanting to know our 'good names', where we were going, whence we came, what we thought of their country, and, inevitably, whether we might like to take some photographs.

On one occasion, our vehicle had the good grace to collapse directly

113

beside a tea bar. With some relief, most of us piled out to stretch our legs and pour tea down our brittle throats, while Sangharakshita stayed behind to work on his lecture notes. As we squeezed back aboard, I asked whether he had discovered the cause of our breakdown.

'I don't really know for certain,' he replied, 'but the repair seemed to involve the use of some matches and a piece of string.' He wheezed with silent laughter for the rest of the trip.

They were hard miles, but they were fascinating. Our circuit took us through a number of distinct regions. For days there might be nothing to see but sugar-cane and cotton: fields upon fields, miles upon miles of it. Here the landscape was quite flat, while away in the distance, dominating the area, rose the drab, imposing outlines and smoke-plumes of the sugar refineries. Dotted about in the fields were the temporary abodes of itinerant cane harvesters: tiny wigwams made from cane leaves. The roads here would be busy with bullock carts, often riding in convoys of twenty or more, all loaded with cane. At night our lights hurled ghost-story shadows into the dust-laden darkness as they picked out the animals' horned heads.

We rode for days through parched scrub, occasionally corkscrewing up into lonely ghats. Even up here there was nothing to see but infinities of bare, arid grassland. And yet, no matter how inhospitable the terrain, there were always people somewhere, usually walking sedately in ones and twos across the vast wasteland, brass pots twinkling on their heads.

Then the ghats became distant lumps and needles, set in chequerboard plains of meadow-land, millet fields, and banana groves. Mangoes added the finishing touch, round-topped and green like the trees children paint.

There were villages and hamlets everywhere: silent, sleepy places of mud, stone, and thatch, clustered around their central compounds. Their children played in the dirt with sticks and hoops, animals grazed on dry grass, the women called to each other as they washed clothes and sorted grains, the men laboured in fields nearby; nobody ever looked at us.

Frequently, usually on the flattest and straightest stretches of road, we came across lorries sprawled on their sides like vandalized fair-ground machines. Dismal confusions of sacks, boxes, pipes, or whatever, lay around the happy colours of their cabs and trailers. Miraculously, the drivers were invariably conscious and whole, and stood arguing tetchily with unconcerned policemen, while bystanders ogled the wreckage.

But we did see death, sometimes. In one place, some dogs toyed with the grotesque remains of a giant buffalo, while their glutted companions dozed in the sun close by; elsewhere, another gang of dogs, tied together with a length of wire, bared their teeth at the sun, and lay stone dead in the gutter. We passed the corpse of a monkey the size of a small man, lying face down in the road; once, we came upon the disquieting spectacle of a headless dog.

And there was also the time when, as our train was pulling out of a station, I heard a terrible scream. I looked up to see the face of a woman, perfectly framed in my window. Her eyes wide with fear and disbelief, she was running along the platform, keeping pace with us as we drew away. At length she slowed, and stopped—too terrified to go any further—and stood wailing, clutching a baby to her breast. As we rolled past the end of the platform I caught sight of a hastily draped body; the white sheet that covered it bloomed crimson with blood.

Altogether, life here appeared to be pretty uncertain—a fact that seemed to make people more, rather than less, careless of it. They drove at night without lights, crossed roads without a glance in any direction, careered down hills without brakes, cleared forest paths with fires in mid-summer, and rode on top of the trains and buses as much as inside them. Initially, I supposed they knew what they were doing, and felt humble, foolishly lacking in the regional brand of *savoir faire*. But then I would read the local papers and discover that they were dying in hundreds every week: in bus crashes and railway accidents, in fires and pointless skirmishes. They did *not* know what they were doing. It was a sobering thought.

Of course, in order to travel you have first to set out, a species of endeavour fraught with its own deadly traps and pitfalls. Most of our journeys began with hours of confused, mind-numbing waiting. We waited for cars that failed to arrive, for buses that were late, for trains that did not run, and for people who had forgotten us. We waited in car parks and stations, in market squares and hotel reception rooms, always guarding that mass of books, always wondering where 'they' had got to: the people who had insisted they would be here, waiting for *us*.

To be fair, this was something that rankled the Western visitors far more acutely than it did our Indian companions. They were used to 'Indian time'.

One morning, when we were waiting to leave Sangamner, I told Lokamitra how sorry I was not to have been able to get any pictures of the place in daylight.

'Why don't you go and take some now?' he said, 'We've got plenty of time.'

'But it's nine o'clock. They said they'd be here at quarter past.'

'Oh, don't worry about that. We'll never leave before eleven.'

I looked at him closely. Had the fay mood come over him? Or was he trying to get me lost?

But at eleven o'clock sharp, exactly as predicted, our managers buzzed up the drive in an overloaded rickshaw, freshly shaved and ironed, smelling inexplicably of paraffin.

More typically, though, whenever I had the temerity to ask Lokamitra when something—anything—was likely to happen, he would throw out his arms and exclaim 'How should *I* know?'

'Well, you made the arrangements.'

'Yes, but this is *India*.'

Soon after arriving in India, Lokamitra had instituted something he called 'Buddhist time'. This was actually clock time. It was now common to hear TBMSG people concluding discussions about arrangements thus: '. . . So, is that two o'clock *Indian* time, or *Buddhist* time?' Unfortunately, TBMSG was still no more than a drop in the ocean of Indian time.

Soon after our tour came to an end I was to find myself arriving at the Foreigners' Registration Office in Calcutta, in hot pursuit of a permit to visit Darjeeling. It was nine in the morning; a soldier in a uniform some two sizes too big for him, and with an ancient Lee Enfield on his shoulder, seemed to be guarding a sign which announced:

'HOURS OF BUSINESS: 10AM—1.00PM'

'Closed, sir,' he said, 'Come back at eleven, sir.'

'But it says ten on the sign.'

He shifted his rifle uneasily, and gave an apologetic waggle of the head, 'Yes, sir. India, sir.'

Of course, we were not always kept waiting by 'them'. As often as not, it was ourselves. A van once broke down in the heart of a sugar cane plantation. While waiting for it to be fixed, some of our number disappeared into the lush, cool depths of the cane forest. When the van was ready, the horn was sounded to bring them back, and off we went. About ten minutes later:

'Where's Munindra?'

The van was halted and thoroughly searched, but there was no sign of Munindra, a records clerk from the Poona munitions depot, a lover of meditation, solitude, and silence.

We drove back to the scene of our breakdown, turned the van round and stopped, just as Munindra was emerging from the cane. Without a word, he let himself in, gnawing happily on a piece of cane. The rest of us looked at each other, arrived at a silent consensus to say nothing of our twenty minute round-trip, and continued on our way.

A recurring thrill of the trip was never knowing where we would end up for the night. Once or twice we stayed in cheap hotels: seedy, airless, lightless places in the heart of town, usually right next to the railway station, whose denizens hissed, hooted, and wailed from dusk until dawn. Occasionally we would find ourselves in the stations themselves, crammed together in their surprisingly well appointed 'retiring rooms'.

When you know that you are actually *in* a railway station and not just close to it, the noises don't seem quite so bad, or so it seemed to me. Sangharakshita, being particularly unenamoured of trains, slept elsewhere whenever possible. This came as something of a shock to the railway engineer who paid us an early morning call in Sholapur.

'But where is Sangharakshita?' he demanded.

I explained that *Bhanteji*, being a light sleeper, preferred a quieter billet.

'Hmph!' he exclaimed, 'Can a man of his Enlightenment not stand a little of such disturbance?'

I tried to convince him that spiritual development did not necessarily remove one's vulnerability to things like noise, overcrowding, and the like, and reminded him that even the Buddha liked to get away from people, from time to time, and enjoy a little peace and quiet.

He smiled condescendingly at my efforts, but remained unconvinced. I pressed on, assuring him that a Buddha, and even *Bhanteji*, could put up with these things, when necessary, and probably with far better grace than could he or I; but this did not mean that they actually enjoyed them, or found them conducive to the needs of lecture writing.

My interrogator's gentle smirk suggested that he was still not happy. He was, after all, a Senior Engineer, and thus qualified to pronounce on all matters, including these, with some authority. I then suggested that he was still rooted in his old Hindu assumptions, expecting a 'holy' man to be a miracle worker, a super-human being from the story books. Perhaps my point went home, for he eyed me shrewdly for a while, asked, as casually as possible, whether we had taken breakfast, and promptly disappeared from the room.

Most of our nights were spent in a succession of 'Government Inspection bungalows'. These were pleasant complexes of low slung buildings with well tended gardens, usually placed on the towns' fringes. They provided board and lodging for itinerant tax inspectors, pump-station foremen, weights-and-measures officials, and municipal engineers—that army of semi-VIP administrators who constituted an apparently crucial, and intriguingly pampered, sector of the Indian work-force.

The rooms were large and commodious; liveried staff padded about their carpets, ministering with po-faced deference to the needs of their passing masters. These latter strutted about importantly, armed with thickly stuffed leather briefcases and heavy-framed spectacles, or patrolled the gardens in open shirts and braces, yawning frankly in the morning air, until their drivers came to take them off to their next appointment.

It was usually possible to hire rooms in these places, or, if you knew someone with a bit of influence—and if there were no gas meter checkers in town—you could borrow a couple of rooms for the night. And that is exactly what we got: a couple of rooms, one for Sangharakshita, and one for the rest of us. It seemed best to be tactful, and avoid quips about black holes, though these were what sprang to mind as we crammed ourselves in, turning their entire floor areas into what were effectively vast, communal beds.

But bed-time was still a long way off. For the first hour or so, these rooms became nerve centres for our travelling enterprise. Books had to be unloaded and sorted, the recording equipment checked, money counted, and the evening's arrangements confirmed with the local organizers, who piled in the moment we arrived, to sit or stand wherever they could find a little space.

Lokamitra became a blur, bouncing from one knot of activity to another, occasionally launching himself across the room to head off an over-enthusiastic visitor about to enter Sangharakshita's room. Officially, they were there to confirm the logistics of the evening's event: when it was meant to start, when it would end, who was to speak, who was to make offerings of garlands, when the taxi was to arrive. . . . Unofficially, they often came armed with lists of their own, more personal requests: Would *Bhanteji* like to come and take tea at their homes? Would he please bless their new vihara? Would he visit another locality to give just a nice, little talk before, after, or even instead of the main event? Sometimes these requests were offered tentatively, delicately; at other times they were presented as quite menacing demands.

One local politician, radiant in his shimmering silk pyjama suit, informed us that he had arranged a procession to the site of the talk, complete with a good band. Thousands of people would accompany us on our march through town, and Sangharakshita would be asked to place just one garland on the statue of Dr Ambedkar in the square. However, on that occasion Sangharakshita's throat was giving him some trouble and Lokamitra had to explain that he would only be able to talk for a short while—and then only if he could avoid as much contact with the dust as possible.

This was not good enough for our politician, who protested and argued for twenty minutes before storming off in a sulk. Half-an-hour later he was back, this time with his band and some thousand people.

'Doctor Babasaheb Ambedkar-ki. . . .'

'JAI SO!!!'

The crowd surged into the driveway and began its slogans and chants, the drums started to beat. The politician re-presented himself at our door, beaming affably as if oblivious of the earlier discussion.

'See? We have come. Everyone is so very pleased that *Bhanteji* is here. They are very pleased that we shall all take part in the march. Shall we go now?'

Lokamitra, clamping a public smile over his frustration, firmly closed the door, bolted it, then quickly issued instructions that the windows should be shut and bolted. Not a moment too soon either, for a few people were already trying to climb through—though with what final intention, I could not tell.

Part of the problem was that we had no idea whether our politician had anything at all to do with the event to which we were committed. For all we knew, he had plans of his own; the procession could end up anywhere: in a rival locality, on a rival stage at the opposite end of town to where we were officially expected. We were adrift upon a traditionally turbulent and stormy sea.

One thing was certain, Sangharakshita was not well enough to take part in a procession. We sat around the place, three to a bed, toying with ideas, wondering what on earth to do, while salvoes of cheers and chants, friendly enough in themselves, battered the walls and filled the air. In the end we fielded a compromise. Mustering as many 'robes' as we could, we set off, minus Sangharakshita, but with such purpose and pomp that the procession was obliged to accompany us. Sangharakshita came along later, by taxi.

The regional promoters were a mixed bunch. In some places they were politicians, while in others they were the henchmen of the henchmen of politicians. Sometimes they represented the local branch of 'Bharatiya Bauddha Mahasabbha', the Buddhist Society founded by Ambedkar, elsewhere they were neither one thing nor the other, simply local Buddhist people who tried to take an initiative in their area, to ensure that at least something of the Dhamma occasionally came their way.

It was inevitable that a few of them would become slightly intoxicated by the extra prominence our visit gave them and, by and large, it was impossible to begrudge our hosts the occasional self-important strut, or the odd flash of bossiness. But for obvious reasons there was rarely much of an effective organizational basis to add glory to their lustre. Many were finding the situation difficult. After all, they had all of us to transport, house, and feed; a stage, loudspeaker system, and lights to procure, a field or hall to hire, garlands to buy, flags to arrange, taxis to reserve. . . . It was a considerable undertaking for people with little education, or confidence.

Once he had joined our party, there was one man, apart from Lokamitra, who had free access to Sangharakshita's room at all times; that was Dharmarakshita.

Dharmarakshita had many singular qualities: an irrepressibly cheerful nature, a beautiful singing voice, a prodigious memory, and the ability to see the bright side of even the greatest calamity. But he had another virtue beside which all others paled into insignificance: that of always being in the right place at the right time. There was always a Dharmarakshita around when you needed one. I put it that way since it was often impossible to believe that there was only one of him. How else could he have appeared with such perfect timing in such different situations?

It was Dharmarakshita, you will remember, who was waiting for us at the bus-stop in Panchgani, with the day's organizer already under his wing. But that was a mere five-finger exercise in his art.

I was once walking in as bland and unfrequented a backstreet of Poona as you could hope to find, worrying about my date with Dharmarakshita. A few days earlier, he and I had arranged to have lunch, but had not arranged where and when to meet. It was now eleven o'clock, and I had had no response to any of the notes I had sent his way. What was I to do?

Even as I pondered, there, incredibly, was Dharmarakshita, drawing up beside me on his bicycle, shooing off my cries of amazement, and telling me about one of Sangharakshita's poems he was rendering into Hindi. The thing was, and it is essential that this is understood: *he had not been looking for me.*

But, as far as I was concerned, his masterpiece was Jaipur. When we took our tour up north to Ahmedabad, Ajmer, and Delhi, I slipped off alone to visit Jaipur. My plan was to meet up with the others at midnight, as the 'Delhi Mail' passed through the Pink City. There, my reserved bench would be waiting for me, guarded, at cost of life and limb if necessary, by my fellows.

Midnight found me extremely cold but cheerful on the blacked-out station platform. Cheerful, that is, until the train pulled in. There was about half a mile of it and, owing to an oversight, none of the carriages were marked, numbered, or identified in any way. The prospect of locating the right berth in the right compartment in the right carriage was so daunting that I froze to the spot while the populations of Ahmedabad and Jaipur noisily changed places around me, along with their furniture and possessions.

But then:

'Yes! See! I have come!' Dharmarakshita was at my side in a trice, his bubbling laughter causing him to trip over his words.

'Yes. It is difficult without numbers. Somebody has made a slip-up, I think. But here I am, and there you are; the train is here, and we will now get onto it. You thought you were alone. But no: I am here with you. Let us go!'

To have found me so quickly, on that blacked-out platform, in all that chaos, was not difficult: it was impossible. I remain baffled even now.

Of all the Indian Order members, Dharmarakshita was the only one to be present at the historic rally where Dr Ambedkar became a Buddhist. He was there, in that half-million strong crowd, and recited the Refuges and Precepts along with everyone else. And yet, unlike most of the other older Order members, he had had no particular interest in Ambedkar beforehand. He had no personal memories of caste-oppression, was not at all militant, and was not particularly concerned with Scheduled Caste affairs. So why was he at the *Diksha* Ground on that October day? Well, he just happened to be in Nagpur visiting a friend at the time and, seeing all the crowds, tagged along to find out what was going on. Once there, he simply joined in with everyone else when they started chanting. By the end of the night he was a Buddhist.

During the late fifties and early sixties, he became Sangharakshita's interpreter and companion in the Poona region. How?

One day, while staying in Poona, he happened to see a sign advertising a talk by an English monk, and decided to go along. The man who had been booked to interpret the talk failed to turn up, and it looked as if the event was going to be a flop. Then someone recognized Dharmarakshita, and called out that here was a young student who spoke English. He could do the interpreting! Fighting, remonstrating, and protesting all the way, Dharmarakshita was literally passed—hand to hand—from the back to the front of the audience, and hauled up onto the stage. Thus began a firm friendship, which led, eventually, to his becoming the first Indian Order member, in 1979.

But that occasion was not Dharmarakshita's first encounter with Sangharakshita. The reason the poster for the Poona talk had caught his eye was that it set him wondering whether this English monk might be the one he had seen speaking in Nagpur on the night of Ambedkar's death. During the four days that followed the traumatic event, Dharmarakshita had attended a few of Sangharakshita's thirty-five talks, including the one where he had addressed the crowd from the seat of a rickshaw.

Sangharakshita's talk had made an enormous impact, he told me, not just because Sangharakshita had been the only man able to speak at all, but because he spoke about Buddhism.

'At that moment, we didn't want to hear about politics or anything of that sort. People were very much afraid that Babasaheb's death might be some kind of punishment. There was a conversion, yes? And then, suddenly, there was a death, yes? People had great fear. They wanted more than anything to be given some confidence in the Dhamma.'

Having met properly, at the talk in Poona, Sangharakshita and Dharmarakshita acted from then on as a two-man touring team during the winter months, visiting the towns we were now visiting on our tour, and more besides. The invitations would come pouring in, and they would go out. Dharmarakshita couldn't remember how many hundreds of talks they had given, in cities, towns, and villages wherever there were Buddhists. There were hardly any other Buddhist monks in Maharashtra at the time, and few of them knew enough about Buddhism to be of any use to the new converts.

In those very early days, the Buddhist world was quite straightforward and unified. In time, once the initial shock of Ambedkar's death had worn off, divisions and factions began to form. Sangharakshita wanted nothing to do with politics, and played a cautious hand, resolving to stay on good terms with everyone. To obviate the risk of appearing partisan he stayed with Parsee friends in Poona, and accepted invitations to speak on any platform. I wondered whether this had ever struck anyone as eccentric.

'Oh no!' Dharmarakshita laughed, 'None of us had any money or food, so he was doing us a favour by finding his own lodgings. Anyway, so long as we could use him, why should we worry where he stayed?'

But didn't it seem strange that one of the most most prominent monks on the scene should have been an Englishman?

'Why should it seem strange? Very few monks were Indian anyway. They came from Burma, Thailand, Sri Lanka. . . . Naturally, we assumed they came from England also.'

In those days Sangharakshita was a powerhouse of energy. As soon as he arrived in a new town, he would head straight for the stage to give his talk, walking so fast that none of the organizers could keep up with him. He was happy to travel long distances in bullock-carts, he could eat any kind of food, and sleep on coarse stubble in the open fields. 'It was quite remarkable. Not even our local bhikkhus could do that!'

He would go anywhere, speak to any kind of audience, always without notes. Never once did Dharmarakshita see him get angry when things went wrong, not even when they found themselves forgotten and deserted by the organizers after a talk, miles from anywhere, with no means of getting home.

'. . . But then,' pondered Dharmarakshita, 'who could he get angry with? I was the only one there, and it wasn't *my* fault!'

Had he, I wondered, ever held Sangharakshita in awe?

'How could I? We were just two friends. He was just he, and I was just I. Yes? There was never any feeling that he was the boss, and that I was just the translator, or anything like that. No: he was the buffalo, and I was the cart; where he went, I went. But I never felt any special kind of respect for him.'

Suddenly squawking with laughter, Dharmarakshita rolled over onto his back, 'But don't you see? That has always been my problem!'

He was a good man to travel with.

twelve

The air is still warm and soft, scented with an aroma of burning wood from supper fires in the nearby hutments. Lorries and scooters grind past two sides of our field, yet the scene is transfigured by a sunset of staggering beauty—courtesy of the dust and pollution that haunts the town.

Tonight we have a whole field, but sometimes we have to set up on roundabouts, at T-junctions, or even in dead-end streets.

People are arriving, sinking in talkative groups onto the grass, or onto heavy brown tarpaulins that flow out from the stage. Some come from the town itself; others have trekked in from the surrounding villages, travelling for a day or more just to be here.

Peanut and chick-pea vendors are doing brisk trade, selling their wares in cones of newsprint by the flickering, yellow-brown light of their lamps. The night is riddled with music: film scores, Ambedkarite anthems, and a 'pop' version of the Three Refuges. Later, maybe, we'll get a live band. . . .

Bodhisen and Mr Landgay are working fast, piling books onto trestle tables. Tonight there could be five thousand people here, and Bodhisen won't be happy unless he sells at least three thousand rupees worth of books. From time to time he casts a glowering eye towards the gate where a man is crouched in the dirt, a pile of books and posters spread around him. No one will admit to having let *him* in. . . . Anyway, he's here now, so there's not much we can do about it. At least he's got some of our publications in stock. I approach the 'official' bookstall; Mr Landgay stops for a moment to shake my hand. 'You have taken tea?' he asks, apropos of nothing in particular. Bodhisen heaves up another sack of books, notices me, shakes his head in a happy way, and says 'Yes!'

Over by the stage, Purna and Bippin are checking the recording equipment. There's a desperate glint in Purna's eye. Perhaps, tonight, everything will be all right. Perhaps not. Since the tour began he's been dogged by a particularly virulent form of mains hum. It's followed him from Poona, through Bombay, and all the way round Marathwada, pursuing him like a fury. He gets mains hum indoors; he gets it in the fields and on the streets; he gets it in the city, and out in the country; he gets it in the day time, he gets it at night. It even comes when he's running on batteries! It usually starts about ten minutes into the talk, just as he's beginning to relax, even thinking of removing the headphones from the pale dome of his shaven head. . . .

I join them at their table and proceed to unload my bag. Might as well check my gear too. One camera with black-and-white, another with colour-slide, one 8mm movie camera, a miniature tape recorder. The batteries seem fresh, the motors are turning, the little red lights are glowing. But this simple job has takes ten minutes, since we are being overwhelmed by a buffeting tide of children. Startled eyes pop from their skulls at the sight of so much costly and forbidden fruit. I'd feel better if I could explain that I've borrowed one camera from a friend, the movie-camera from my dad, and I'll probably have to hock the tape recorder at the end of all this to pay my rent. Mind you, nobody would be listening; all they want is that I should take their picture.

'Please! Just one? One only!'

Anticipating compliance, they line up in groups, preen themselves, push interlopers out of frame, and throw themselves into poses lifted from the Kung-Fu movie posters. It's like this everywhere; I'm travelling through India like an ice-breaker, cutting a jagged path through walls of stiff, saluting children.

The scene is dominated by the stage, assembled by a team of *pandal-wallahs* this afternoon. Its bones are rough bamboo poles; a few planks have been arranged to give it a floor, and lengths of canvass and cloth have been draped around to give it a skirt, back-cloth, and awning. It looks great, but they are still decorating it. Paper cut-outs of stars and flowers are beginning to twinkle and bloom on the drapes, a huge portrait of Dr Ambedkar is being fixed to the proscenium arch; multi-coloured Buddhist flags hang limply from lines that reach out to the loudspeaker columns; cascades of tinsel shimmer in every corner.

Basic lighting comes from bare fluorescent tubes tied to the roof supports, and planted here and there out in the field. Up on posts, a little way off, a couple of football-sized bulbs, moored in battered tin reflectors, stand ready to offer some extra candle-power when the big moment comes. Sometimes we have strings of fairy lights festooned around the stage, even spread out beyond to cover part of the audience, like a canopy. In Latur, Sangharakshita had to give his talk standing directly in front of a spinning 'Dhammachakra Wheel' made entirely of light

The police are here, of course, standing by their jeep. They come to all our meetings, but so far there hasn't been any trouble. Sometimes a nearby factory hooter will go off at an unlikely hour, or a scooter will fizz past, its horn blaring. Maybe this sort of thing is harassment; maybe not. A bit of noise, more or less, hardly makes any difference. We tend to come expecting the worst.

Official stewards, sporting outsized Ambedkar rosettes, circulate in the crowd, telling people where to sit. A few disciplinarians have planted themselves at the very front among the kids, and cast fierce glances in every direction. Each holds a thick, long stick.

The crowd is getting bigger all the time now. I try to see whether there is anyone I can recognize from this afternoon's procession. The moment we arrived in town, we were ushered into jeeps and driven slowly through the streets while two thousand people, armed with flags and banners, walked before and behind us, chanting the Refuges. No doubt they're all here now. But it's hard to recognize anyone; even with all the lights on, it's still pretty dark beyond the stage.

Now the last arrangements are being made: a cheerleader dashes from one part of the throng to another, explaining which slogans will be chanted when Sangharakshita arrives, and how he is going to lead them. A hundred women in white, blue-fringed saris—members of local *mahila mandals*, or 'women's circles'—have begun to form a human arcade from the stage to the entrance gate. They chat excitedly, craning their necks towards the entrance, all the time guarding frail candle flames, and keeping sticks of incense upright on their silver trays. Up on stage, a couple of organizers and an unknown monk are taking turns to call out through the PA system that the moment is almost upon us. Down behind the stage, himself surrounded by admiring children, a 'loudspeaker-wallah' fiddles with knobs, dials, and wires, trying to eliminate the unearthly noises which all but drown the announcements.

But, whether we're ready or not, the taxi has come. The lime-green Ambassador drifts to a halt beside the entrance, and there is Sangharakshita!

He climbs out, beaming warmly, directly into an outheld garland. Lokamitra follows behind, smiling too, but fully alert, looking to check that the key organizer is here, receiving his own garland and exchanging greetings, while a host of well-wishers thrust posies into Sangharakshita's hands and kneel at his feet.

I am still finding it hard to accommodate myself to the way people treat him here. As he passes by, at last on his way to the stage, showered as he goes with rice grains and rose petals, he offers an almost imperceptible wink, and murmurs an aside: 'We don't do things like this in England, do we?'

Photographers—private and professional—dart out into the arcade ahead of him and the flash bulbs pop. Now the slogans have erupted and the applause is deafening. The moment he reaches the stage, however, chaos reigns as the arcade dissolves into an undisciplined scramble for the best places.

Once everyone is settled, Sangharakshita is invited to garland a bust of Dr Ambedkar and a painting of the Buddha, while a flustered MC offers a running commentary over the sound-system. The stage itself is now packed, but at least it is comfortable, since the entire surface has been spread with mattresses. Sangharakshita is there, with Lokamitra and Vimalakirti beside him. Then there is a squad of local organizers, and also, it would seem, a few monks whom the organizers have failed to move to the chairs below. Naturally, all this can lead to serious overcrowding. In Kannad we arrived to discover about twenty-five organizers and monks already planted on the stage; there was actually no room left for any of us. It took half an hour, and some extremely sensitive negotiating on Purna's part, to have just enough people removed to make room for the speakers.

At any Dhamma event in Maharashtra, the monks enjoy a kind of traditional right to be at the centre of the action—and the limelight. They are usually, though not always, friendly folk, and seem content with their lot in a worldly sort of way. For all that, even the chummiest of them give the impression that they are searching for a role—that of Dhamma teaching being denied them by their lack of knowledge and experience. Few have received any training, and most have little idea, if any, of what the spiritual life is about. Some of the older ones, I heard, were Hindu sannyassis before the conversions; afterwards they simply got themselves ordained as monks so that they could continue their undemanding lives undisturbed.

The trouble with having them up on stage is that they will distract people from the fact that this talk is a gateway to TBMSG—which has something practical to offer in the way of instruction, facilities, and follow-up. If they are moved by the talk a few people will probably invite an Order member to come and lead a meditation course in their locality, or even try out a retreat. The long-term effects could be profound. But if they fail to realize that there is a distinction between TBMSG and other elements in the local Buddhist world, then their response to the talk might go no further than feeding a few monks for a day.

Having himself garlanded Dr Ambedkar and the Buddha, it is now Sangharakshita's turn to be garlanded. This can be a prolonged affair. Individuals, families, Buddhist organizations, women's circles, all kinds of associations have brought their garlands, and now the MC must read out their names as they step forward to offer their loops of marigold and tuberose. Sometimes there can be as many as forty of these offerings, and Sangharakshita will spend the rest of the evening beside a colourful heap of fast-wilting blooms. He always insists that they are brought back to our digs at the end of the evening, and then festooned over chairs, fans, light-fittings, window ledges, and coat hooks. But the word will get around; people will know that their gifts have been fully registered and appreciated; only a politician, He once scoffed, would be so insensitive as to leave his garlands behind.

Sangharakshita is not the only person to be garlanded. Each of the organizers receive one, Lokamitra and Vimalakirti get a few each, and sometimes even the rest of us get a share. There was an exceptionally wholehearted session in Nanded. The MC needed a couple of assistants to help him at the microphone, correcting his errors and handing him 'stop press' details of last minute 'unreserved' offerings, as people rushed out into the street to buy more. The scene on stage resembled closing time on the last day of a flower show, as hosts of garlanders stumbled about, as if drunk on the scent of marigolds, trying to fit the right garlands over the right necks.

At last things quieten down. Mahadhammavir takes the microphone to lead the crowd through a recitation of the Refuges and Precepts, the final and most important 'preliminary'. Then, after a few words from the chairman, and a brief introduction from one of the Order members, Sangharakshita and Vimalakirti get up and take their places at neighbouring microphones.

In the background the traffic continues to rumble and toot, temple bells clang, and the air vibrates to the shiver of crickets. The sky is now full of stars; from the back of the audience, the stage stands out in the darkness like the theatre of an eccentric puppeteer.

Standing in the warm yellow light, Sangharakshita and Vimalakirti open up their broadside of words, each English sentence being hammered swiftly into place by the high-pitched echo of Vimalakirti's Marathi translation. A rapport develops as they speak, Vimalakirti's response coming so fast that, before long, the translation seems to overlap—and even precede—the original.

Sangharakshita holds a fat wad of paper sheets, each covered with his neat, red handwriting. These are thorough, detailed notes, a line of script for each sentence of speech. . . . And yet his eyes rarely seem to leave the audience.

It happens every night: the moment he starts to talk, an electric thrill passes through the assembly, for the fact of the matter is that all these people really want to hear what he has to say. Everyone and everything quietens down; mothers lean forward, forgetting the babies they are squeezing into their laps; the disciplinarians cast sharp, threatening looks about them, brandishing their sticks and clipping the odd ear if the boys are still frisky.

Perhaps, like Ambedkar, Sangharakshita sees his listeners in a paradoxical, twofold aspect. On the one hand, they are poor, uneducated, mainly illiterate. Even as they sit listening, their bodies express an air of physically ingrained humility. Most of them have known hard lives, some of them heartbreaking ones. They need prosperity, material comfort, and ease; they need the self-respect that a bit of worldly success could bring. And perhaps they still need to win a few political battles.

But they have also struggled out of a trap that ensnares most of the world: they have thrown away their gods and forsaken superstition. They know that life holds greater purpose than placid obedience to some divine plan. Then again, because they are poor, culturally isolated people, they are relatively untainted by the notion that life is about little more than consuming, about acquiring and heaping up material treasures. They are a community of people with the freedom, and just a little time, to think things out for themselves.

Their leader told them that they should look for their dignity and their destiny in their own inner riches. He believed in them, believed that they could give birth to an ideal society if they would only dig deeply enough into themselves. This is why they have come tonight, and come in their thousands. For all the carnival atmosphere, this is a serious audience.

Sangharakshita usually begins by explaining who he is, and how he came to know Dr Ambedkar. He thanks them for the warmth of their reception and, if he has been here before—and if it is appropriate—will express delight in seeing them looking more prosperous than they were last time.

He explains how and where he has spent the past two decades since he left India, and tells them a little about the Buddhist movement he has established in the West. This news acts as a visible source of encouragement. They never thought there could be so many practising Buddhists in the prosperous West.

He points out that these Western Buddhists are all 'New Buddhists', like themselves, and reminds them that whatever people may say about 'New Buddhists' being 'second-class Buddhists'—and such slights are frequently used as a weapon to undermine their confidence—the Dhamma *can* only be practised by new Buddhists. You have to decide to be a Buddhist: no one can be born a Buddhist. The very notion is absurd.

'*I* am a New Buddhist; Dr Babasaheb Ambedkar was a New Buddhist; the great Emperor Ashoka was a New Buddhist; even Gautama the Buddha himself was a New Buddhist! The *only* good Buddhist is a New Buddhist!'

There is laughter and delighted applause. In the front ranks, kids gaze up wide eyed, carelessly poking fingers into their cheeks as they open and close silent mouths.

In the West, he says, many people have lost faith in God, and in the superstition-rooted conventions of the church. Yet they still feel that there must be a deeper purpose to life—something that their old religion perhaps hinted at. They are rich: many of them have cars, televisions, washing machines, refrigerators, things that can make life much easier. And yet they are not happy; they feel frustrated because their lives are based on nothing more than material goals and achievements. They want the world to be a better place, but no longer believe that the politicians have the clarity or the vision to change things in any radical way. And they feel trapped by narrow convention, impotent in the face of the deeply entrenched power-groups that dominate society. They want their individuality back: they want to feel their own potency and effectiveness.

He tells them how he started his movement, and proclaims that the movement has centres in Britain, America, New Zealand, Australia, and India. He touches on the communities and the workers' co-operatives that are making the movement self-sufficient, and points out that all this has happened in just fourteen years, even though there were few people, and no money, when it all began. The Dhamma is effective. It brings results. The 'Dhamma Revolution' here really could be a revolution. If people are prepared to work for it, it will happen: it will change every section and aspect of society. But it will not come about unless everyone takes responsibility for it, unless everybody works for it. And, of course, because this is a *Dhamma* Revolution, they

Jai Bhim!

can only do that by practising the Dhamma.

It is not enough to chant the Refuges and Precepts thinking that that alone makes you a Buddhist. Dr Ambedkar didn't want to turn his people into Buddhist parrots! He wanted them to become real Buddhists, 'one hundred percent Buddhists'. Someone who calls himself a Buddhist, and then does nothing about it, is like a donkey pretending he's a horse. His over-sized head is inflated with knowledge; his big ears allow him to hear more than he understands; his loud 'Hee-Haw' is just words without action, and his useless little tail betrays his lack of any real qualities. Finally, he is obstinate, unreceptive, and lazy.

The crowd roars with laughter. Someone takes it upon himself to lead a slogan chant, not fully understanding what is going on, probably because he's been drinking. The children laugh too, and try to catch the eyes of the people up on stage. If they ever succeed, they curl up in embarrassed delight.

Now the commotion has woken a goat that's been asleep in the middle of the throng since long before the talk began. We wait while she is slapped and shooed on her way.

The Dhamma leads to change. It is about change. Some people say that, because the Buddha taught 'impermanence', Buddhism must be gloomy and pessimistic. But it is wonderful that things are impermanent: it means that they change. And if things have to change, then why should they not change for the better. People are changing all the time, so people can become better. Society is changing, so society can become better. Nature is changing, in a process of constant evolution. Human beings too can change, with effort, in a process of 'higher' evolution. A bad man can become a good man; a good man can become a better man; a better man can become a Buddha. This is why we practise the Dhamma. This is its purpose: to help those who want to change for the better, and who want to make the world a better place.

Each night Sangharakshita introduces a fresh range of teachings, and explains aspects of Buddhist practice, basing his commentaries on a host of traditional formulations: the Four Noble Truths, the Eightfold Path, the Threefold Way, the Seven Limbs of Enlightenment, the Five Spiritual Faculties. . . . His discourses are peppered with stories, jokes, anecdotes, and examples from the life of the Buddha and Dr Ambedkar, or simply from Indian village life. His words are straightforward and clear, and leave no one behind.

Purna's tape recorder hums and whirrs, picking up his words. Before long they will be transcribed, edited, translated, and published in the Marathi, Gujerati, and English-medium magazines that circulate within

130

the Buddhist community. During the course of this visit Sangha-rakshita is creating a legacy of teachings that will keep those publications stocked for years.

Again and again, he returns to the theme of morality. Ambedkar once said, 'Morality is Dhamma; Dhamma is Morality'. Sangharakshita distinguishes 'conventional morality'—the morality of the group or caste—from 'natural morality'. In terms of *natural* morality, some actions—of body, speech, or mind—express lower, less human, even animal mental states. Others express truly human states, express our distinctively human capacity for wisdom, love, and unselfishness. Our first task, therefore, is to become truly human and to get beyond the animal realm of blind craving, blind instinct, and self-centredness.

To be truly human is to recognize that actions have consequences, for ourselves, for others, and for our environment—and to take full responsibilty for our actions. The five Precepts help because they offer a kind of blueprint for more truly human actions and states of mind. These precepts don't take their sanction from a god, or from the group, but from our innate potential to develop, and from our deep yearning to do so. For this reason 'natural' morality is the foundation of human life itself, whether individual or collective. Naturally, if we live a truly ethical life we will be free from conflicts and confusion; we'll get on well with others, and we'll know how to help them. Our lives will be clear, free from worry, free from anxiety. . . .

For some reason, almost every night, at around the half-way point, there is a major disturbance. Tonight we've got a man who wants to drive his bullock cart through the audience. He can't be bothered to go the long way round, and thinks he can just trundle across our field. A argument has erupted at the gate.

Sometimes, a circle of ladies will arrive late, and come floating into the proceedings with their trays of lighted candles and incense, like spirits from a dream. But every night, no matter where we are, a moment comes when the young mothers realize it's time to put their little ones to bed. As soon as they get up, they seem to disconnect from the event completely, and enter a new dimension. They talk at the tops of their voices, call across to each other, and berate their children, while other members of the audience shout at them, hiss, wave their arms, and try to calm them down. If things get really bad Sangharakshita will take a few discrete steps back and study his notes while Vimalakirti joins in from the microphone. It can take ten minutes for the ripples to subside.

Sangharakshita goes on to explain how mental and emotional freedom, the fruits of ethical conduct, provide the basis for meditation practice. Meditation, he says, opens the way to the higher development

131

of the mind which Ambedkar upheld as the indispensable requirement
for a decent life. Ambedkar repeatedly spoke of his faith in the 'energy',
'enthusiasm', and 'inspiration' that lie within us. These qualities can be
contacted directly, through meditation. In a mind that is concentrated
and focussed, distractions have no place, the various 'aspects' and
'selves' that make up a person are brought into harmony. The result is
that we begin to feel quite different: we have more energy because
none of it is being drained by confusion or vagueness; we can reach
down into our depths and discover tremendous power, limitless
enthusiasm, and a fundamental level of confidence.

He teaches the practice of *anapana sati*, or 'mindfulness of breathing',
a meditation which brings about this kind of concentration. Anyone
who practises it will begin to see their life more clearly and find out
what they need to do to make it better. It is a practice that can carry us
into realms of thought, feeling, and imagination far richer than those
we experience most of the time. This is where the fresh vision will arise,
helping us to take our lives and ambitions onto an ever higher
level.

He also teaches the *maitri bhavana*—the 'development of universal
loving-kindness'. Emotions like love, fraternity, and compassion *can* be
developed, he says. We tend to think that they arise solely as a matter of
chance or passing mood, but our emotional states need not depend on
outside circumstances at all. Someone who has worked to develop
even a little *maitri* can stand firm in the face of difficulties. He won't be
discouraged by the knocks he receives, he will be able to think clearly
and positively—remain in a good state to find a way of beating the
obstacles that confront him. If all the members of a Buddhist locality
were to practise *maitri bhavana*, they would not just get on well with
each other, they would be able to work effectively together: they would
be strong, and they would have an incalculable effect on the localities
around them.

It surprises me to see Sangharakshita teaching meditation this way.
In England I've never once heard him explain how to practise
meditation at a public talk. But here, in this town, there is no public
centre for anyone to visit for a follow-up class, and Poona is a long way
away. Even while he speaks, I can sense the urgency he feels. Even if
just one person here manages to get somewhere with meditation as a
result of this talk, he or she will make an impact on the others, another
seed will have been sown.

There is a *vihara* in this locality: a small, rectangular, one-roomed
building. It has a Buddha-shrine, and is used as a lodging by visiting
monks. Most of the time, though, it serves as a sort of social club.
Sangharakshita asks his listeners to keep their vihara beautiful and

clean, and use it only for Buddhist activities:

'A Vihara should be a peaceful place, a place where you can make a special effort to practise the Precepts, a place where you can meditate. If you treat your vihara well, and use it properly, you will have no need to make the costly pilgrimage to Bodh Gaya. You will have the Buddha right here in your own neighbourhood, reminding you of the real purpose of life, inspiring you to make further efforts.'

Meditation, practised successfully and deeply, he continues, provides the foundation for wisdom. In this context wisdom is not something we get from books. Of course it is important to study the Dhamma; that is how we find out what the Buddha actually did and said, and what he advised us to do. But even that kind of book learning is not wisdom; Wisdom is the way we see things when we are living on a higher level. And this kind of wisdom can express itself in a number of ways: as fearlessness, as generosity, as patience, and, of course, as 'insight'—seeing things as they really are. He offers an illustration:

'Once upon a time there was a lion cub who had lost his parents. In fact, he became completely separated from the other lions, and strayed into a flock of sheep. He lived with the sheep for years, and grew up among them—thinking, after a while, that he was himself just another sheep.

'One day while out grazing, the sheep/lion came across a big, wild lion. At first he was terrified, and tried to run away, but because he only knew how to run like a sheep, the lion soon caught up with him, and asked him why he was so frightened.

' "Baa!" said the sheep/lion, "I am afraid because I have been told that lions are dangerous to us sheep. You will want to eat me up."

' "*Us* sheep?" stammered the lion, "But you are not a sheep at all! You are a lion like me."

' "Baa! Oh no. I am not a lion. I am a sheep. Why are you trying to confuse me?"

'The lion had never encountered anything like this before. There was no doubting it, though: here was a lion who thought he was a sheep! Then he had an idea, and led the sheep/lion by the scruff of the neck to a pool of clear water and forced him to look at his reflection. There, the sheep/lion didn't see a sheep at all—but a lion! He immediately "woke up", and realized that for all those years he'd been living under an illusion.

'We are like that lion cub. We think we are sheep when really we are lions. We think we are weak when really we are strong. We need to see for ourselves what we *really* are.

'Of course, like that lion cub, we may need a friend to come along and remind us about our true selves. But in this respect we are very lucky.

Jai Bhim!

We have had *two* friends, two lions, in the not too distant past. First there was Gautama the Buddha. And then—even more recently—there was Dr Babasaheb Ambedkar!'

Repeatedly, Sangharakshita embroiders his stories with references to Ambedkar, and recapitulates the man's qualities and significance. Whenever Ambedkar is mentioned in this way there is an explosion of applause. The official cheerleader—one of the village elders—sets up a few chants; the atmosphere is jubilant.

One night, after a talk, I asked Sangharakshita about these continual references. It was all so different to the Buddhism I was used to. Were all these references, and the general preoccupation with the social dimension of things, anything more than a 'skilful means'?

'What do you mean?' Sangharakshita was perplexed.

'Well, in the West, you explain Buddhism far more in terms of individual, even psychological, development. Isn't that where all this must lead in the end, to individual Buddhists working on themselves to develop Enlightened qualities?'

He laughed. 'Well, in the West, people are far more individualistic and psychologically oriented. I therefore have to talk in those more "psychological" terms. Here, people are more community oriented; they *experience* themselves more as members of a community or family. So here I talk in more, as it were, social terms. But, actually, I'm using a skilful means in both situations. You must not assume that either approach is any closer to the fundamental Dhamma than the other. The Dhamma is whatever helps people to grow. They may choose to work on themselves first, or they may choose to work in society. Either way they will be growing, and setting up the conditions for their own further development—and that of their society.

'If anything, you *could* say that the language of social uplift is *more* effective—though both approaches have their advantages and limitations, of course. If Enlightenment consists in overcoming the "self-other dichotomy", we can progress towards it by working on the "other" end of things just as effectively as we can by working simply on ourselves.'

Night after night, he instructs, uplifts, and befriends. If there is any one element that I will recollect above all others, it will be the bond of warmth and intimacy that grows between him and his audience as each talk progresses. No wonder there are people here who remember his last visit, twenty years ago. And no wonder he has never forgotten them.

In the little town of Kurdu Wadi, he compared Ambedkar's Dhamma Revolution to the 'Green Revolution' that had brought water, crops, and prosperity to the backward, famine-stricken regions of India.

'Water helps things to grow. Yet every tree, flower, and crop grows in its own way, according to its own inner pattern. The Dhamma helps people to grow, but they too must each grow in their own unique way, according to their nature, according to their own inner potential.'

The Buddha once compared himself to a mighty rain cloud, pouring forth the nourishing rain of the Dhamma. I think of Sangharakshita, of our entire party: we have been passing over Maharashtra like a rain cloud. Who knows what roots are now stirring, what shoots are quickening with life? Ambedkar has sometimes been compared to Moses, leading his people out of servitude, delivering the Holy Word into their midst. But perhaps it would be more appropriate to think of him as a rainmaker: the man who conjured up rainclouds in the middle of a desert.

In the old days, when Sangharakshita gave his talks, the talks were all he had to give. There were no tape recorders to pick up his words and, but for Dharmarakshita, he was alone. Now things are different. He concludes his talk by saying a little about the team of Dhamma workers that Lokamitra has established. He mentions that his talks will soon appear in issues of *Buddhayan* and *Dhammamegha*, and that Order members are available to come and give more talks, or to lead courses. There are centres in a few cities, and there are retreats. From now on his listeners can get as deeply involved in the Dhamma as they wish. The opportunity exists; the Dhamma doesn't have to be an occasional treat. In time they could even think about setting up special Dhamma communities, even getting a co-operative off the ground. In time they could be living as 'one hundred percent Buddhists'.

The talk ends on a recapitulatory high-note. Sangharakshita hopes that everyone will remember his words, and that they will now try to practise the Dhamma with new enthusiasm. He urges them to work together and avoid energy-wasting disputes. He tells them that if they can do even that, then they will become happier, they will find their way to dignity and prosperity, their communities will become 'new societies', and Ambedkar's dream of a Dhamma Revolution will move closer to fulfilment.

Vimalakirti renders these last words into Marathi, and then, bringing his hands together, adds a final 'Jai Bhim' of his own.

Normally, at the end of a Dhamma talk in Maharashtra, people come forward to give the visiting monk some *dana*—or money. But on our tour this only happens when the arrangements have gone wrong. Sangharakshita would rather people spent their money on Dhamma books for their community.

So, once the chairman has given a vote of thanks, and once Lokamitra has finished his sales pitch for the books that Bodhisen is selling, the

Jai Bhim!

Dhammapalam Gatha is chanted, and the programme is over.

Crowds now form around each of the bookstalls and around the stage. Sangharakshita is shaking hands, talking, signing autographs. A diminutive man squeezes his way through the throng, hammering open a path with the tiny baby he carries in his arms. He thrusts the dazed infant under Sangharakshita's nose.

'Name! Please, *Bhanteji*! Name!'

Sangharakshita looks at the well-wrapped child. 'Is it a boy or a girl?'

'Girl, *Bhanteji.*'

He takes another look, smiles, '*Bodhipushpa*—Flower of Enlightenment.'

Overcome with rapture, the father spins on his heels and batters his way back through the crowd, his eyes wildly seeking out the rest of his group. The entire affair has lasted no more than fifteen seconds, but that name will go with the girl for the rest of her life—among a few others no doubt—as a highly prized talisman. Meanwhile, with an anxious eye on his watch, Lokamitra sends off relays of messengers to find out what has happened to the taxi. It is eleven o'clock.

The books are selling well. Bodhisen and his helpers are answering questions, explaining what the books are about, trying to enlist subscriptions for *Buddhayan*. Even if they only manage to pick up a couple, a link will have been formed, since each copy will be read—or heard—by tens, if not hundreds, of people.

The book-selling team will stay on for another hour or so. When they finally return to base, Bodhisen will write up his accounts and check his stock lists. He never leaves anything until the morrow. When you suggest that he could do with some food, or sleep, he just laughs in his determined way, says 'Yes!' and goes back to his work.

Sangharakshita will need to get back as soon as possible to ensure a good night's sleep, but the rest of us are now scooped up and taken off to someone's home for a meal. There, wife, daughters, grannie, and some of the neighbours too, will have been up since dawn preparing the feast, pounding spices, sifting rice and lentils, chopping vegetables, making chapatis and puris. It will be around midnight when we arrive. They will be, by stages, bewildered, upset, and finally happily resigned to Sangharakshita's absence.

The women usually make a brief, silent appearance when we arrive, and just before we leave, but that is all we'll see of them. They will be out in the kitchen the rest of the time, slapping chapatis from hand to hand, frying the puris, keeping the whole operation going. After we've left they will serve the menfolk. Heaven knows when *they* will get to eat.

Our hosts rarely make much effort to get us talking. It seems perfectly acceptable that we should just eat and chat among ourselves while they serve us. Everyone is happy and excited; the evening has gone well, right up to this last detail. Who needs more talk?

It is a relief to be able to eat in this way, just chatting easily among ourselves. This has been a long, demanding day: another long and demanding day! We'll be up at six-thirty tomorrow to do it all again.

We talk about the lecture, about the day's journey, about the delays, about Sangharakshita. We share stories about our backgrounds and outlooks. But mainly we talk about the Dhamma Revolution. After all, this is not just any kind of journey we are making together: it is an adventure of almost mythic proportions, a shared enterprise. We are savouring the essence of 'Fraternity'.

One night, in Ambad, Buddhapriya, Vimalakirti, Purna, and I sat in a café, just an hour before the programme was due to start. As we teased Buddhapriya about some slip-up in the arrangements, I realized that the other patrons were watching and commenting on us among themselves. Their looks were inquisitive but friendly, even encouraging. Then the penny dropped. They were intrigued by the fact that we were a mixed group of Indians and 'white' men.

Our easy cameraderie seemed to please them, but their reaction still took me by surprise. Until that moment such a thought had never even crossed my mind.

thirteen

'We wuz holed up at Ol' Paw Dongray's.'

Bent double, Jyotipala hovered at my side, skewering a sunblotched face into mine as he handed over a cup of coffee.

'No. If someone ever writes a book about all this, that's how they should begin this bit: "We wuz holed up at Ol' Paw Dongray's. . . ." '

He headed back towards the house, polishing his dreadful blend of Yorkshire and Hillbilly.

'Yup! Hawoled oop aiyat Ol' Paower Dawngray's.' As a rule, Jyotipala said things thrice.

Nevertheless, we were, so I have.

There were three phases to the tour: constant travel and one-night stopovers at the beginning and end, and, here in the middle, ten days of relative stability in Aurangabad. The talks went on of course, in Aurangabad and its surrounding villages, but for a spell we were able to enjoy the luxury of a permanent base—an ancient military bungalow on the extreme edge of the cantonment district. Our host was Mr Dongray, a retired army recruitment officer.

It was a fascinating abode: dark, shadowy, musty, stuffed with decrepit furniture, piles of faded magazines, and heaps of bric-a-brac, like a complex of interconnecting attics badly in need of a sort-out, yet lacking a house beneath. Mr Dongray had his nest in a small, fluorescent-lit room at the very heart of the place, and suffered from a number of age-related ailments. He spent much of the time lying on his rickety four-poster bed, enveloped in cigarette smoke and electrical buzz, but got up occasionally to take meals with us; he even came to our programmes when he felt up to it. He was a great talker, and filled the nooks and crannies of his ever-shuttered domain with the nursery-rhyme rhythms of his cracked but kindly, resonant voice. The rhythms had lost much of their bounce now, and most of his sentences tended to peter out as they neared their end, as if the trusty clockwork motor behind them was running down.

The pride of his life was the garden, a fenced-off enclosure of miniature pathways and irrigation channels, over which loomed an immense variety of trees, shrubs, geraniums, and an eye-assaulting riot of red and mauve bougainvillaea. The garden gave onto an arid, grassy plain, in the centre of which stood a perfect replica of an English country church, faithful in every detail but for its overcoat of brilliant white paint. A little beyond the church ran the narrow highway which linked Aurangabad with Poona. But for a few bicycles and buses it was a quiet road, though, from time to time, goods lorries would nose their way along it, piercing the air with epically nostalgic wails from their two-tone horns. Then—beyond the fields, the road, and the plains—rose the ghats, soft and pale in the dazzling sunshine.

The firm trunk of a peepul, or 'Bodhi' tree, rose from the earth beside a room-sized porch, and spread its mass of heart-shaped leaves over the balcony above, creating a shady retreat for Sangharakshita who had been given the one upstairs room—the very room where Ambedkar used to stay when visiting Aurangabad.

It was a time of arrivals and departures. Some of our number returned to Poona: temporarily, to pick up more books, or permanently, to rejoin families and jobs. Others joined us at this point, either for the duration of our stay in Aurangabad, or for the rest of the tour. There were but three beds in the entire place, so at night we camped around the house and out in the garden, unrolling matresses and mosquito nets before turning in, then stowing them away again for the day.

Fearing that this 'break' might lead to a loss of momentum in our enterprise, Lokamitra kept us constantly busy, cleaning out the house, cooking and washing up, transcribing the tapes of Sangharakshita's talks. Purna now busied himself with the frightful task of knitting his recordings together, for in his attempts to shake off mains hum, he had been switching microphones and tape-recorders several times during the course of each lecture.

However, our real boss and absolute dictator at this juncture, enjoying the all-transcending power of a ship's captain on the open sea, was our housekeeper, Jyotipala. He had arrived in Aurangabad a few days before us and had worked hard to make the place as neat and welcoming as possible. But from the moment we arrived he ruled us with a rod of iron.

Jyotipala was the first to admit that the world could count itself lucky that he had spent so much of his adult life in institutions: two Catholic monasteries, the army, and a marriage. He was one of the warmest, funniest, and kindest people I had ever met, yet none of these virtues could quite conceal the fact that somewhere within him lurked a killer. He had, for example, a way of pointing out that you had forgotten to wash your tea cup, failed to sweep the floor thoroughly, or purchased the wrong variety of biscuit, which was subtly but seriously menacing. At such times you could only hope that the 'outer' Jyotipala—who would be affectionately laughing and enfolding you in his arm, poking a little fun—would be firm enough to protect you from the 'inner' Jyotipala whose secret eyes surveyed you with cold scorn . . . whom you could almost hear saying 'Why don't we just kill him now boss?' Clearly, his two years as a motel janitor in Las Vegas had also played their part in giving shape to his personality.

His manner could be as uneven and unpredictable as the skin-tones of his face. He would work himself and others into the ground, as if conducting a rite of mass-expiation, yet at other times he could fill the place with lunacy and laughter. His voice could be coarse and rough one moment, almost curdled with mincing piety the next. He blamed it on his Catholic conditioning, and in the meantime kept a very tight ship.

This had its advantages. At last we were eating simple, regular meals. Those we had been taking on our travels had been fabulous affairs, but they had come at irregular times and in terrifying quantities. It had not been uncommon to eat a substantial meal in one house, before getting shunted next door, where an even bigger one would be waiting. In

India, and especially among poor people who have gone to great trouble and expense to lay on a good spread, one has a certain duty, and that duty is to eat. And one must eat everything that finds its way onto one's plate. This is all further complicated by an Indian ritual of etiquette according to which one says 'no' when one really means 'yes'. I soon learned that to avoid being faced with second, third, and even forth helpings, I had to eat extremely slowly, with at least one hand poised to fend off the in-bound delicacies. My hosts, of course, were far more adept at the game than was I, so by the time we reached Aurangabad, my stomach was crying out for a rest.

We also wallowed in the luxury of a good-sized room for meditation, and enough space in our daily programme to use it. Trying to meditate, crammed into those government bungalows, already anxious about the coming day's arrangements, had been challenging to say the least. Here we could gather in our spacious room knowing there was plenty of time before anything was going to happen.

It may seem strange that we tried to meditate at all under the conditions of the tour. But nobody ever skipped a day if it was at all possible. On the highest level—assuming we managed to attain such heights—it was our meditation practice that ensured we were functioning from inspiration rather than a sense of duty or sheer doggedness. On a lower level, the daily meditations went some way towards preventing the clutter of our physical circumstances from infecting our minds, but, by and large, we kept meditating because that was what we were used to doing.

In the Buddhist scheme of things one does not meditate solely to enjoy blissful 'experiences', or even, for that matter, states of refreshing relaxation. One meditates in order to maintain and deepen a thread of connection between the surface and the depths of one's mind. Sometimes this *can* bear fruit in the form of a special experience, but more often it is simply good hard work. The day is always better for it, even when your meditation seems to have been a pretty fruitless struggle against distractions, and, perhaps surprisingly, many people find that their 'best' meditations can take place under the most trying conditions. But, above all, it is simply worth pressing on, for, in doing so, one is planting mental seeds, strengthening familiarity with the various aspects of one's being, filling out, going deeper. . . .

There were, of course, the mosquitoes. These were the biggest, meanest, most malevolent tykes I had ever come across. We were accordingly obliged to meditate shrouded from head to toe in sheets, towels, and veils of lungi material, praying that none of the beasts would penetrate our defences. Had a passing stranger looked into the room at such times, he would have probably mistaken our motionless forms for a suite of chairs, covered for the winter to keep the dust off while the owners were away.

The relatively quiet, travel-free days also gave us an opportunity to do a bit of sightseeing; we made trips to an impressive but necessarily second-rate imitation of the Taj Mahal, just outside Aurangabad, to the ancient fort-city of Daulatabad, and, of course, to the Buddhist cave temples at Ajanta and Ellora.

Those roomy, cool temples and halls, carved out of the living rock, were truly impressive. The sculpted Buddhas and Bodhisattvas which sat, stood, and reclined within them, as well as their faded frescoes, were works of art in themselves, still communicating, as effectively as ever, their powerful appeal to the highest values and the most sublime ideal. But it was the sheer grandeur of the complexes: the total achievement that each one represented, which really took the breath away. How much work, how many labourers, artists, and artisans must have been involved in their creation? And how many generations of monks had kept their echoing chambers aboom with chants?

Just a couple of days after our visit to Ellora, Sangharakshita spoke to an assembly of Buddhist teachers and students at Milind College, an establishment founded and designed by Ambedkar, and named after the king who plied the monk Nagasena with penetrating questions in the *Milinda Pannha*, or 'Questions of King Milinda'. In his talk, Sangharakshita referred to the caves, reminding his listeners that in becoming Buddhists they had become heirs to a magnificent legacy. He went on to warn them against dismissing Buddhism as an ancient relic whose proper place lay in the distant past, and urged them not to be deceived by the archaic dress of the monks, the temple ruins, or the 'dead' language of the Pali texts. If they could only dig deep into the Dhamma they would unearth basic principles—principles which were as valid today as ever. The Dhamma still had the power to change people, and to transform society.

It was a clarion-call of a talk, aimed very directly at this materially ambitious, youthful audience. In India, as Vimalakirti had explained to me, the spiritual life, and certainly any full-time involvement with it, was considered to be something of an old man's occupation, to be undertaken only when life's battle was over. It was the final stage in the (Caste-)Hindu's journey through the world. Vimalakirti had added with a laugh that many young people were reluctant to have anything to do with meditation, since there was a belief abroad that it made one impotent.

Milind College was itself something of a legacy. Established during the fifties by Ambedkar's 'People's Education Society', its six thousand students lived and worked in surroundings that had been consciously designed to enhance their self respect and sharpen their ambition. Although never properly completed for lack of funds, the entire complex had a noble, even classical, air, with its domed roofs, and sweeping, columned arcades.

The new college made such a stir when it was opened that Aurangabad, formerly something of an educational backwater, began to sprout more and yet more schools and colleges, as Hindu, Christian, and Muslim institutions sought to compete with Ambedkar's creation. A crowning honour almost came when the Chief Minister of Maharashtra indicated that he was planning to name a new university being built in Aurangabad 'Dr Ambedkar University', to commemorate the man responsible for the region's academic renaissance. A number of vocal Hindu pressure groups resisted this move, however, and demanded that the university should instead be known as the 'University of Marathwada'.

There were marches, demonstrations, violent confrontations. A few people lost their lives, women were raped, thousands of people were imprisoned; Buddhists were forced by mobs to urinate over statues of the Buddha and Dr Ambedkar. In the end, the Ambedkarites lost their fight: the university would be known as The University of Marathwada. Now, several years on, grudges remained fierce. In Aurangabad still, as in many other Maharashtran towns, Ambedkar's statues and busts lived behind wire cages, protected from hammers, shoes, buckets of pitch, and even excrement.

But the picture was not all black. A few days later, Sangharakshita was invited to address an assembly of liberal-minded Caste-Hindus. The talk he gave was a carefully argued exploration of the implications of life in a secular state. In establishing herself on such terms, he said, India had made the implicit undertaking to allow her citizens the right and freedom to practise the religions of their choice. Her laws favoured and discriminated against no one. If the Constitution was to work, then India's many religious communities would have to learn to co-exist in peace. Her people would have to recognize each other, first and foremost, as people, and not as Hindus, Moslems, Sikhs, Christians, or whatever. In India, as in any secular state, the human being, not God, would have to come first.

This, he acknowledged, presented the followers of theistic religions with something of a problem. If they were to get along with each other, as well as with those who followed non-theistic religions, then those who were in the habit of putting God and his Will first would have to change.

In the case of Hinduism, for example, the God-given doctrine of the caste system declared that people were not equal, and insisted that they should be treated unequally. But this, as was now clear, militated against the fundamental principles of a secular state. India would therefore be a secular state only when the caste system was no longer practised. How was this to come about?

The answer was really quite obvious, he said, for there was really only one effective way in which the caste system could be eradicated for good and all. The root of the system was the *hereditary principle*: endogamy; the scriptures forbade any marriage between members of different castes. The destruction of the caste system could consequently be brought about only by the overthrow of that hereditary principle. More marriages would have to take place between Hindus of different castes, and all Indians who accepted the principles enshrined in their own constitution were implicitly committed to the practice of inter-caste marriage.

Politely suggesting that, as India became more truly sec 'ar—in fact as well as in law—then she might well find herself turning again towards the reasonable, tolerant principles of Buddhism, he brought his talk to an end.

* * *

Ambedkar married twice, first at the age of fourteen, and again at the age of fifty-six—his first wife having died in 1935. The first marriage was arranged by his father and was, quite naturally, within his own caste. But his second marriage was, as he put it, 'the best match' he could arrange for himself. He married a Brahmin doctor.

This inter-caste marriage gave him considerable satisfaction. In his *Who's Who* entry, he starkly recorded the fact that he, 'an Untouchable by birth', was married to a lady, 'Brahmin by birth'.

But the match was not popular among his followers. Again and again I saw the same photograph of his first wife—perhaps the only one ever taken—mounted on the walls of Buddhist households. She was revered as an archetype of loyalty, patience, and devotion. But the popular mind turned sharply, even vindictively, against his second wife, even though she had nursed and cared for Ambedkar ceaselessly throughout his last, increasingly painful years. When he died, there was a public dispute between her and his one surviving son, which had finally to be settled in a court of law. This was just the beginning of a depressing series of conflicts that followed Ambedkar's death.

For all his strengths and virtues, and despite his numerous achievements, Ambedkar's life was beset by a nagging handicap. He was admired, respected, and considered indispensable even by some of his enemies, but his need to deploy—almost constantly—the qualities of aggression and bull-headedness in his work drove him repeatedly into painful clashes, even with his allies, and distanced him from people. He lamented the habitual scowl that scarred his features—partly physical accident and partly a testament to the battles with which his life was fraught. Sometimes, he would even admit to feeling more at ease in the company of books than with his fellow humans. As a public figure he was worshipped and adored, but as a man, one feels, he lived very much alone. It is, perhaps, a common paradox: here was a man who overflowed with hot, altruistic feelings, and yet his emotional energies were so sharply channelled into the causes for which he fought that he had little left to invest in more personal affairs.

This imbalance was probably responsible for the one serious omission in his life's work. He left disciples, devotees, and admirers, but he left no team.

Clearly, there was no one man able to replace him; intellectually he stood like 'a titan among dwarves', as one of his followers put it to me. But had he been able to weld his closest lieutenants into an harmonious, mutually supportive team with clearly established goals, then things might have turned out very differently.

For, within just a few years of his death, many of his colleagues were arguing over what he had really wanted, what he had really meant to say, each able to cite contradictory quotations and references to support their claims. A price had now to be paid for those 'inconsistencies'. Soon they were splitting into factions, establishing rival parties and organizations, diverting energy and strength into mutual criticism and competition. The wider Buddhist community became so divided, confused, politically castrated, and, above all, so dazzled by all the fireworks, that it lost sight of Ambedkar's vision of a Dhamma Revolution.

There were those who blamed the Congress Party, claiming that the machiavellian Hindus at its helm had snatched away the Buddhist initiative, raising the old doubts about the Buddha as an incarnation of Vishnu, or offering 'puppet' Buddhists at the polls who attracted votes but then did nothing once elected. Perhaps so. But there is no doubt that the Buddhist community itself engendered a good crop of its own 'new leaders', each of them after a share of the freely available limelight, each vying to assume 'Babasaheb's' mantle. But they were none of them Ambedkars. They lacked his education, his experience, his vision; they lacked his stature. Each had his short day, before fading back into obscurity, taking with him yet another quantum of trust and hope.

This fragmentation affected the more directly Buddhist side of things too. Political leaders, appreciating the propaganda value—if little else—of the Buddhist initiative, started setting up their own Buddhist groups and organizations. In no time, these were clashing with one another in their attempts to direct the flock.

All these trends were escalating during the years that Sangharakshita was working in Maharashtra. Soon, he found himself having to watch his every step, guard his words, and, above all, avoid allowing himself to become 'appropriated' by any one faction or party.

As an example, he told me of an occasion when he gave a talk at the *Diksha Bhumi* or 'Initiation Ground' in Nagpur, the very place where Ambedkar's conversion rally had taken place. Naturally, this plot of land had an immense symbolic value for the entire Buddhist community, and it was believed that the government was considering giving it to the Buddhists in a gesture of friendship.

When his talk came to an end, Sangharakshita was asked to plant a Bodhi tree sapling, as a momento of the occasion. This was a trap. Were he to plant the tree, the group responsible for this particular meeting would probably use it to enhance their political prestige, even as evidence in their claim for some eventual right to the land. And yet there would be an unpleasant scene if he refused.

What he did was admire the sapling, take up the proffered shovel, though asking as he did so: 'I suppose this is a cutting from the *real* Bodhi Tree, the one at Bodh Gaya?'

Embarrassed, his hosts had to admit that it was not. Then, without having to appear as anything more than a stickler for symbolic detail, Sangharakshita played his card.

'Well, as it would take so little time and trouble to get such a cutting, a cutting from the descendant of the very tree beneath which the Buddha gained Enlightenment. . . .'

The organizers of course suspected that he knew what he was doing, and he knew that they suspected this. But nobody could say a word, and the issue was promptly dropped amid murmurs of delighted accord. He once said of that era that he managed to keep himself out of trouble, and avoid compromising himself, only by putting forth the wisdom of the serpent.

In the course of the tour we had a few opportunities to watch that serpent wisdom at work. He was fluent in the ways of Indian social politics. He could enthuse and encourage, even gasp with wonder as politicians showed him drawings and designs, or painted pictures with their words, and generally sought to impress him with their plans and visions—for temples, viharas, schools, and so on. But he would sign, so to speak, nothing. He was a master at the art of 'limited concurrence', offering wholehearted encouragement—and thus satisfying honour— but withholding commitment, unless totally confident that no attempt was being made to exploit his name for suspect reasons. What was remarkable was how he always managed to do this in a thoroughly friendly way. No one could ever take offence, no one could ever be quite certain that he was not at all as innocent as he seemed.

He told me that one of the main reasons behind his decision to leave India and work in the West was his growing conviction that he could do very little in India until this period of disintegration and politicking had come to an end. As things stood, none of the politicians were equipped to give a lead, none of them could reunify the movement, none of them had clear enough aims, nor the skill and integrity required to realize them. They lacked precisely those qualities which Ambedkar had hoped they would develop by practising Buddhism.

Yet it was precisely Buddhism that everyone ignored during this period. If anything, Buddhism became little more than a rallying call, a banner, a symbolic totem of the group.

Vimalakirti was an active Ambedkarite during this period. He dabbled with politics, but soon became disillusioned by the amount of corruption and confusion he saw around him. So far as he knew, he had read, quite literally, every word that Ambedkar ever wrote, and had formed his own view that Buddhism held the key to Ambedkar's manifesto.

'This is what I thought. And I wanted other people to understand it too. But when I contacted the others, they gave me a very difficult time. I tried to convince them that we must make the Dhamma our top priority, try to become good Buddhists first of all, and then try to do everything else. In time, the Dhamma would give us the strength to do things properly—in the political field, in the social field, and so on. But let us first muster our strength together in the Dhamma!

'These people could not understand. They would create difficulties. All they cared about was politics. Of course, they did take Dr Ambedkar seriously, but they were so confused. As far as Buddhism was concerned, they thought that it just meant doing some chanting and arranging the ceremonies in the right way. They could not see how relevant it was for our struggle.'

For their part, the monks—the full time Buddhists—offered nothing more than the Buddhism of the group: Buddhist weddings, Buddhist funerals, Buddhist festivals. And, whenever possible, the politicians would be up on stage with them at meetings, sometimes dressed in robes, having got themselves ordained as shramaneras for one- or two-week periods—particularly at election times.

The Dhamma Revolution ground to a standstill. The Buddhists still enjoyed some of the safeguards that Ambedkar had won for the Scheduled Castes. In Maharashtra, at least, they could still take advantage of the 'Reservations' in education and State government employment; in other states, and in all central government services, they were required to register themselves not as Buddhists but as Scheduled Caste Hindus if they wanted to make any headway.

Meanwhile, India was becoming more prosperous. In the towns and cities the most blatant features of caste discrimination were beginning to weaken. Some Buddhists were achieving a slightly higher standard of living and a little more self-respect as their sons made progress in the world. But there was no Dhamma Revolution, no real transcendence of old attitudes and ideas, nothing to compare even faintly with the dream that Ambedkar had entertained.

The Buddhist community could hardly be blamed for this state of affairs. Who was there to guide and inspire them, or to help them interpret Ambedkar's vision? Vimalakirti, Buddhapriya, and most of the older Order members were still volubly bitter about the monks' failure to offer any real lead.

During the tour we were to have our own unfortunate glimpse of this syndrome in the form of a lively young Maharashtrian monk. He had made contact with TBMSG about a year before Sangharakshita's visit and had been deeply impressed by all he saw. Since then he'd thrown himself into the practices and ambience of the movement like any keen newcomer. When Sangharakshita arrived, he asked whether he could accompany us on tour; as well as wanting to spend time around Sangharakshita, he mentioned that he had a number of contacts who might be helpful as we travelled around. He added that he was thinking seriously about disrobing after the tour, and training himself towards ordination into our Order.

To begin with, he was extremely helpful and cheerful: good, interesting company; we liked him a lot. But as the tour progressed, his appetite for the big crowds and the bright lights became more obvious. Somehow, he always managed to get himself up onto the stage, and usually managed to grab hold of the microphone at some point in the proceedings.

At first we just teased him. But as his pursuit of glory became more obvious, it became cruder, even distasteful. He stopped helping with the work, began to distance himself, and then tried to order us about.

We begged him to wake up to what was happening, tried to point out how he was becoming a victim of his robes. But he refused to acknowledge it, refused to see it. He was, after all, a bhikkhu!

In terms of any real Buddhist practice, he was a beginner. He was a promising and sincere one to be sure, but still new to everything, and very obviously so, as was clearly indicated by the transparent worldliness of his ambitions. But those few folds of orange cloth gave him automatic importance and position. He could boss the ladies around at programmes, and even make his own private arrangements with the organizers. In time, we discovered that it was he who had been responsible for many of those 'unscheduled' stops on our journeys.

In the end he left us, and returned to his native town where he would soon establish a movement of his own, a shallow duplicate of TBMSG, aping its techniques and organizational structure. Of course, any new Buddhist movement in Maharashtra dedicated to practice should have been a source of joy, and relief. But, considering his motivation, we could only wonder.

Our monk friend did at least meditate, and he now had some knowledge of Buddhism. In time the little he knew might have a transforming effect on him. In the meantime, those qualifications alone would make him more useful than most of the other monks. But like so many of them, and like so many of the politicians, he was just too vulnerable to the pull of the vaccuum left by the demise of Dr Ambedkar.

There is some irony in all this. Ambedkar hated idols and hero worship. He viewed the Indian tendency to set people on pedestals and worship them like gods as a terrible betrayal of weakness. He held that their religious conditioning made Indians wait passively for *avatars* and messiahs to come and shoulder their worries and fight their fights for them. Believing thus, when would they ever take the initiative themselves?

And yet he could not prevent his followers from treating him in practically the same way, and consequently depotentiating themselves. Nor could he foster a sense of team spirit among them, which might have acted as a substitute for his own physical presence.

Speaking again at Milind College, but this time to a public gathering out in the grounds, Sangharakshita launched a strong plea for harmony and teamwork among Buddhists. He talked about TBMSG, explaining that the movement was successful because people were prepared to work together, prepared to take the initiative. Such reminders had a particular relevance here, for a degree of factionalism had infiltrated the local Buddhist community. Aurangabad lay in the heart of the Marathwada region of Maharashtra, but many good posts in government service and in the local education establishments had been filled by Buddhists from the Vidharba region to the east. The Marathwadans resented the success of the Vidharbans, and thus divisions and enmities had formed.

As a matter of fact, some of the first people to make contact with TBMSG in Aurangabad had been Vidharbans, some professors from

Milind College. They were an extraordinary bunch of men. Mutually
infected with a delightful brand of eccentricity, they took an enormous
relish in our visit. Zooming back and forth on their scooters and
bicycles, they turned up at the bungalow at all hours, intercepted us on
our walks through town, accompanied us on sight-seeing tours, and
constantly belaboured us with back-slaps, hand-squeezes, hugs, and
shoulder-shaking laughter. They competed energetically with each
other—and with our schedule—to entertain us, almost bullying us into
visiting their homes for breakfast, lunch, and dinner. They were a
phenomenon.

In their more serious moments, they shared their dreams with us.
Inspired by what they had heard of the movement in England, they
wanted to set up some co-operative businesses and other 'Right-
Livelihood' ventures. They envisaged a six-month training course in
practical skills like motor maintenance and scooter repair; they wanted
to start schools for children from the backward classes. . . . There were
all kinds of visions, and they were impatient to get going, unaware,
perhaps, that they would first have to spend a while learning how to
concentrate their energies, and developing clearer plans.

Nevertheless, they were drawing obvious encouragement from the
arrival of two more Order members from England, two people with
something of a special mission. Vajraketu and Padmashuri were soon to
start working on TBMSG's first 'social welfare' project, in Dapodi, a
squalid hutment district on the edge of Poona.

Sangharakshita and Lokamitra had always had it in mind that
TBMSG should one day develop a social wing, directed specifically
towards the material uplift of the poorer and more helpless members of
the community. No matter how important the gift of the Dhamma may
be, it is hard for people to take advantage of it if they are constantly
preoccupied with poverty, hunger, or sickness.

Many of those who made up the inner core of TBMSG came from a
sort of lower-middle class. Those who had achieved more success in
life than that were generally too distracted by purely material goals to
get at all interested in the Dhamma; many of them even tried to sever
links with their Buddhist background altogether, filling their homes
with images of Hindu gods in the hope that their neighbours and
professional friends would mistake them for Caste-Hindus. The very
poor had no time or energy to spare for Buddhism at all. The 'Poona
Project'—as we called it in the UK—was therefore to be a prototype,
offering medical care, education, and livelihood to people who lived in
the slums.

Padmashuri was an experienced nurse, Vajraketu was to provide
administrative talent, and in a few weeks they would be joined by

Virabhadra, a doctor. In Dapodi, the land purchase negotiations seemed well under way, while in England a new charity called 'Aid For India' had been created to raise money for this work, and had already raised half a million pounds.

I sympathized with the professors. Why shouldn't they feel inspired by the progress of the movement. So much had happened in a very short time. It was a formidable achievement, and an eloquent testament to Lokamitra's abilities. One evening, up on his balcony, Sangharakshita mused on this:

'You know, it really is quite remarkable what he has done in just a few years. To think that things could already be so well established in Poona—and that it has been possible to arrange a tour like this. It really is something! I honestly can't think of anyone else who could have done what he has done.' Then he laughed, 'You know, I'm not even sure that *I* could have done it!'

It was curious. Outwardly, Sangharakshita and Lokamitra were like chalk and cheese. Unless you got to know Sangharakshita a little, you could be forgiven for wondering whether he would survive a hot curry, let alone the strains of living and working in India! India was for the tigers like Lokamitra. But when, and if, you got to know Sangharakshita better, you would begin to see that all the necessary power, the fierce creative energy, and the formidable determination were there, unshakeably established. The extraordinary, and superficially deceptive, thing about him was that he never wasted a drop of it.

Sometimes, when he phoned me from his eyrie in Norfolk, drawing my attention to a typographical error he had discovered in the magazine I edited for the movement, I would wonder in exasperation how on earth such a man could have managed to do all the things he had done. But then I would have to acknowledge that it was precisely because he *was* so meticulously attentive to detail, so mindful, that he had achieved so much. His drive and his energy never manifested in rush, sloppiness, or in action for its own sake. Instead, it pulsed steadily, directly, and appropriately into everything he did, and bore him, like a tamed lion, towards his consciously chosen destination.

Someone once asked him whether he ever thought about what might have happened to him had he not discovered Buddhism.

'I told them that I would most probably have gone mad. It was as if all the forces of my nature were so strong, and sometimes so seemingly contradictory, that had I not been able to commit myself to something as powerful, as worthy, and as all-consuming as the Three Jewels, then I think those forces might have ripped me apart.'

Lokamitra, in the meantime, was ceaselessly busy. All manner of folk were turning up at the bungalow to discuss arrangements for the tour, usually trying to eke out another lecture or another meal-taking. Some came to buy books, or to talk about land which could be made available to TBMSG. These meetings often kept him up until one in the morning.

He was under considerable, and occasionally visible, strain. He could get annoyed, be a little sharp with people, and drive them hard. It was easy to be critical of his tenser moods. And yet, he would be awake before any of us, meditating at five, practising Yoga from six until seven. If he had any spare time, he would seek out his friends for long, confessional talks. He was working on himself as hard as anyone else—perhaps much harder.

Above all, he was investing himself unstintingly in something he believed in: something which he knew was important. There was nothing one-dimensional or fragmented about his spiritual life; because he put the whole of himself into it, he never felt the need—as some of us did—to break off for a while and establish contact with his 'neglected selves'. They were all in there, fighting for the cause, for better and, very occasionally, for worse. He never took a day off, never enjoyed a holiday; his energy welled uninterruptedly up and out. He was still taming his lion, but he was something considerable even then.

I once asked him what kept him going. Was it the pressure of knowing himself to be the man responsible for carrying out Sangharakshita's 'Indian vision'?

'That's very much how I saw it when I first came out. I just wanted to do whatever I could to help Sangharakshita with his work. But it's different now. I've been in India for three years and I've made a lot of friends. As I get to understand the situation for myself, I realize that I'm working more from my own commitment.'

He laughed. 'You know, I originally took this on as a ten year job. I wouldn't even think of leaving now. This is my life.'

Sangharakshita put it a little differently, but it added up to the same thing:

'At the moment, people still think of Lokamitra as "Sangharakshita's disciple". But in just a few years time, I'm certain they'll just think of me as "Lokamitra's teacher".'

2
Transformations

fourteen

The two old ladies stood in the doorway, exchanging anxious murmurs. At their feet, on a thin mattress, lay the writhing form of a long white ghoul: the man who had moved into their spare room just the night before.

It was December 1984. I was back in India.

I had been warned that a second visit could throw a harder punch than the first, and I was now discovering that this really was the case. As I thrashed about in the throes of a high fever, my brain spouted images like a punctured water-main: fat black pigs, leprous beggars, heaped platefuls of mouth-scorching food, tangled roadways, and festering hutments. I had returned to write a book, but was already wondering whether I would ever even walk again.

It occurred to me that I could blame Sangharakshita; but it was really my own fault. I had been the one who had made the suggestion, one evening while we were staying in Aurangabad, that I should try to write a book about our tour. I had reminded him of that conversation a year later, when he was staying in London.

'Well, it's quite a good idea. I think you should definitely try to find the time one day to make it possible.'

Even so, the dream had begun to fade. After two busy years in England it was fast becoming a might-have-been: something I would mention occasionally to my friends with a wry, nostalgic smile.

But then I got Lokamitra's letter.

I was surprised to hear from him at all at that particular time. Sangharakshita was back in India for a short visit, giving a few talks and conducting some ordinations. Lokamitra should have been far too busy to think of me.

'You'll be delighted to know', he wrote, 'Bhante has just committed you to that book.' That was all. There were no details, no further explanations.

155

Jai Bhim!

I got the full story a few days later from the director of Aid For India, who had just returned from a three month visit to Poona.

'Oh yes!' he said, 'Did you ever go to Worli?'

In my mind's eye I instantly beheld those light-bedecked chawls, a sea of faces—and jewels.

'Well, Sangharakshita was there a couple of weeks ago, and told them you would be out by the end of this year, to write a book on the Dhamma Revolution—'

'—About the Dhamma Revolution? Who was he talking to?' I asked.

'Well, it was hard to tell, but I reckon there were about five thousand in the crowd.'

* * *

Thankfully, I was through customs and immigration in no time; almost before I knew what was happening I found myself face to face with Lokamitra, Bodhisen, and Jyotipala.

'Nagabodhi! Jai Bhim! How are you?' Smiling warmly, Bodhisen somehow managed to take all my bags from me and hug me half to death at the same time. 'When are you coming to visit us "Bombay boys"?' He had not only been ordained—though he had retained his old, already Buddhist, name, but now spoke passably fluent English. Otherwise he was the same as ever: a storm of smiles and laughter. I struggled to stop him bearing off with my luggage; it didn't seem fair on the others to let him do all the work.

Jyotipala was sorting out a ride into town. Last time I'd arrived in India, Jyotipala had spent half an hour arguing with the driver at the end of our journey to Dadar. Now, within moments of leaving us, he was calling over his shoulder, nagging us along, with a pre-paid taxi ticket in his fist.

Lokamitra steered me into the taxi, and then began to extract news from me. They all wanted news: about their friends in England, about developments in the movement, about Sangharakshita's plans for another visit. . . . In the past two days I had had little more than four hours sleep, and the plane's air-conditioning system had wrecked my throat, but I offered what titbits I could, while trying at the same time to get a few peeps out of the window.

There it was again! The filthy soaring palms, the tawdry kiosks, the kids playing in the rubble, endless hutment encampments, and people everywhere, spilling out of the shops, houses, and huts onto the pavements, off the pavements into the road.

Almost to the day, three years had passed since I last landed in India.

156

On that occasion I had sat staring out of the cab window in dazed silence, barely believing my eyes, blankly wondering why so many people were having picnics on the roadside at eight in the morning. Now, I found myself grappling with the strange feeling that I had never really left India at all, that all the time I had just spent in England was only a dream. With a deafening report, a tyre exploded and we skidded to a halt in the middle of the 'Expressway'. Waves of beggars engulfed us as we waited for the driver to fit the gnarled monstrosity which served as a spare wheel. Yes, things were much the same as ever.

Jyotipala was in Bombay for just a few weeks. These days he spent most of his time in Aurangabad, living with Mr Dongray and Mahadhammavir. He had come to Bombay to give some talks and lead a few classes, and was staying at TBMSG's new Bombay centre. Only Lokamitra and I were going on to Poona, but Bodhisen and Jyotipala came along to the station with us, laughed uproariously as the fires of my first *Idli Sambar* consumed me, and waved us off as the 'Hyderabad Express' bore us away towards the ghats.

In the days of the tour, Lokamitra had been something of a beginner in his efforts with the Marathi language. Although he could understand most of what was being said, his attempts to speak were distinctly ponderous. During these two years he had taken giant strides, and proceeded to demonstrate his prowess the moment we arrived in Poona. A rabble of rickshaw drivers, catching sight of my cases, competed noisily to make the highest bid for the ride from the station to Sahakar Nagar where I was to spend my first few days. Haggling all the way, Lokamitra led me to a vehicle, entered into an animated exchange with the driver as to whether or not the meter was working properly, called a policeman, explained our plight, got justice, and parried the driver's bitter complaints for twenty long minutes as we weaved and dodged through the evening traffic. They parted the best of friends, while I staggered away, impressed but shell-shocked.

I should perhaps note at this point that Lokamitra was no longer in robes, and upstairs, waiting to greet us, was his wife Ranjana.

This was not the first time I had seen him since my last visit. He had spent a few weeks in England the previous year, and had talked a lot about his impending decision to disrobe. He had been wearing robes right up to the moment of his departure from India, but had more or less decided to return in 'civvies'.

He had worn the robe, and observed celibacy, for six years, but now felt the need for a change—in his own life, and also in his 'image'. No doubt his more personal reasons can be taken as read, but as he spoke to me in London, it was clear that other factors loomed as large in his mind.

Just as Sangharakshita had found that his robes inhibited communication with people in the West, so Lokamitra had come to experience similar difficulties in India. People tended to see him as a 'robe', rather than as a human being. He wanted to connect much more directly, and on a deeper personal level with his friends and colleagues, but the robes got in the way, even in his dealings with some Order members.—They too had received a strong dose of Buddhist cultural conditioning.

He was also anxious to know whether TBMSG could stand a little more clearly on its own feet, without requiring a berobed leader-figure to give it credibility in the wider Buddhist world. By quitting the robe, yet retaining his obviously crucial role in the movement, both as organizer and spiritual adviser, he hoped to challenge some of the more counter-productive conventional assumptions and expectations.

'It's incredibly hard to get people to *practise* the Dhamma here,' he once told me, 'They tend to think of Buddhism in entirely institutional terms. They may chant Buddhist chants, and arrange Buddhist weddings and funerals, but they can't connect with Buddhism as a *path*, as something which can have an effect on them. They've been told again and again that that side of things is only for the monks—not that many of *them* are doing much in the way of practice!'

There was a risk involved, which was why he pondered his decision for so long. There could be all kinds of gossip and back-chat, which could be damaging to TBMSG; the scene in Maharashtra was still volatile. But in the end, he omitted his short visit to the airport washroom, where in the past he would have slipped back into his robes, and walked out into the Bombay sunlight in smart trousers and a pale blue shirt.

Naturally, there were a few gasps of surprise. When Buddhapriya paid his welcoming visit, he sat in a daze for ten minutes, staring at Lokamitra across the table. Then, breaking into a smile, he rose, walked around him, laughed, and finally pronounced: 'Yes. Much better now!'

There was some gossip too, but much less that Lokamitra had feared, and it died down remarkably quickly. Within a month, the whole issue seemed forgotten. Naturally, he was working as hard as ever, and received the same respect as before, both within and beyond the movement. To his delight, he also experienced a noticeable change in his communication with others, and was astonished to see how much freer and more honest people were prepared to be with him now.

The next, more or less inevitable, step was marriage, since, as he put it, 'There's only one way of not being celibate in India.'

In true Indian style, his friends arranged everything; though in true

Lokamitra style, he insisted on having some say in the matter. He was married, to my intense aggravation, just ten days before I arrived in the country, to Ranjana, a woman from Ambedkar Society, endowed, we fervently hoped, with all the virtues of heroism and forbearance that life with a man like Lokamitra would require of her.

A thousand guests attended the wedding, and expressed unanimous enthusiasm for it; in their eyes, Lokamitra was not only sealing a bond with his spouse, but with India herself. They were never going to lose him now! Constant to form, he swept his new bride off to Panchgani for a honeymoon, and swept her back twenty-four hours later, already worrying that he had been away from work too long.

Of course, the movement was not completely lacking in robes. Jyotipala and Mahadhammavir still kept theirs, and Ashvajit, an Order member from London, who had arrived just after my departure in 1982, was also there to add orange lustre to the Poona scene. But Purna was no more: he had returned to New Zealand.

'Does he wear his robes still?' Buddhapriya was steering me through the narrow lanes at Ambedkar society.

'Oh no,' I replied, 'Nobody would understand the robe over there.'

'Ha! They don't here either. Put a donkey in robes and everyone would bow to it.'

We were on our way to visit the two elderly ladies who had a room for me, just around the corner from 'Dhammavijay', the Poona Centre. I was anxious to get a close-up view of TBMSG in action, having spent my first week living *en famille* with Lokamitra, Ranjana, and Lokamitra's sister, Rachel.

Back in England, Lokamitra had managed to entice three sisters and a brother-in-law into the movement. Two of them were now ordained. Rachel had started going to classes at the centre in Brighton while a student at Sussex University. Now, after a period of 'training' in the offices of Aid For India, she was over on a six month visit, working in the accounts department, and doing whatever she could to smooth Lokamitra's transition to the 'householder' state by acting as a kind of companion-cum-cultural-interpreter for Ranjana. The three of them lived in the pleasant flat where Sangharakshita once stayed, still on loan from the days of the tour.

If I was keen to get over to Ambedkar Society, where most of the action took place, so, for that matter, was Lokamitra, who was urgently looking for a home in the Yerawada area, eager to shift camp as soon as possible.

With showers of 'Jai Bhim's, my two hostesses greeted me and showed me to my room. 'My room', it turned out, was in fact *their* room.

159

They seemed perfectly content to live and sleep, along with a fifteen-year-old niece, on the kitchen floor of their tiny dwelling, though whether out of devotion to TBMSG, or because the extra rent money came in handy, I never did find out. Within twenty-four hours of moving in I was back at Sahakar Nagar, moaning deliriously while Rachel—who had bundled my useless frame into a rickshaw—and Ranjana, fed me drugs, cups of tea, and some wonderfully bland food. I remained with them, feeble as a kitten, for another week, but finally made the move to Ambedkar Society on Christmas Day.

The Housing Society had not changed at all. Fresh generations of goats and pigs wandered its lanes and alley-ways, but among them the children still played their endless games of cricket. The hawkers ululated their haunting cries; the *chowkeydhar* dragged his heavy stick through the gravel, calling out the hours as the night unfolded. An unbroken procession of women still walked to and from the Sikh family's buffalo farm, carrying on their heads—with the grace of goddesses—shallow pans piled high with steaming dung.

Dhammavijay, the public centre, was still situated at number 32, though a shiny corrugated-iron extension had been tacked onto its rear to serve as a main operations room. Like any Indian office it was stacked to the ceiling with newspaper-wrapped bundles of letters, documents, and publications. It already looked a hundred years old.

Lokamitra's room was quite unchanged. A huge wooden bed occupied half its area. Lokamitra had slept and worked in here for six years, until his marriage demanded more spacious surroundings. The pungent pink walls had peeled a little further, but the writing desk was as rickety as ever, since it was incapable of going further downhill. For this reason, the bright yellow electric typewriter that Rachel had brought over from England lived on the bed, along with a clutter of files, notebooks, reference works, and a silver crash-helmet.

At nine o'clock each morning, the room's incumbent would arrive on his lime-green scooter, and come bursting in on a scene of activity that had been brewing since the public meditation session at six-thirty. Office life began at eight, which meant that Lokamitra not only found the place abustle, but already crammed with people hoping to see him.

I followed him around one morning, just to see what he got up to.

On that occasion he was greeted by a bent old man from Vidharba. His head, weighed down by a gigantic pair of spectacles, drooped into his chest as he explained that he wanted someone to come and give a talk in his locality. Effusively sympathetic, Lokamitra explained that although everyone was very busy, something could perhaps be arranged in February, or March. Content, the visitor left. Lokamitra, looking slightly dangerous, sent Mahendra, his PA, to find Vimalakirti.

'Why did that man come to see *me*?' he asked of no one in particular, 'It's Vimalakirti's job to deal with that sort of thing.'

There was no time to contemplate Vimalakirti's lapse, however, for we had already been joined by another fellow—heavily garbed in the uniform of the 'Mahar Regiment'—who was collecting funds for an Ambedkarite charity. Slapping his hand as much as shaking it, Lokamitra pierced the man with energetic, twinkling eyes. 'You want *us* to give *you* money? What's in it for *us*?'

The soldier's robust frame shook with laughter, and for a few minutes the two of them chatted affably in Marathi, until Buddhapriya appeared, wondering when would be a good time for him to return with Vaijnath to sort out a few details. An appointment set, he went off, taking the military man with him in search of tea.

Mahendra returned with Vimalakirti in tow, the latter looking dark and irritable. He liked to spend his mornings buried in the donnish clutter of his living room, translating Sangharakshita's English lectures into Marathi. But he was also responsible for 'Triratna Grantha Mala', the movement's publishing wing. In the early days, it was Lokamitra who had rushed around Poona's printing and binding establishments, fighting for the best deals, struggling against impossible odds, to get booklets and magazines out on schedule and within budget. This was now Vimalakirti's arena of activity. I didn't envy him.

The Vidharban visitor clearly lost among his brain-cells, Lokamitra proceeded to quiz Vimalakirti on a different issue. Some time ago, some money had been transferred from the main TBMSG account into the publishing account. Now, no one was quite sure why the transfer had been made, how there had happened to be so much 'loose' money available in the main account, and, above all, how this had happened without the necessary authorization.

While the three of them speculated and argued, a blood-curdling commotion erupted outside. For fifteen minutes all talk was overlaid by the piteous screams of pigs. I had always assumed those ubiquitous animals to be wild. I was wrong: they belonged, I was told, to some Christian farmers—who had come, even now, to conduct one of their periodic round-ups, dragging off those that had attained the requisite size and weight.

The details of the transfer business soon had me lost. I appealed for an explanation.

'Don't ask!' Lokamitra retorted, 'It will make your head hurt horribly.' Vimalakirti cradled my head in a paternal way, while Mahendra disappeared into the back office to consult the ledgers. A minute or two later we joined him.

The extension measured some ten feet by twenty. I never did quite work out who was actually meant to be working in there, for there were six desks but rarely less than nine or ten people in the room, perched in its alcoves and darker corners, as well as sitting at or on the desks. At any one time there were three loud conversations in progress.

'Lokamitra. Please! I must have a room of my own if I am going to do all these things.' Planted at his document smothered table, Bodhidharma launched his sally the moment we entered. Since his ordination, he had become—as expected—a central and indispensable figure in the movement, taking on all tasks that called for expert administrative wheeler-dealing and red-tape cutting. He was expert in the art of working with politicians, businessmen, and village elders. He told me that the more deeply he meditated, the better he found himself able to deal with the mighty and pompous. High up on a bright green filing cabinet sat a red telephone, a living testament to his skills. By winning the good offices of a central government minister he had got the device installed after a mere two year wait.

He had recently resigned from his well paid job to work full-time for TBMSG. His wife had worried at first about the dramatic plunge in income that the shift would involve, and his fervently Ambedkarite parents had thought him mad. But he was loving his new life, brazenly confident that 'the Dhamma would look after him'.

His crash helmet lay beside him. Soon he would be taking his trusty scooter—onto the spare wheel of which he had written his Buddhist name in flowing golden script—and charging off to fix something new, while Lokamitra awaited his return, already anxious for him to be fixing *more*.

'Ahem. Excuse me.'

I turned to see who was tapping me on the shoulder. He was a man with thinning grey hair, an athletic body, despite his fifty-plus years, an impish smile, and a hearing-aid which whined and whistled as he adjusted it before addressing me.

Pravinbhai was about to deliver one of his impromptu lectures.

'One moment, please? You know, I have one son. He is twenty-six. Twenty-six years old. When my first wife died, twenty years ago, I started to look for something. My son is a Hindu. My father is a Hindu: a Brahmin. I did not want these false religions in my house. I was looking for something that was Truth!

'I had one bungalow worth seven, eight lakhs, and my sweet-meat business in Surat was very successful, bringing in an income of five to six thousand rupees per month. But I spoke with my son. I asked his permission to leave the householder life.'

So Pravinbhai, the Gujerati Brahmin, had tramped his way to Ahmedabad, where he made contact with Bakula, and thus with TBMSG. Now he was living here in Poona, sleeping on his wooden office desk, and insisting, in his flamboyant way, that he wanted nothing more than a handful of grain per day—enough only to keep body and mind together. Like another great Gujerati, Mahatma Gandhi, he was an energetic advocate of the simple life, and had covered the office walls with laboriously calligraphed slogans on the virtues of thrift. With very little hesitation, Lokamitra had made him treasurer.

My lecture was not yet over.

'I am here for the Dhamma only, not for the sake of my comfort or for the food. Only for the Dhamma. I am of the opinion that we must guard every *paisa*. I think we should have one little book, and enter into it even the smallest items of expenditure. Then if one man wants to buy a ball-pen, we will be able to say "Ah! But you bought one ball-pen only fifteen days ago!" ' At this point, he enacted an elaborate mime of a man carelessly losing a ball-point pen.

'We are not a garment undertaking! I think we should be living as if we were a poor family, and not like a garment undertaking.' He went over to the wall and switched on a light. The dim yellow bulb glowed uncertainly in the harsh daylight. 'Often I see this at midday in garment undertakings. No one thinks of the expense because they think the garment will pay for everything.' I suddenly realized that by 'garment' he meant 'government'.

'We have a responsibility to the Sangha for every penny. If we are wise with regard to the pennies, then there will be no problem regarding the pounds!' Bestowing upon me a genial smile, he indicated that I was at liberty to go, and returned to his desk. Q.E.D.

Digamber looked up from his desk, twisting his cramped features into a sympathetic smile. He dealt with a wide range of secretarial chores, and spent much of his time in post offices, mailing things out and sending off telegrams. This was no light task in a country where posting a letter could involve up to four separate interviews, each one preceded by an interminable fight for the clerk's attention.

Altogether, there were now about a dozen Order members and regulars financially supported to work full-time for TBMSG; almost as many again worked part-time.

In England, when the movement was young, it had been relatively easy for a few of us to take the leap into full-time involvement. We were mostly unmarried, and under no obligation to support our mothers, fathers, or sisters and brothers. Some of us had managed to save money quite easily, to support ourselves until the time the movement itself would be in a position to pay us.—And, of course, there had always been the safety-net of State allowances, should things go wrong.'

But in India it was different. Most men were married by the age of twenty-five, and most women even earlier. Parents expected their sons to support them in their old age, and at the age of thirty an elder son could easily find himself the main bread-winner of a family which extended far beyond its nuclear core. There was effectively no State support for the unemployed, so a career slot in a government office, a small business, or even as the cleaner of a back-street café, would be guarded with a grip of iron.

Vimalakirti had been the first person to forsake his job to work for TBMSG, closely followed by a young man called Dharmananda, who now ran the little book kiosk next to Ambedkar's statue down in Poona city. They, and the people who followed them, had shown a remarkable degree of courage and faith. TBMSG had no impressive buildings or bank accounts to underpin their confidence. Any of them could have been forgiven for deciding to avoid the uncertainties that lay ahead. Yet one by one they had made their commitments, and now, as more people joined them, a team of dedicated Dhamma workers was beginning to emerge.

Rachel's voice suddenly pierced the office, 'Pravinbhai! Where should we enter the expenditure for manure at Bhaja?'

Working beside Pravinbhai, sorting out the books for the annual audit, was doing wonders for her lungs. There were few who could get their words registered in his ears.

'Well, Rachel, I think it is best we enter it under "Fund-raising".'

'Fund-raising! How on earth do you come to that conclusion?'

'Well, if we are putting manure on the fields, more rice will grow. More rice equals more money when it is sold at the market. It is therefore an investment.'

'But you could say that about everything! Everything we spend money on is making things grow. You could say that the money we pay ourselves is an investment. If there are people working for the Dhamma, then some of the things that happen as a result will bring in money. Maybe we should put down all of our expenses under fund-raising! We are all just like manure!'

Pravinbhai's eyes began to radiate visionary joy, 'Oh Rachel. That is a beautiful thought!'

Meanwhile, the three ledger sleuths had tracked down an explanation for the rupee transfer mystery, and seemed happy with their conclusions. The phone was ringing in Lokamitra's room when we returned. It was Dipak Agaley, the warden of the newly opened children's hostel in Lohagaon. Lokamitra called out for Bodhidharma.

'It's Mr Agaley. He's got back trouble and needs someone to stand in for him while he sees a doctor. Can you sort it out?'

As Bodhidharma took the phone and began murmuring quietly into it, a smart gentleman, equipped with a bulging briefcase, placed himself among us. Lokamitra was temporarily immersed in a fat tome on Indian charity law, reluctant to be distracted until he had found the reference he needed. The stranger therefore addressed himself to me.

'Good morning. My name is Unwalla. I spent forty-eight years of my life in Burma. I like Burmese people. They have no pretensions. They see everybody as being quite equal. Even a government minister whom I have met for just five minutes will put his arms around me and take me for a cup of tea.

'I prefer the average Burmese to the average Indian. I once told this thing to an Indian diplomat. He said that I was not a good Indian. "No!" I said, "If that was the case then I would have cancelled my Indian citizenship!" '

Lokamitra looked up, but before dealing with Mr Unwalla, stopped Bodhidharma who was passing through the office on his way out. Dancing over to his writing desk and opening a drawer, he extracted a small brown paper bag stuffed full of bank-notes, and handed it to him.

'Ah, yes,' said Bodhidharma with a wide grin, and rushed back into the main office, to return a moment later with his crash helmet, 'I'll be about an hour.'

Soon it was time for Buddhapriya's appointment. He arrived with Vaijnath, the caretaker at 'Sadhamma Pradeep', the Retreat Centre at Bhaja. Vaijnath, whose visage shone with a kind of radiant timidity, had with him a list of requirements, and had made the pilgrimage to Poona to place them before Lokamitra. How was he to get the grass cut? Where would he find a labourer to water all the new trees? How was he going to get the opportunity to study the Dhamma with others when he lived so far from town? Finally, he was finding the nights cold, and wondered whether there were any sleeping bags available. Buddhapriya, champion of the Bhaja land-purchase, stood beside him, translating his little speech.

Lokamitra sorted out the cold nights, the water, and the Dhamma study, but could not understand why cutting the grass should be a problem.

'But what does *he* do all day?' he asked Buddhapriya.

Vaijnath launched into an explanation. 'He gets up at three forty-five in the morning so that he will have time to meditate, then . . .'

'—Oh, all right. All right.' An able politician, Lokamitra knew when

165

to concede defeat.

The Bhaja Centre really had been a success story. The land negotiations had after all gone smoothly and quickly. Water had been found and a bore-hole dug, the construction work had kept very nearly to schedule, and the Centre had ended up looking very similar to the one in the plans. There were countless hiccups and near-disasters, but the roof was in place just before the rains began. In fact, soon after my arrival, there was to be a special day to celebrate the first anniversary of its gala opening by Sangharakshita a year ago. Lokamitra took me out a day early so that I could see the place before the crowds arrived.

It was a fine building, a long, capacious bungalow, brightly painted in blue and white. It had a large, cool shrine room, a few rooms off for accommodation, a kitchen of sorts, and even enough toilets to cater for the numbers that used the place. It sat right at the foot of the ghats, with nothing behind it save a steep, densely forested hillside. Before it stretched a smooth vista of fields and mango groves, broken finally by the light-softened humps of the opposing ghats four miles across the valley floor. It was quiet, peaceful, and remote, a twenty minute scramble over cracked earth and crumbling footpaths from the nearest road. Now, fifty or more people at a time could have a retreat in relative comfort, and in ideal conditions.

But that was only the beginning. As soon as we arrived, Lokamitra led me through the surrounding fields and meadows.

'We have just bought this field, and Buddhapriya is trying to buy the land between here and those trees over on the hillock there. We also want to get hold of the fields between those mangoes, there, and the banyan over there.' I gasped, partly out of wonder, and partly with the exhaustion that Lokamitra's break-neck pace was inducing. In the distance buffalo herdsmen, their voices sharp with outrage and reproach, called to their wandering wards.

'But why do we need so much land?'

'This is nothing! In time, the centre we've built here will only be used for accommodation. We're going to build the *real* centre on that hill over there. In the meantime we are trying to buy up as much of the surrounding land as we can while it's still cheap, to make sure that we don't get encroached upon. This whole area has become very popular with rich Bombayites. They're building weekend houses all over the place. Anyway, Sangharakshita is keen that we grow some of our own food. None of this land is going to be idle.'

Then he froze.

'How did that cow get in there? I've *told* Vaijnath to keep those fences in good order. Oh no! It's going to eat all the trees.'

By 'trees' he meant the pathetic little shoots that had recently been planted around the grounds, each one sitting in its own crater of well-watered mud. We approached the trespasser.

'How did *you* get in here?' Lokamitra stared the cow in the face. There was nothing sentimental in his manner as he addressed the beast; he was absolutely serious, and seemed to be waiting for an answer. Bellowing in fright, the cow ran off, searching the walls and fences for a way out. Finally she dragged her bulk over a low gate.

'And don't let me *ever* see you in here again!'

My guided tour was over. Lokamitra was already on his way to find Vaijnath.

The next morning we stood out on the veranda and watched the far-off trains creeping across the valley floor, pausing briefly at Malavli station. Half an hour later our guests began to arrive, in a long colourful line which threaded its way across the fields to disappear behind hedges and mounds. Lokamitra stood at the gate, with Vimalakirti, Buddhapriya, and Bodhidharma, welcoming people as they entered the property in laughing knots. Soon, some four hundred had arrived.

At exactly the same time, a bullock cart, loaded with bamboo poles and heavy swathes of canvass, came lumbering out of the landscape. Buddhapriya had arranged for a stage and canopy to be erected alongside the building but, the night before, the *pandal-wallahs* had mistakenly erected their awning two miles away, outside another, unused, vihara belonging to a different Buddhist organization. Now, having come so far with all their paraphernalia, they were determined to set it up.

Reasonably enough, Lokamitra pointed out that our event was about to begin, and that by the time they had completed their work, our day would be over. This simple argument took some time to register, and the pandal crew spent the rest of the morning grumpily perched on their cart, talking darkly among themselves and resisting Buddhapriya's occasional attempts to jolly them away.

Inside, once everyone was ready, Chandrabodhi gave a short talk on the history of TBMSG and the building of the retreat centre. A few years before, I had watched him introducing Sangharakshita in his home town of Pimpri. Almost paralysed with nerves, he had seemed on the point of choking on his tongue as he fumbled with the buttons of his shirt. Now he spoke with practised ease, bringing forth torrents of laughter from a spellbound audience.

Then it was my turn to give a talk on the value of meditation. I had already given a few talks in India. During the first week of the Marathwada tour, when Sangharakshita's throat was giving him trouble, a few of us had had to stand in on a couple of occasions. Once again I felt myself awed by the concentration and enthusiasm with which these people listened, and gratified by the full-blooded roars of laughter which greeted my jokes. As I spoke, a little girl in the front row, wearing a mauve, Paisley patterned dress, fiddled abstractedly with my bare toes. It was good to be back.

We spent the afternoon out on the gravelled forecourt, watching an eccentric cocktail of entertainments, the like of which had probably never appeared on any stage in history. Dharmarakshita and Lokamitra had long nursed the hope that TBMSG would one day develop a cultural wing, which could serve as a bridge between the movement and the wider Buddhist community. Now, for this event, Dharmarakshita had organized a programme of fifteen acts, to be performed by the movement's friends from Poona, Bombay, and some of the villagers around the Retreat Centre. There were Buddhist devotional chants and songs, a magician, two stand-up comics, a classical dancer with a tabla accompanist, a moral tale which featured a brahmin, a drunk, and Charlie Chaplin, some rousing Ambedkarite anthems, and a kind of song-poem, composed by a bard from one of the neighbouring hamlets. As he half spoke, half sang, Bodhidharma explained the story of his song. It dealt with the history of the Untouchables, the heroic life and deeds of Dr Ambedkar, the mass conversions and the appearance of TBMSG, and concluded with some verses in praise of Lokamitra's recent wedding.

I looked across to see Lokamitra laughing in the middle of an ocean of loving faces. He and his six-year-old project were already a legend: elements in a still unfolding myth. Sangharakshita's prophecy was coming true.

* * *

A few days later, however, when the 'Poona Activities Committee' met, the post mortem was less than self-congratulatory. What had happened to the loudspeakers? Why had there been all that trouble over the stage? Dharmaditya, the master of ceremonies, had introduced my talk but not Chandrabodhi's; how could we expect people to develop confidence in our Order when we only treated the foreigners in that way? And Chandrabodhi had spent far too long poking fun at monks. This wasn't necessary in the company of our own people, and to go on and on about that sort of thing was unnecessarily negative.

For an hour or more, they chipped away at each other. The day had been good, but it could have been, and should have been, better.

'It is not enough to do things in a half-hearted way,' said Vimalakirti. 'Everything must be followed through to the last detail. If you take on a responsibility, you must honour it totally.'

Bodhidharma was quite upset. 'These events are so important. We must either do them perfectly or not at all. Because of our reputation, people come to our events expecting something really special. It reflects very badly on us if anything goes wrong.'

Dharmarakshita was roundly upbraided. He had been wanting an opportunity like this for years; but when he got the chance to do something, he had not held nearly enough meetings or rehearsals. It had all been far too chaotic. . .

Despite all the hard words and uncompromising judgements, I noticed that they managed to remain friendly throughout the discussion, and fundamentally loyal to each other. All the same, a few nights later, Buddhapriya took his reactions to that session to an Order meeting. It was the practice that, each week, after an opening period of meditation, one Order member would have the floor, to report-in on some aspect of his life or practice with which he wanted help. Taking his turn, Buddhapriya confessed that he was finding life hard. Since giving up his job he had never stopped working and rushing about. He was involved in the land purchase at Bhaja, but he was also meant to be helping out in Dapodi. Then there were all those business meetings he had to attend. He knew he ended up getting things wrong, or not seeing some of his jobs through to completion—like the pandal business at Bhaja—but that was because he was finding it impossible to be always in the right place at the right time.

It was an obvious plea for sympathy, made even more effective by the tears which coursed down his cheeks as he spoke. But for half an hour he was taken to task again as his friends tried to make him see that he simply did not plan his life carefully enough.

'What about all those days when you disappear to your village?' asked Vimalakirti, 'Or the weekends you spend with your children when you've said you'll perform some task? No one ever knows where you are or when you'll be back!' Buddhapriya sheepishly admitted that this was true. Yes, he did have a habit of coming and going.

'And what about all those marriages you keep getting involved in?— When we've agreed time and time again that we won't act as marriage brokers.' Yes, that was true as well. As a universally respected elder, Buddhapriya was often asked to act as a match-maker, and, being soft-hearted, he never liked to refuse.

Gradually, Buddhapriya began to acknowledge his own part in the 'problem', and agreed that he needed to live and function in a more disciplined way—for his own good as well as for the good of his work. But by now people were pointing out his strengths and rejoicing in his merits, which seemed to make him cry even more.

A week later, when it was his turn, Munindra talked about some difficulties he had been having with his work at the munitions factory. While he was away on sick leave, one of his colleagues had interfered with his files. The result had been a wasted morning as he went through everything, sorting it all out again. He had been angry, but did not feel it right to inflict his anger on the people he worked with. He had had a number of similar experiences, and still did not know how to be true to himself and honest with others, without sometimes acting 'unskilfully'.

On his evening, Dharmananda turned on his fellows. He was unhappy that so few books were being sold, and felt that the others could be doing far more than they were. He wanted them to go round the Buddhist localities selling *Buddhayan* from door to door, expected them to attend big meetings in order to sell books. . . . He felt he was doing everything he could, but that it wasn't nearly enough. He needed more support.

These hot, cramped, mosquito-infested meetings were simple, human affairs; but they were crucial. In a way they were the very heart of the Dhamma Revolution, perhaps much more so than the big rallies and the exciting building projects. Here it was possible to see people changing, or coming to terms with the strains of change, almost from week to week, and to see their spirit of 'fraternity' growing stronger all the time. One thing that had struck me when I arrived back in Poona was that the Order members I had known before looked not only clearer and more confident, but younger too.

They were still very new to their responsibilities; mistakes would be made as people disappeared into clouds of vagueness, sentiment, or self-doubt. But they were all aware of what they had to do, and working as hard as they could to make progress. Perhaps this was just one tiny element in their revolution, but it was an essential one. Meditating together, holding up mirrors to each other's strengths and weaknesses, pooling their resources of experience and inspiration, they were not only enjoying a special kind of friendship, but turning themselves, by degrees, into people who could be more effective in the world.

When his turn came to report-in, Jayaditya—a fierce-eyed young man from the nearby hutments—had a rather special problem.

'I live in a very mixed locality. There are many Hindus and Sikhs, as well as our people. A little while ago, my wife and my mother suddenly became very sick. They could not eat, they were confined to their beds, and yet they could not tell me what was the matter. I asked the doctor to come and see them, but he could find nothing wrong with them at all.

'In the end, my mother confessed to me. She said that she and my wife have to spend much of their time with the Hindu women. "They all have images of the gods in their houses," she said, "They do *puja*, they go to the temple; but because we are a Buddhist family you do not let us do these things!" She and my wife are afraid that they will be punished for not worshipping the gods. I told them that the gods do not exist—I told them to stop this superstition. But they are still deeply afraid.'

Later, Padmashuri told me that this was a common syndrome. In many Buddhist homes, the pictures of Dr Ambedkar and the Buddha would have a prominent place in the main room, but back in the women's world of the kitchen area, tucked away somewhere close to the cooking range, there were usually a few small representations of the elephant-headed Ganesh, or the 'monkey-god' Hanuman.

And yet, at Dapodi, she and Virabhadra had found that it was the women who took much of the initiative in Buddhist affairs. It had been through the medium of the women's circles that they had first developed links with people in the traditionally insular slum localities. And most of their regular helpers had been women. The first attempts to establish some 'Right Livelihood' schemes had been conducted by women.

In Ambedkar's day it had often been the women who caught the excitement of his vision before the men. For his part, he had devoted a tremendous amount of work to the uplift of women at all levels of Hindu society. Even when his Hindu Code Bill was clearly doomed, he had tried to salvage at least those sections which gave some basic rights to women. It was Bodhidharma's mother, and not his father, who determined that he should get an education, at no matter what cost of hardship to the rest of the family. And when Sangharakshita worked in Maharashṭra during the fifties and sixties it was often the women's groups and societies that were responsible for his invitations and engagements.

Even so, most Indian women still lived their lives in a virtual cage of unending housework and underlying subordination to the men-folk. It was still an exceptional woman who even came to hear about any other options that life might hold, and perhaps an even more exceptional husband—or father—who allowed her to explore them.

Padmashuri suggested to Jayaditya that he should make a Buddha-shrine for his home, so that the women could find an outlet for their devotional feelings. He should ensure that they made more contacts among the Buddhist women—bring them to events like the Bhaja anniversary celebration, so that they could acquire confidence in the Buddhist community. Above all, he should let them come to the classes for women that she led at the centre, and encourage them to come on some of the women's retreats.

After three years, Padmashuri had reached the point where she now found her time divided between nursing at Dapodi, and her more directly Buddhist work among women. She was leading a good number of retreats at Bhaja now, some of them very fully attended, and travelled around the state giving talks and holding classes. Although their husbands often brought them to the retreat centre's gate— carrying their baggage across the fields—and insisted that Vaijnath should never leave the premises, to protect them while they were there, Padmashuri laughingly pointed out that most of her women were more than able to look after themselves. Built like Amazons, a great many of them had been leaders in their own hutment communities, battling with the municipal authorities to get water, electricity, and latrines installed. A few of them had even spent time in prison for taking part in demonstrations. Now, some of the most deeply involved women were leading classes and study groups in their own home towns, and setting their sights on ordination. As a consequence, Padmashuri was thinking of giving up nursing altogether, to concentrate full-time on Dhamma teaching. Through those classes and retreats she would be helping to create leaders among the women, and a few exemplary figures. The potential effect was incalculable.

The possibilities seemed limitless. The movement was spreading and deepening in a variety of ways. At any time of day or night there always seemed to be a class taking place in the little shrine room at Dhammavijay: beginners' meditation classes, talks and study groups for the regulars, women's classes, children's classes, and study groups. . . . It was impossible to count how many people passed through the place each week. Amritbodhi was taking classes over on his side of town, and Vimalakirti was building up a group in an area close to the railway station. Chandrabodhi had established a branch in Pimpri, and was already making plans for the day when he would move on to Nanded, to start activities there.

Almost every day I would hear the names of towns we had visited on our tour. Sangharakshita's talk had led to more contacts, and then to more, and finally to regular activities. The network was extending. The centres in Bombay, Aurangabad, and Ahmedabad were now established and throwing out subsidiary shoots. All the time, invitations kept coming in, and anyone with the time and speaking skill was going off to honour them. It was now possible to see the makings of another quantum leap; it was as if a kind of critical mass had been attained, and the chain reaction was just about to begin.

Going over to the community house for lunch one day, I found an old monk seated in the dining area. He was as thin as the proverbial rake and, when the food was served, ate hungrily and copiously, oblivious of anything else.

Nobody seemed to know quite who he was, but when Lokamitra joined us, he explained that our guest was the incumbent at a vihara just a few miles outside Poona. A group of Buddhist politicians and businessmen had donated money, raised some more, and built a fine vihara. But now that it was finished, with a monk installed, nobody knew what to do with it. The monk had therefore come along, with the trustees' blessing, he said, to ask whether TBMSG could take it over, since he believed it was the only movement capable of putting the facility to good use.

A few days later I found another monk at our lunch-time gathering. In bold contrast to the first, this gentleman was huge of bulk, highly jovial, but remarkably sparing in his appetites. Once upon a time he had been a famous singer-bard figure in Maharashtra. Even as a monk he still liked to work through the medium of 'music programmes'. A few years ago, after one such programme, a millionaire had dropped a small fortune into his lap as a gesture of devotion. He had used the money to buy some land, but since then nothing more had been done. Now he wanted TBMSG to take the land over, perhaps to build a vihara, or a hostel for students from poor families.

Similar offers had been made in Ahmedabad, Aurangabad, and Hyderabad. The land on which the hostel in Lohagaon was being built had also been a gift; TBMSG seemed to be winning a particularly advantageous form of respect. But this dramatic opportunity-boom was causing some strain. There were still only twenty-eight Order members, and only a handful of them were free to work full-time. There was also an acute shortage of people with the skills and qualities that Vimalakirti and Bodhidharma could mobilize. Dealing with legalities, government departments, political upsets, and overseeing construction projects, called for a kind of confidence and aptitude not traditionally associated with the Buddhist community. People were having to develop these qualities as they went along—but that was what it was all about.

Lokamitra tried to seize every opportunity that arose. Along with many of the others, he believed that the movement needed to expand its base as quickly as possible. The sooner it became widespread, well known, and materially secure, the sooner it would be able to weather the storms that could still erupt from time to time on the Buddhist scene. Many of the older Buddhist organizations and societies now felt threatened by the success and dynamism of TBMSG, and feared that they were about to lose members and funds to this new movement. TBMSG was therefore becoming a target for periodic attacks: it was run by foreigners who did not understand Ambedkarism; it was a CIA plant, its foreign members actually spies; it was a covert attempt to restore the 'Raj' . . .

Lokamitra made tremendous demands on his colleagues, and watched vigilantly for gaps between their words and actions, between intentions and fulfilment. In his own life he made no distinction between the 'inner' and the 'outer' aspects of the spiritual path, and did everything he could to turn the demands thrown up by the movement's progress into spiritual challenges. He urged, inspired, and occasionally goaded people, not just onto the next level of efficiency and effectiveness, but onto the next stage in their own development. He wanted nothing more than to be made redundant, and saw this rash of opportunities as a chance to move things further in that direction. As had been the case in London all those years before, there were those who could occasionally find him overbearing. It seems to be in the nature of things that those who try to to offer the highest form of friendship are not always easy to take.

The laws governing the success or failure of a spiritual community are quite different to those governing a 'worldly' enterprise. There are none of the usual sticks and carrots, no brilliant 'career prospects' or salary increases to strive for, and no fear of dismissal. In Poona, as in London, people were creating this new movement because it was something they believed in; it was entirely up to them how urgently, how efficiently, or even how responsibly, they went about it. Those looking on from the outside might envy them for doing something they really cared about, and assumed it to be easy to work with such motivation. But it was never that easy.

When your primary motivating force is a vision, and an often painfully won commitment to that vision, then woe betide you when you lose contact with it! From time to time, anyone can pass through months of arid meditations, find too little time or mental space to study the texts that inspire them, or simply fall victim to the gravitational pull of their earlier conditioning. At such times they may find themselves wondering why on earth they are doing all this, why they are making all this effort to create a 'movement', when what they really want is an easier life with more time to meditate, study, or simply relax and enjoy themselves. Unfortunately, to develop a commitment to the ideals of Buddhism is not quite the same thing as becoming a Buddha!

What was special about Lokamitra—and what was so bracing about him—was the way he would use day-to-day situations to help people take responsibility for their vision. If you were late for a meeting, forgot to ask a shop-keeper for a receipt, gave an ill-prepared talk, or did anything that implied carelessness, a lapse of responsibility, or satisfaction with mediocrity, then, in no time, he would be stabbing you with his finger—metaphorically and occasionally physically—demanding that you look into your state of mind, even warning you that you were on some kind of dangerous downward slope. At such times he took on the aspect of a wrathful demon from the Tibetan pantheon, a hair-raising force out of a nightmare. But, like those awesome demons, he was—or was at least doing his best to become—nothing more nor less than a messenger from the realm of truth. He was trying to act like a *kalyana mitra*, a 'spiritual friend', someone who helps you in whatever way he can to take the next step along the path, simply because he cares about you.

There are many beautiful literary accounts of 'first encounters' between gurus and their disciples in which the guru gives just a little smile, or offers a gentle touch, and sends his chosen man soaring into dimensions of bliss and light? I must confess that, whenever I have had the good fortune to meet a highly developed human being, the feeling I have experienced has been one of being hit very hard on the undersides of my feet by the planet Earth.

Only one of the developments unfolding in Poona when I arrived was distressing. Subsequent to the uprising by Sikh extremists in Amritsar, the Indian authorities had tightened immigration procedures immeasurably; the holder of a UK passport was no longer free to enter or live in the country without a visa. While it was still easy to get a three month tourist pass, we were discovering that anything else was going to be difficult. The Western Order members had applied for their visas, having already spent some years in India. When I arrived, most of them were still waiting to hear their fate. After a few weeks Lokamitra was asked to 'tidy up his affairs' and be gone in six months.

Vajraketu had not even been that lucky.

* * *

If anyone went to India thinking he would be providing a bit of Western know-how and efficiency, then perhaps it was Vajraketu. With a Cambridge degree under his belt, a few prosperous years spent on the fringes of the popular music trade, a co-operative business success story to his credit, and freshly ordained, Vajraketu burst onto the sub-continent in January 1982—while our roadshow was halted in Aurangabad—confident that he would have everything sorted out in a couple of years. The taxi ride from the airport to the centre of Bombay was, he later admitted, something of a revelation. He was not prepared for the sights that his eyes transmitted to his brain. It was the *scale* of the poverty and squalor that shocked him, the sight of acres upon acres of

175

hutments and shabby tenements.

Even so, he threw himself into his work with dazzling verve, and joined us in Aurangabad after he had been in India for just a week. Already he had taken himself to Dapodi and met several members of the local Buddhist community, he'd made contact with the land-owners and strolled around the place, plans in hand, familiarizing himself with the layout. He descended on our party like a comet falling from the sky, hustling Lokamitra and Vimalakirti away for discussions at every opportunity, impatient at any hint of delay or obstruction.

He was poised for a fall.

One evening, after a talk in a village twenty-five miles out of Aurangabad, a few of us had slipped from the hall to check that everything was all right with our van. It was not. There was no sign of it, nor any trace of the driver. A man we met in the road helpfully suggested that he had gone off on another job.

By now people were leaving the hall and had begun to gather round us, smiling sympathetically at our predicament.

'This is preposterous!' Vajraketu bristled, 'This is absurd! He *can't* just go off like that. It's completely irresponsible! What are we going to do?' He looked about him, taking in the forest of waggling heads. Then he called Buddhapriya across.

'We can't let Sangharakshita get stranded like this. It's terrible. Can't you ask someone here to take him back in their car?'

Buddhapriya looked uneasy.

'Vajraketu,' I said, 'I doubt whether anyone here owns a bicycle, let alone a car. I think we're going to have to try another tack.'

Then and there, Vajraketu seemed to run out of steam. His mouth sagged as the implications of working—of trying to get anything done quickly—in this alien world, dawned on him.

Such early traumas alerted Vajraketu to the fact that he didn't like India. He was also afraid of it, and afraid of what it was telling him about himself. He hated the dirt; he hated the noise; he hated the chaos and the constant struggles involved in buying a railway ticket or a stamp. He began to think that he'd made a mistake in placing himself there.

By then, being about to leave for London, I took him out to a juice bar and asked him whether he thought he would be staying much longer.

'How can I leave?' he replied, 'My reasons just aren't good enough, are they? I mean, here I am feeling sorry for myself because we live in a noisy street, or because I want jam on my bread. When I realize that, I just can't look some of the Indian Order members in the face.'

At that time we all thought that the Dapodi land negotiations were close to completion. Vajraketu took comfort in the fact that he would soon be too busy too think about himself. Until then, his pride—if nothing else—would keep him loyal to his assignment.

But the land negotiations turned out to be the most complicated, convoluted, and protracted affairs in the history of bureaucratic endeavour. It emerged that some thirty members of the ancient family who owned the land we were trying to buy had some title to it. Every one of them had to sign forms and take part in the negotiations. And as new family members were being born all the time, each with some hereditary claim on the land, the situation became ever further entangled. Then there was a 'Land Ceiling' restriction to overcome and planning permission to win. The affair dragged on and on.

Left high and dry, Vajraketu became more miserable as each day passed. He remained in Poona, falling ill, going to classes, learning a little Marathi, and writing anguished letters to his friends in England, most of them bitterly lamenting his own lack of compassion and impotence in the face of so much human misery. Each time he discovered something new about the hardships his fellow Order members had suffered, he disliked himself more. He felt pampered, culturally over-indulged: a non-starter in the altruism stakes.

It was the 'Bombay boys' who turned him round in the end. These were Bodhisen's friends, an energetic and determined bunch of men from the Bombay tenement and hutment areas. They came to Poona from time to time, and finally persuaded Vajraketu to lead a regular weekly class in Ulhasnagar, a semi-rural suburb of Bombay, about an hour's train ride from the centre of town. In no time at all, he had fallen under their spell. To the astonishment of his friends, Vajraketu abruptly announced that he was going to start work in Bombay—at least until the Dapodi situation was clearer.

And so he moved to Bombay where for a year he led an entirely nomadic existence, sleeping in corridors, on staircases, very occasionally in a friend's house, and in the Buddha-Hall at Siddharth College, one of the People's Education Society's establishments in a run-down sector of the city. Bodhisen roamed with him, though he preferred to sleep on the street near a Japanese cemetery, since there was a public water tap nearby where he could take his morning bath.

On this shaky basis, Vajraketu took up a life of public speaking and Dhamma teaching. He held meetings in the gloomy, betel stained corridors of the tenements, and in the rubbish-filled gorges and ravines that separated the grimy buildings. He stood on pavements and in railway yards, each week making contact with about a thousand people.

'A thousand people a week probably sounds quite impressive,' he wrote, 'but at that rate it will take me twenty years to meet every Buddhist in Bombay—just once. There are a million of them here! And they all seem to want to know more about Buddhism!'

His wanderings came to an end when he received a tip-off about a vacant flat in a small block run by a Buddhist housing society. For £10,000, an exceptionally low price for Bombay, he could have a place big enough for classes, and permanent enough to act as a contact-point for 'TBMSG Bombay'.

The money had to be found in just one week, or the deal would fall through. In England his friends rushed around organizing collections at centres, digging into their pockets, sounding out possible benefactors. . . . The money was found.

By now, Vajraketu had come to love Bombay. He and Bodhisen were virtually inseparable, and between them acted like a magnet, attracting an ever-widening circle of friends and followers. By the time Sangha-rakshita paid his next visit to India, Bodhisen and two more Bombayites were ready for ordination.

Their apartment block stood four-square and dirty, like an abandoned galleon, adrift on a sea of hutments. The flat was ten soul-destroying flights of stairs from the ground, so when I arrived for a short stay, it was the coolness of the marble-dash tiling on which I lay, and the hurricane generated by a five-speed ceiling fan, that really endeared me to the place. As consciousness returned, I became aware of the 'Bombay boys'.

Two of them at least, Prakash and Siddharth, both in their early twenties, were leaping around my supine form, doing a sort of war dance, laughing deliriously and chanting, 'Sri, Sri, Sri! Nagabodhi—Ji!' over and over. Clearly my fame had gone before me; but then, so had theirs. I already knew that they were two of the brightest people Vajraketu had ever met. I had been warned that Prakash had a tendency to let his unquenchable exuberance overshadow an as yet rudimentary stock of sensitivity, but that Siddharth was 'the perfect person to go for a walk with when you just needed a bit of peace and quiet'. I also knew that they both lived in the hutments nearby, and I had seen slides of Siddharth's home: a blue box, about eight feet by ten, where he lived with his mother and father, wife, sisters, and brothers, and an enormous stack of urns in which the daily half-hour's worth of running water was stored.

They not only worked in the same glass factory, as packers, but actually held down the same job. To avoid meeting certain rules and regulations designed to ensure his workers' basic rights and amenities, their boss operated the fairly common system of employing his staff as casual labourers: one month on, the next month off. Therefore, whenever Prakash was working, Siddharth was free, and when Siddharth was doing his stint, Prakash would be on leave. Their earnings averaged out to three hundred rupees per month—about twenty pounds—each. Although they were both looking forward to the day when they would set up a TBMSG bookshop in Bombay, which would give them permanent work and a better income, neither ever complained about his lot. They more or less managed to scrape by, and had plenty of free time, much of which they spent in Poona, helping out with the office work at the centre, and all of which they devoted, in some way, to the spread of Buddhism.

Prakash had played Charlie Chaplin at our Bhaja cabaret. He was a diminutive fellow, about four feet ten inches high, with a slightly wider than regulation moustache. He was currently engaged in a tense struggle with his parents who were trying to marry him off before he felt ready, to a girl whom he did not like, and who was fiercely in love with his brother. He had a highly developed capacity for creating and worshipping heroes. Any mention of Vajraketu left him speechless and dreamy eyed; Jyotipala was 'such a very, very fine man! Like a father, so very damn fine!' Lokamitra was the greatest mortal ever to breathe the air, and he still bristled with satisfaction because he had managed, a year before, to dash up to Sangharakshita at the Bhaja opening ceremony, and spend *six seconds* talking to him before Lokamitra hustled him away. But he was not incapable of seeing his own merits and strengths. I lost count of the number of times he told me about his thirty-six hour, non-stop bookselling marathon at a recent convention of militant Scheduled Caste activists. 'Four thousand, three hundred rupees books sold! And no sleep! No food! Just selling! Four thousand, three hundred rupees!'

Siddharth was the perfect foil to Prakash's ceaseless effervescence. Tall, slim, and handsome, he exuded an air of almost palpable 'spirituality'. At times his moods and feelings seemed to hover lightly around and above him, rather than living solidly in his being. I couldn't help wondering whether, when he was a bit older, we might not perhaps export him to the West, where he would doubtless make a small killing in the spiritual supermarket as a 'Realized Saint'. To some extent, this aura was an accident of physical appearance, though his personality went some way towards confirming it. He was sensitive, warm, and obviously familiar with the fruits of meditation practice. He was, for all that, youthful and lively, as willing to fool about as was Prakash, and equally boisterous in his eagerness to do anything which might take the Dhamma Revolution another notch further. If Poona was the 'General Headquarters', then these two firmly believed themselves to be stationed on the front line.

A little later I met Prabhakar, a cleaner of Bombay buses, a wiry man, built like a fly-weight wrestler, with a tendency to reach for his comb and slick back his hair whenever confronted by something reflective. Crackling with organizational energy and a native air of calculation, he was the outfit's roadie-cum-manager. Within seconds of meeting me he wanted to know how long I would be in Bombay—and then whether I had meant that I was leaving Thursday *morning* or Thursday *afternoon*. As we spoke, he eyed me over, fitting me into slots and categories so that he could set me up with the most appropriate engagements, and have me invited to the right homes for lunches and dinners. I soon began to feel slightly afraid of him.

Because of my schedule, and the demands of their jobs, I met Chandrasil and Vajrasil, the two other Order members, only fleetingly, just long enough to see that despite their more advanced years, and their heavier family and career responsibilities, they displayed the same raw edge of excited enthusiasm as the others. Vajrasil, who must have had one of the highest-pitched voices in India, and certainly the squeakiest laugh I have ever heard, translated a talk I gave at Siddharth Vihar. I couldn't help noticing that most of his sentences were far longer than my English originals.

For six days I accompanied this little circus around the town, to talks in echoing railway sheds and courtyards, in living rooms and school classrooms. I went wherever they went, and watched them filling the hours in between back at the flat, counting up their books, listening to Sangharakshita's tape-recorded talks, and immersed in meditation. It was easy to see how Vajraketu had become so attached to Bombay. Even if it was, as he put it, a 'Bodhisattva's playground'—a place where someone endowed with infinite quantities of compassion and wisdom could go on giving, without ever exhausting the need to give more— the company was excellent.

I heard Vajraketu's name a hundred times each day, and slept at night in a room filled with his books and possessions. But he himself was not among us. He had flown over to England several months before, and was now trapped there.

While it had been quite easy for Aid For India to raise considerable amounts for the social projects at Dapodi and Lohagaon, it was not so easy to raise funds for the directly Buddhist work that TBMSG was doing—which actually provided the indispensable basis for the social projects. So Vajraketu was invited over to England, and his tour was a reasonable success, raising about £40,000 in four weeks. We had just one problem left when it was all over. How were we going to get him back into India?

There were those who said he never should have left India in the first place; the visa restrictions had just been imposed when he flew to London. Perhaps it would have been better to delay his tour until we had a clearer picture of how things stood. But the publicity had already been prepared, the radio interviews arranged, everything was ready to roll. So he came. As his tour neared its end, he applied for a residential visa, and was refused.

When I left England, he was still trying to find a way of getting back to India. By chance, I bumped into him just as I was leaving for the airport. His eyes brimmed with tears as he raised his hands, folded in an Indian salutation. My suitcase was half filled with presents he had asked me to take out to his friends.

'Jai Bhim,' he said.

'Jai Bhim,' I said.

fifteen

'GODAMGURU'

I rubbed myself a little to check I was awake. But that really was what the sign on the platform said.

Beside me, wrapped in heavy blankets, Lokamitra and Vimalakirti lay asleep on the smooth wooden benches of our second-class compartment. We were now in Andhra Pradesh, but the 'Hyderabad Express' was running two hours late; it would be at least nine when we arrived.

Outside, the luminous beginnings of an overcast morning revealed a panorama of verdant millet and wheat fields. These were generously criss-crossed with irrigation channels, and spouts of water pulsed sparkling from fat grey pipes. The farm labourers resembled medieval friars, with their white shirts and dhotis almost hidden beneath brown, cowl-like, over-blankets. Here and there, young boys perched on flimsy platforms, and whirled slings over their heads to keep the birds at bay. The entire scene was cluttered with a chaotic jumble of immense black boulders, as if a giant-child had attacked a mountain with his mallet, and left the mess behind.

Lokamitra and Vimalakirti were visiting Hyderabad to sign a few documents; some local Buddhists wanted to give TBMSG a piece of land close to the heart of the city. A small vihara had been standing there for years, but very little was happening. Now they were hoping that TBMSG would build a student's hostel and organize regular Buddhist activities.

They had also invited their visitors to give some talks that night, and had asked them them to deal specifically with the theme of 'Buddhism and Communism'. Once awake, Lokamitra and Vimalakirti took advantage of our delay to prepare for the engagement.

Hyderabad was clumsily festooned with the relics of a general election. As Mr Prem Rao, a frantically friendly lawyer, sped me away from the station on the back of his scooter, we passed beneath the beatific gaze of a forty foot high cut-out of N. T. Rama Rao, the upstart, ex-actor, Sannyassi politician, whose Telugu Dessam party had all but annihilated the Congress (I) at the polls in Andhra Pradesh. A few blocks later, we zipped beneath the protective effigies of Rajiv and Indira Gandhi. The competition must have been lively: every scrap of wall space and bill-boarding, every stretch of water pipeline, even the roads and pavements, were buried beneath names, slogans, and picture symbols. 'Please vote for Hand. (Congress (I))', 'Kindly register your Mark for Lotus. (Bharatiya Janata Party)', and so on. Such endearing supplications contrasted ironically with the crudeness of a campaign that had given an entire city the air of a sleazy back-street lavatory. But democracy had triumphed. The local David had vanquished the national Goliath, and the Lok Sabha had been given something of an opposition.

We took breakfast in the kind of hotel where you need an overcoat and torch to survive the air conditioning system and find your food. Mr Rastrapal, the silver-haired president of the local Buddhist Society, explained why he felt the evening's meeting to be so important.

'This issue of Buddhism and Communism is a very crucial one in our town. Many people here are impatient. They think that Buddhism is just a waste of time. They want to look for the answers in politics, in Communism.'

He was a calm, gentle man, and talked about the current tensions with benign but weary resignation.

'You know, they have changed Babasaheb's old slogan. He said "Educate, Agitate, Organize!" Now they are saying "Educate, Organize, Agitate." It is only a little difference, I know, but it changes everything. Nobody thinks of changing attitudes or changing consciousness. They think only about rushing in and changing society. And they are prepared to use violence if necessary.

'A little while ago I was invited to a rally. Just after I arrived there was some trouble, and people started to fight with the police. They were throwing stones, and the police were making lathi charges. It all seemed completely wrong to me. I felt very uncomfortable to be taking part in it. Just at that moment I encountered an old friend, a man whom I had worked with in the police-force. I said to him "What are *we* doing here?" He laughed, and said that he did not know. So we took each other by the hand and made our way out of the crowd.

'You see, nobody can understand how the Dhamma itself might change things. We have had some bhikkhus here. They gave very nice talks. But when people asked difficult questions afterwards, they seemed to get rather confused.

'Unless something can be done to educate people more, I am telling you that things will get much worse. Already some of our young people are forming themselves into a "Dalit Liberation Army"—an army of the oppressed.'

This was a familiar story. Ever since the conversions there had been a background rumble of doubt. There had been many leaders—from the Scheduled Castes that did not convert, and even from among the Buddhists—who could not understand why Ambedkar rejected the option of a Communist revolution. Many of the leaders to emerge in past decades had prescribed far sterner measures for social change than had their 'Babasaheb'.

In 1982 it was possible to identify Buddhist hutment localities by the red and black flags which fluttered from their roof-tops. These flags were the emblem of the 'Dalit Panthers', a sort of para-military youth organization modelled on the American 'Black Panther' movement. Already, three years later, those flags were hardly to be seen anywhere. Like so many other parties and splinter groups, the Panthers were on the wane, disintegrating through internal disagreements, haziness of intention, and weak leadership.

But as Mr Rastrapal indicated, the militant outlook was still popular. After all, caste prejudice was still strong in many areas; atrocities were being committed. Now, as material conditions changed, caste divisions were gradually becoming overlaid by class divisions. Poor Caste-Hindus resented the 'preferential treatment' handed out to people from the Scheduled Castes, perhaps forgetting that the 'dalits' still had to overcome the handicap of thousands of years of oppression. The reservations policy was coming under bitter attack, Ambedkar's safeguards could soon be lost.

And so the debate continued. Had Ambedkar been duped by Hindu manipulators and diverted first from militant Islam, then from Communism, and finally steered towards the stagnant backwaters of a dead religion? Or was he simply outraged that the Communist Party of India had been infiltrated by high-caste Hindus? There were many who believed that, had he really been true to himself, he would have urged his followers to take up the hammer and sickle.

At big Ambedkarite rallies one could pick up any number of tracts and pamphlets on this theme. Through their pages writers gave vent to their frustration: 'Look at our meetings. Every year people come together in hundreds of thousands: for *Buddha Jayanti, Ambedkar Jayanti*. . . . Our meetings are disciplined. No one has to worry about such things as theft or molestation of women. We are still united in the memory of Dr Babasaheb Ambedkar. Why is all this energy and enthusiasm not being harnessed?'

It must have been frustrating indeed for the politicians and demagogues to discover, time and time again, that those vast reservoirs of power, which shimmered so tantalizingly before their eyes, would dissolve to dust the moment they reached out to claim them.

Ideologically, Ambedkar was a state socialist. He believed that a social economy rooted in *laissez-faire* capitalism and private ownership—and the network of exploitative relationships issuing therefrom—was a key cause of human suffering and degradation.

In his view, the ideal society would be one in which the state owned and controlled all major industries, regulated the price and supply of essential goods, controlled and co-ordinated imports and exports, and maintained a policy of full employment. All land would belong to the state, which would 'sub-let' it to local collectives; their responsibility would be to tend that land to its full advantage for the good of all, while at the same time shaping themselves into microcosms of the ideal society, based, of course, on the principles of Liberty, Equality, and Fraternity. There would be no class, no caste, no bosses, no servants, and no such thing as landless labour. It would be the duty of the central administration to ensure a constant movement towards cultural refinement throughout the land, something it would achieve by giving each of its citizens the right and freedom to explore his or her highest capabilities to the full. In his view, this was the only system of government which would have a hope of correcting the imbalances and inequalities that so plagued Indian society. But how was such a state to come into being? And how, once created, could it be preserved?

Ambedkar's love of 'Liberty, Equality, and Fraternity' naturally drew him to the conviction that an ideal state should be democratic. But the democratic process—particularly in a country like India, whose traditions were so profoundly undemocratic—could take decades to establish itself. In the mean time it would almost inevitably function as a source of instability, with basic issues constantly at the mercy of a tug of war between powerful and strongly opposed interest groups. How could one possibly legislate for social change, or create an entirely new economic order, in such conditions?

The Marxist answer—resorted to by all existing socialist states—was the dictatorship of the proletariat, the absolute (if 'provisional') tyranny of the state. But to Ambedkar this was no solution at all. He held that unless people's hearts and minds were transformed, all the old patterns of rich and poor, exploiters and exploited, would return the moment the state dismantled its instruments of control. The forces of ignorance, and greed for wealth or power, were proven survivors, ever primed to reassert themselves.

'There is no use in pursuing a certain path', he once said, 'if that path is not going to be a lasting path. If it is going to lead you into the jungle; if it is going to lead you to anarchy, there is no use pursuing it. But if you are assured that the path you are asked to follow is slow, maybe devious, maybe with long detours, yet if it ultimately makes you reach a safe, sound ground so that the ideals are there to help you to mould your life permanently, it is much better, in judgement, to follow the slower path . . . rather than to rush up and take what we call short cuts. Short cuts in life are dangerous, very dangerous.'

His slow and devious path consisted in the creation of a democratic state whose socialistic orientation would be guaranteed by the constitution, and conversion to Buddhism.

He pointed to the example set by the Buddha's followers. They had almost no personal possessions: just a robe or two, a water strainer, a needle, and a begging bowl. He wondered whether any so-called Communist state imposed such harsh strictures on its citizens! And yet the Buddha's disciples accepted their discipline willingly, even chose to accept it, because they were trying to cultivate the qualities of wisdom and compassion. If enough people could only transform their most deeply rooted habits and attitudes, then all else would follow.

He seriously believed that if the practice of Buddhism could spread among the ex-Untouchables, and even to the communities beyond, it would quite naturally foment an authentically socialistic mood in the nation. As people awoke to the truth of impermanence, for example, they would cast off the snare of attachment to private property; if they could make serious efforts to *develop* the virtues of loving kindness and compassion, then the evils of exploitation and oppression—even caste-oppression—would disappear. 'The Touchables and the Untouchables', he said, 'cannot be held together by law. . . . The only thing that can hold them together is love.'

For all his distrust of *mahatmas*, there were times when Ambedkar could sound rather like one himself. He believed that if people were prepared to make the effort to change, then an ideal society would emerge as the inevitable and securely established result. In one of his last speeches he declared 'I am quite confident that if we all become one tenth as enlightened as the Buddha was, we can bring about the same results [as those envisaged by the Communists] by the methods of love, of justice and goodwill.'

* * *

Lokamitra and Vimalakirti had been asked to speak for half an hour each. Their audience, comfortably seated in the conference hall of the 'Press Club of Hyderabad', contrasted noticeably with those generally found in Maharashtra. To begin with, most of them seemed well-dressed and relatively affluent. Then, apart from a handful of Maharashtran immigrants, very few of them were Buddhists. Coming from the Scheduled Castes, however, they had an obvious respect for Ambedkar: 'We are not even fit to touch his bootlaces!' cried the chairman in his opening remarks. Nobody present seemed to find the suggestion offensive or contentious.

To my initial surprise, neither Lokamitra nor Vimalakirti tackled the 'Buddhism *versus* Communism' issue head-on. While both paid heed to Ambedkar's views on the limitations and dangers of an exclusively Marxist approach to social change, they chose, by and large, to give their listeners a taste of Buddhism itself, though clearly proposing it as an essential catalyst for the transformation of the individual and society.

Their listeners gave them a good hearing, screwing up their eyes in concentration, nudging each other and laughing, much like any Maharashtrian audience. But, looking around the room, I had the strange feeling that they were somehow frozen in time, caught in the early fifties, still prevaricating over whether or not to take the plunge into conversion. For them, the issue was further complicated by the fact that in Andhra Pradesh there were no reserved quotas of places for Buddhists in government service and higher education, as there were in Maharashtra. To convert, and to declare their conversion publically, could lead to the loss of opportunities and advantages they had gained as members of the 'backward classes'. Many of them looked well accustomed to their middle-class lives. They would be in no hurry to rock the boat.

Lokamitra spoke about the 'Threefold Way', a traditional formulation of the Buddha's teachings in which the path is seen under the aspects of morality, meditation, and wisdom. He concluded on a more 'direct' note, however, asserting that while it was easy to make noises about the need for change, and to attack the government of the day, it was another thing altogether to try to change yourself. Reminding his listeners that that was the challenge proposed by their leader, he threw down a further gauntlet of his own:

'Please bear in mind when you think about Buddhism and Communism that Dr Ambedkar was an extremely sincere man. He saw, and felt very deeply, the need for social change. He worked for it all his life. He was also a very wise man, and devoted years of reflection and study to the question of conversion. He really thought about Buddhism, and he really thought about Communism. Of course, you will want to think for yourselves, and you may decide in favour of Communism. But if you do this, without giving the matter the same *amount* of thought as did Dr Ambedkar, and the same *depth* of thought as he did, then you will be insulting his memory, and calling him a fool.'

Vimalakirti spoke primarily about another traditional formulation, the Eightfold Path, and set out to demonstrate how its various limbs added up to a blueprint, and even a manifesto, for individual and social change. All the same, he could not resist devoting a little time to the theme of violence. It was unrealistic, he said, to divide the world into just two camps—the exploiters and the exploited—so as to generate hatred between them. All human beings know what it is to suffer. And the root of all suffering is the mind—which can never be changed through violence.

In concluding, he urged his listeners to see life, and their society, as wholes, and to acknowledge that true liberation for all would come about only when people were prepared to work on themselves and work on their mental states.

Lokamitra had made it clear in advance that he did not wish to take part in a debate. He had specifically requested that there should be no speakers other than himself and Vimalakirti, and no concluding question-and-answer session. I knew that he and Vimalakirti were both capable of arguing powerfully and well on this theme. Vimalakirti, with his political background, had felt frankly frustrated by the non-confrontational strategy. In the end, however, they had decided that people should go home, just this once, with nothing more nor less than the Dhamma ringing in their ears.

But this, as Lokamitra liked to say, was India.

The chairman had risen from his seat, and was approaching the lectern to deliver a vote of thanks, when a heavily bespectacled man scuttled up and whispered a few words in his ear. There was a subdued exchange. Finally, casting a helpless glance in Lokamitra's direction, the chairman announced that we had just one more speaker. A very well-known gentleman wished to add a few words to those we had heard so far.

The gentleman in question was actually well-known as a Communist agitator, and took his position at the lectern with practised ease.

'We have just had the honour of listening to two very fine and worthy talks,' he said. 'We should all feel extremely grateful for two such very clear expositions of the Buddha-Dhamma! I feel myself therefore to be most reluctant to spoil anything of this atmosphere that has been created by our speakers. However . . .'

And then he got going.

'We have been told that Dr Ambedkar was not in favour of this violence. He did not want to have anything to do with it! But what is there to be afraid of in violence? What about the violence of the state? What about the violence of the police? What about the violence of the landlords and their paid henchmen? What about the most terrible atrocities that are committed against our people every day? Are we to have nothing to do with this violence? Are we to accept it like sheep? Are we not justified in ourselves taking up violent measures to remedy violence? I don't think our speakers have properly satisfied us on this question!'

He continued in this vein for ten minutes. It was a heartfelt call to arms, born of frustration, impatience, and not a little hatred.

It was not hard to understand his feelings. Caste-connected violence was still commonplace. Every year there were some four hundred murders, and as many rapes, fifteen hundred serious woundings, more than a thousand cases of arson, and ten thousand more miscellaneous indignities meted out on members of the Scheduled Castes, directly attributable to caste prejudice. Almost daily, the newspapers displayed lurid photographs showing the aftermaths of burnings, blindings, and beatings. The police were suspected of taking a wilfully passive role in these matters, and were sometimes even accused of being the instigators. It was only too easy to imagine what feelings of rage and impotence simmered in the breasts of those Scheduled Caste people who kept up with the news.

Our meeting lurched out of control. For forty minutes, speaker after speaker made his way to the lectern. Some sought to stir the flames still higher, while others tried to dampen them with appeals to 'the wider point of view'. Many even paid tribute to the fundamental fairness of the system. After all, Ambedkar himself had played a major role in its formulation. One speaker, typical of this faction, concluded his manifesto for change thus:

'We must first educate our people, and then, using constitutional methods, we must capture the government of this country, and capture the legislature!

'I have suffered. I have witnessed atrocities. But seeking revenge will do us no good. I believe that if we are firm, and stand firm against those who would commit atrocities, we will prevail. But for the time being, we must organize ourselves.'

It was a calmer, more reasoned outlook, but it fell short of Ambedkar's vision.

'Had my mind been seized with hatred and revenge', said Ambedkar, 'I would have brought disaster on this land in five years!' He resented the suggestion that he was motivated by any force so base as the desire for revenge—even though he had suffered his own quota of prejudice.

At his peak, had he chosen to utter the appropriate war-cry, he could have mobilized tens of millions of Untouchables and turned India into a bloodbath. But he did not want revenge, and he did not want a violent revolution either. He certainly did not want a socialist state if its achievement would undermine the core principle of its own ideology, the fundamental sanctity of the individual. He had no personal fear of violence; nor was his rejection of it rooted in sentiment. In his view, violence simply did not work. Hatred never ceases through hatred; hatred ceases only when opposed by love. This law was as valid and inflexible to him as any defined by Marx.

As Vimalakirti had pointed out, Ambedkar saw the whole of Indian society corrupted by a sickness. He hated that sickness, but he could not bring himself to hate the people who were ravaged by it. In a sense, it was secondary to him who had that strain of the disease which manifested as 'exploiter', or 'oppressor', and who had the strain which manifested as 'victim'. He longed to cure the sickness itself, once and for all, and knew that its roots lay in the mind of each individual in the society. No wonder he warned his followers that his would be a long and difficult path! And perhaps it was no wonder that I was witnessing these signs of impatience. The process of transformation had hardly begun, if at all. After twenty-five years, Ambedkar's prescription had still to be given a fair trial.

When speaking on the theme of Buddhism and Communism himself, at a Buddhist convention in Kathmandu, Ambedkar laid crucial stress on the importance of good Dhamma teachers. How could there be any hope for a Dhamma Revolution if people were not given good guidance, and shown how the Dhamma could be used to change their lives?

Up on the stage that night, we were accompanied by a monk. He was a rather peculiar young man, with a mane of well-oiled black hair, who had obtained his position on the dais by appearing at the last moment, climbing onto the stage uninvited, and then causing an embarrassing fuss upon discovering that there was no chair for him. In the end a chair was produced, but only after it had become clear that he had no intention of ceasing his pitiful screeches until he received satisfaction. Once established, he fidgeted nervously throughout the evening. It was obvious to all that he was not only a complete poseur, devoid of any spiritual qualities whatsoever, but quite possibly in need of psychiatric care. One had to feel sorry for him, but at the same time, it was hard not to feel sorry for our audience, who were getting a highly discouraging view of the *Sangha*.

Since everyone else was doing it, I asked whether I could perhaps say a few words.

'Be careful!' said Lokamitra, as I squeezed past on my way to the lectern, 'This is a big issue. Don't go out of your depth.'

'Relax, I'm only going to tell a story.'

Throughout the day, Mr Prem Rao had been petitioning me to tell him something about the Right-Livelihood co-operatives we had set up in England. I decided that this would be an opportunity to satisfy him and, as I explained to my audience, contribute at least something to their debate.

I told them the story of Aryatara Community.

'Aryatara' was an attractive residence in Purley, a suburban town on the extreme southern edge of London. Originally a preparatory school for boys, the house, with its spacious rooms and pleasant garden, had been taken on by some of Sangharakshita's followers and transformed into a rather sleepy community. At weekends it was occasionally used for small retreats and, in the garage, a tiny printing press serviced the movement's modest literary requirements. Even so, the place had a rather dreary atmosphere, and was regarded as something of a joke.

At the beginning of 1976, a few people moved in with the intention of turning Aryatara into an active public centre. Some tentative moves had already been made in this direction: Yoga classes were quite popular among local housewives, but the 'beginners' meditation class rarely attracted even a handful of people; the 'regulars' class, a more decidedly Buddhist evening, drew just a sprinkling of somewhat jaded participants. Sangharakshita suggested that a real attempt be made to 'shake the place up'.

The key members of the new team were myself, my friend Steve from the BBC—now known as Padmaraja, a dreamer of extravagantly vivid dreams named Vessantara, and a newly ordained Yorkshireman called Jyotipala. Between us we could deploy an effective array of qualities and talents, and mobilized everything we had to make the classes hum.

To begin with, we were motivated as much as anything else by our determination to show our more pessimistic friends that we could turn our no-hope community into a lively public centre. Having moved there from busy centres ourselves, we also craved the stimulation that such a centre would offer.

After a few months we began to register success. Twenty or more people were coming to the beginners' classes; our stock of 'regulars' was growing and showing signs of life; some were even asking whether they could join the resident community. The printing press had moved to London, enabling a more appropriate atmosphere to develop, and we encouraged our new friends to turn up at any time of the day or night for a chat, to meditate, or to help with the gardening.

Money was in short supply. We needed it to support ourselves and to keep the place in good repair. We also wanted to contribute towards a number of the movement's more general projects. So we organized sponsored walks, jumble sales, and benefit dinners. The jumble sales were a treat. For a few weeks we would spend our free evenings cruising the streets in borrowed cars and vans, collecting unwanted clothes and bric-a-brac, then carrying out the sales in hired halls. They were laughably small affairs, but the fun lay in the fact that they brought us all together more frequently, and in a more dynamic way. The classes at the centre benefited too, as the spirit of friendship buzzing between those most involved started to infect the rest. We took to redecorating the house—almost as an on-going activity—if for no other reason than that it fed that spirit.

Inevitably we started talking about some kind of permanent business venture. That way we would be able to support ourselves and pay the centre's running costs, and be able to spend more time with each other. Stage by stage, we were stumbling into a kind of Zen-like arena in which work and daily life, approached in the right way, at the right pace, and with the right companions, became a powerful 'technique' for change.

We decided to go in for wholefoods. A wholefoods shop would provide a good ethical basis—though none of us was particularly fanatical about the 'wholefood ideology', even though we were vegetarian. It would also require relatively little start-up cash. Some of our friends in London had been running wholefood market stalls for a number of years; we would be able to draw on their experience when we got our own venture under way.

We just needed a few thousand pounds.

Padmaraja returned to the BBC on a short-term contract. Jyotipala, a painter by trade, bought a few buckets and brushes, hired a ladder, and set up a decorating business. We bought a battered wreck of a van and touted around for light removals jobs, while a few more of our number took to manicuring local gardens. We upgraded our jumble sales—advertised them as 'bazaars'. And we asked our regulars to give money too. This they did, dropping their notes and cheques into the lacquered *dana* bowl that sat beside the front door. As things began to take off, it was obvious that a few of them were thinking of forsaking their jobs and joining us. Giving money on a regular—and sometimes substantial—basis served as a kind of bridge in their progress towards fuller involvement.

Up to this point, we had been giving the treasurer just our rent and a contribution towards the food bills, keeping back the rest of our incomes for ourselves. We now decided to give everything we received into a general pool. The treasurer paid the bills, gave the houskeeper his allowance, and at the end of each week floated around the house depositing a five pound note onto each bed—pocket money.

After a lot of badgering on our part the municipal council offered us the burnt out hulk of a three storey building in the heart of town, directly beside the bus station. They thought we were mad when we accepted it.

It was mid-winter and there was not a single window in the building. We piled into the place, working on it seven days a week. Floors had to be built, walls knocked down, partitions erected. We did all the work ourselves, mobilizing whatever resources of labour, advice, and expertise became available through the classes. For two weeks, without a break, one man worked outside, fixing windows and gutters with his bare hands, while snow lapped at his ears.

People from the local office blocks started popping in for a chat. Some stayed to eat lunch with us, and then appeared at our evening classes back at the centre. Despite the long hours and the hard work, nobody was missing those classes. We knew that the success of our 'total Buddhist life' was necessarily fed by the more directly spiritual practices. We were now getting up even earlier in the mornings in order to fit in two sessions of meditation before work, and took to giving meditation and Yoga classes in nearby social clubs and office blocks at lunchtime. The first part of our new 'complex' to be finished was a pleasant shrine room on the first floor, purpose built for small public sessions.

As regulars and some of our newer contacts moved in, the community at Aryatara grew fuller, and a second community had to be opened in the new building. We also began looking for premises for a women's community. At the centre it was no longer rare to find seventy beginners at the meditation class each week.

Everyone involved in the project had a say. Weekly business

meetings took place in the garden behind the shop's premises, to accommodate all those who wanted to attend. The meetings were friendly, but demanding. As well as deciding who would work where during the coming week, we were now having to apply ourselves to an increasingly wide range of issues. How soon after joining the work-team could a person expect to be financially supported? Should we work six days a week, or seven? When we opened up the shop, would we be selling jams made with animal-based agents, or going for the purely vegetarian, but more expensive, varieties? Would we buy prepacked grains and pulses, or would we do our own packaging—thus giving more people a chance to work with us, even though the work itself would be rather dull?

We took each other to task over failures in responsibility, for adopting too selfish an attitude—or for adopting a too self-denying one. We tried to operate according to the principle of 'give what you can, take what you need', and our attempts to engage with the day-to-day details of that little cliché caused us many fruitful hours of discussion and self-examination! We also subscribed to the ideal of 'perpetual revolution'; nothing was ever fixed; nothing was ever to become a matter of habit or routine. Those more used to 'head' work suddenly found themselves painting or plastering, while someone at home with manual work might be encouraged to serve as assistant treasurer. People began to change dramatically as they came up against, and overcame, their limitations and their limited views of themselves, or developed hidden strengths. It was all very hard work, but intensely rewarding.

We opened our wholefood store on schedule and within budget. But by now we had already decided to turn another section of the building into a vegetarian café. So while the shop got under way, the building work continued next door. We registered ourselves formally, as a worker's co-operative.

It must be confessed that we suffered from a terrible lack of expertise. The shop's finish was cheerful, but cheap and a little rough. And all that 'role-switching' hardly conduced to efficiency. The finances, though healthy enough, were in chaos. A few months after we had opened, when we were turning over £1000 a week, a business consultant appeared at our classes, took a look at our arrangements and blanched. We had moved into an arena of activity for which we had no training or experience. But the revolution continued to unfold: the skills were acquired and mastered; the business consultant retired early—and moved in.

I left Aryatara at around this point. Since then, I told my Hyderabad audience, the community had been through many further transformations, and had gone from strength to strength. The businesses were now housed in a far better part of town, turned over half a million pounds a year, and now supported fifty full-time workers who all lived in communities, and maintained a seven-day-a-week 'Dhamma life'. Aryatara was no longer used as a centre at all, since the public classes now took place in the purpose-built 'Croydon Buddhist Centre'. Surplus funds from the businesses paid the Centre's bills, financed a thriving and increasingly prestigious 'Arts Centre', and had recently purchased a retreat centre in the Sussex countryside. There was even enough left over to make a substantial contribution towards the work of TBMSG in India, and the upkeep of a school for refugee children in West Bengal. In the process of creating all this, most of those early regulars, and many more recent additions to the community, had become Order members.

After my time at Aryatara, I moved on to East London where a parallel development—though on a grander scale—had been taking place. Soon after my arrival, a television company made a little film about our co-operative there, as part of a series on co-operatives in Britain. The presenter was a well-known Communist, and as he talked viewers through the varied case studies, he described ours as the 'most ideologically pure' example of a co-operative he had found.

Without wanting to do anything more than create the best conditions for the practice of Buddhism, we had unwittingly given birth to an ideal Communist state in microcosm!

We had started out with nothing. Now we had financial independence, a rich culture to feed on and share with others, and we were beginning to exert an increasingly significant influence on the world around us. I put it to my listeners at the Press Club that the Dhamma was no soft, escapist option. Practised fully and in depth, it really did have the power to change the world.

As I returned to my seat, I remembered a conversation I'd had with a friend, back in 1974. He had just embarked upon a career of revolutionary agitation, with a sub-sect of the Communist movement, while I was soon to be ordained. He felt that by working primarily in the field of individual consciousness, I was ignoring the importance of external conditions. I argued that in concentrating on group consciousness and the material superstructure of society, he was overlooking the collective effect of individual motivation, individual attitude, and habit. In the end we came to an agreement of sorts. He was prepared to concede that his revolutionary movement would benefit from the institution of a 'spiritual wing', directed towards the uplift of individual consciousness, while I accepted that the Buddhist movement would need to operate in the social and material dimension.

Our paths drifted apart. We met again five years later, by chance, in the vegetarian restaurant which formed part of that East London co-operative. It seemed he had indeed tried to initiate something of a spiritual-cum-philosophical dialogue within his movement, but in so doing had made himself the object of considerable distrust. However, he was confident—and saw some of the current geo-political developments as a sure sign—that the revolution could not be far off. The forces at play in the world were now so polarized that just the smallest injection of class consciousness would trigger off the cataclysm.

'And what then?' I asked.

'Oh, you know . . .' he offered a weak smile, 'Fighting in the streets . . . barricades . . . the dictatorship of the proletariat . . .' He didn't seem at all clear whether this was a prospect he relished, or dreaded.

I showed him our public centre and the large community above. I took him down the road to the typesetting business, the wholefood shop, an import-export business, the offices of Aid For India, and a few more branches of our local complex. He acknowledged that we had developed a 'material wing'.

The people working in those businesses were doing so for a basic level of support, which allowed their business profits to pay for Buddhist activities, both in the UK and in India. Their attempts to overcome the distinction between doing things for themselves and doing them for others had nothing to do with mystical speculation: they were engaging with the minutae of the task on a day-to-day level, in their work and community lives. They were prepared to take the risks that such a transformation required—which was why they had created this situation in the first place. After just four years, there were now a hundred people involved in the 'core' community.

My friend seemed generously impressed, as was my audience in Hyderabad, but I could hardly feel smug. Like him, like them, I suppose, I wondered whether it was still too small and too slow.

The world is on fire. It is burning with famine and oppression, with exploitation, war, and with the madness that makes the nuclear stockpiles grow. Essentially, it is ablaze with the same forces that the Buddha identified two-and-a-half-thousand years ago: greed, hatred, and delusion, with straightforward human weakness and confusion. These are forces that have survived innumerable changes of political system, economic order, and cultural revolution. They are fundamental facts of human existence, and they are raging within each of us.

But to accept that the real Revolution has to start with ourselves, and will not progress a step further until we are prepared to take up the struggle in our own hearts and minds, is daunting. It can also seem rather undramatic and inadequate. It doesn't come naturally to hear news of wars, famines, oppression, or arms-races, and then to conclude that one's most constructive starting point will be a thorough overhaul of one's own attitudes and motivating forces. And yet, unless we are able to think and act with integrity, with clarity, with generosity, and selfless love, what do we hope to achieve?

Such an approach to the transformation of the world is inevitably slow and devious. But short cuts are not only limited in their effect; they are positively dangerous.

A couple of hours before going to the Press Club that day, we had been invited to inspect our new plot of land. The walls of the simple vihara that stood there were almost papered with photographs; there were pictures of Dr Ambedkar, shots of meetings and rallies from years ago, and a vast proliferation of group studies. In one of these I saw a youthful Mr Rastrapal standing with a happy, smiling bunch of friends, one of whom was a monk with pronounced oriental features.

'Ah yes,' sighed Mr Rastrapal, 'He was a Cambodian bhikkhu. He went back to his homeland, soon after this picture was taken, and was unfortunately killed by the Khmer Rouge.'

Once upon a time I was a little defensive about my Buddhism. I couldn't help feeling inadequate when challenged by the serious political types with their big visions and big words. Not any more. I throw in my lot with Dr Ambedkar. I have no faith in revolutions that are thrust upon anyone, which trample rough-shod over their own ideals as they unfold. I do have faith in the 'Dhamma Revolution'; I have seen enough of it in Britain and in India to know that it works, and that its ideals are there to help us as we go along: are in fact the means as well as the end.

It is impossible to know how that revolution will progress. But progress it will as more people become involved and make their own contributions, as more individual genius is unleashed, and as more points of contact are forged with the wider world.

That world has reached a point at which no one can know for sure whether the final curtain will not come down on us before we have built our various utopias. In the mean time, acting with love and clarity, we must do whatever there is time for.

Next morning we were up on another stage, this time giving talks to the pupils of a private girls' school. I stood at the lectern trying to give a lecture on 'What Buddhism Is', while a physics teacher tried to eliminate the feedback from the sound system. Six hundred girls sniggered and flashed their eyes at me, and a flock of pigeons that lived in the proscenium arch swooped and fluttered about my head. Had I been the final act in a sixties rock-concert, things would have been going pretty well. As it was, it was business as usual.

La lutte continue, as we used to say.

s i x t e e n

He stands on the heart of a fully opened lotus, in the midst of a clear blue sky. His limbs are bedecked with jewels, richly clothed in flowing, rainbow silks. Avalokiteshvara, the *Bodhisattva* of Compassion, the 'Lord who looks down', sees everything and everyone, and bestows a smile of unspeakable kindness. His eleven heads survey each region of the universe; a thousand arms radiate from his shoulders; his hands offer books, thunderbolts, rosaries, medicines. . . . He is an archetype of Enlightenment. By visualizing and contemplating him, by entering into an imaginative, spiritual intimacy with him, a resonance develops; we are rewarded with an emotional glimpse of ultimate Compassion, and a vision of what that Compassion may require of us.

The Dhamma has been defined as whatever helps people grow towards ultimate happiness, the catalyst which helps them take the next step on their path towards fulfilment. Some need advice on how to live a more truly human, ethical life, others are ready for guidance in meditation; others still thrive on the stimulation of ideas and insights. But there are also those who need the nourishment of food, education, or just vitamins. . . .

It was impossible to spend time among the poorest people in India without seeing how badly they needed straightforward, material help. Almost incredibly, the Dhamma teaching provided by TBMSG seemed able to inculcate a joy and excitement in life that would make many prosperous Westerners envious, but this did not mean that material circumstances could be overlooked. A great many of these people were simply too worn down by poverty and sickness, too worried about their jobs and debts, to give much thought to the notion of 'higher development'. Among the crowds at Sangharakshita's meetings it had been easy to recognize the dull, listless expressions of the anaemic and malnourished, or the extra strain on the faces of the illiterate.

Soon after Lokamitra arrived in India he enlisted undertakings from two medically qualified Order members, Virabhadra and Padmashuri, to follow him out and initiate some kind of welfare project. He also wrote to friends in England about the kind of money such a project would require.

So, while Lokamitra was establishing a Buddhist movement in India, building up a network of friends and contacts, winning trust and credibility, Virabhadra was poring over microscope slides, taking a course in tropical medicine, Padmashuri had stopped nursing and was managing a women's co-operative business in London, learning how to work with others in a way which helped them give of their best. Meanwhile, Aid For India's fund-raisers were learning how to knock on doors and ask the British public for substantial amounts of money.

When I had left India in 1982, Padmashuri was relatively new to India and still acclimatizing; Vajraketu was trying to decide whether or not he wanted to acclimatize at all; and Virabhadra was mostly sleeping. He had just arrived, and insisted—with all the authority of his medical training—that the human metabolism needed ten days to adjust from the April climate of England to that of India.

Three years later he was still the last person to appear in the shrine room for his morning meditation, and always arrived at breakfast just as everyone else was clearing up. He was never at his best at this time of day, and it could be fascinating to watch him wind himself up, passing from pained silence, through a phase of gently cynical exchanges with whomever he could get to play along, until, at length, he achieved a level of warm humanity just in time to mount his scooter and face the day.

Like Lokamitra, he had become a competent scooter driver, knowing instinctively how to weave through the tinkling flocks of cyclists, careening onto the verge to avoid pot-holes, or crossing over to the 'wrong' side when confronted by a wayward lorry or a stray herd of buffaloes. By now he knew every bend and every crack in the road between Ambedkar Society and Dapodi, and was therefore happy to take me along as his passenger, 'to keep the boredom away' as he put it.

Dapodi formed one link in a chain of industrial developments and suburbs that spilt out from Poona, fifteen miles along the Bombay road. Once upon a time it had been a separate rural village, just within the bounds of Poona municipality, an ideal dormitory for people who were moving in from outlying villages, attracted by burgeoning job opportunities in town. Over the years, the fields and meadows around Dapodi had therefore sprouted what the untrained beheld as a single, tangled wasteland of tin huts and primitive shelters. In the eyes of its inhabitants, however, the area was actually a 'conurbation' of four separate localities whose boundaries were rarely crossed: Jai Bhim

Nagar, Mahatma Phule Nagar, 'Arun Talkies', and 'Railway'.

It took Virabhadra and I twenty-five alarming minutes to get there from Ambedkar Society, but at length we turned off the main highway, passed over a level-crossing, dodged our way through the bazaar, and came to a halt outside the office, scattering a flurry of children, goats, and chickens in every direction.

I had been to Dapodi once before, in 1982, to get some pictures for Aid For India's publicity brochures. I'd gone along with Padmashuri, Vajraketu, and—in one of his rare waking moments—Virabhadra. In those days, the hutments were still something new for all of us.

There are no films or photographs that can possibly prepare you for the experience of entering one of these places. The dirt and the squalor is all there, as well as the sickness and overcrowding. But don't expect anyone to approach you with baleful eyes and outstretched hands. People do not sit passively in the dirt, emanating gloom while waiting for the documentary film makers to arrive; they are up and about, as busy and preoccupied as anyone else, fetching water, rooting through piles of rubbish, cooking, playing cards, and shouting at the children who run barefoot over tangled mounds of waste, chasing dogs or playing cricket. These are real people, living day to day lives. They may not seem to be taking any great delight in their circumstances, but neither do they seem particularly crushed by them. Don't imagine that it's some mystical acceptance of a Divine Plan that keeps them going: it is habit, ignorance of any alternative, the need to survive, and the very natural impulse to get whatever pleasure there is to be had out of life.

If you are going to feel anything like pity or compassion, then you will have to put forth the 'discriminating wisdom', and look at the particulars, separating them from the hurly-burly that presents itself. You'll have to look hard, and think about what you see, to notice that many of the people are thin and undernourished. For their part, they are walking around the place laughing and joking with each other. You may see someone with two elbows on one arm, or limping along on twisted legs. But they are probably on their way to catch a bus to work; they are not moaning with pain or need. If you think about it, you will realize that their bodies have turned out that way because of polio, or because they couldn't afford medical attention after a childhood accident. The woman washing clothes over by the taps may not look any different from the others. There's no easy way of knowing that she has just lost one of her children to measles or dehydration.

Again and again you have to take an 'emotional initiative'. Otherwise, as you walk into a hutment area for the first time, you'll be disturbed only by the smell. The people who live there will watch you, scoffing at your clumsy attempts to avoid the filth on the ground, exchanging sly winks among themselves, and jokes at your expense. Unless you can see this world through the eyes of Avalokiteshvara, you will feel no compassion; you will probably feel nothing more upsetting than embarrassment and awkwardness.

It was in this world that Virabhadra and Padmashuri now spent their days. Their purpose-built medical centre was still a building site, but in the meantime they had the use of a modest, two-roomed building on the very edge of the hutment zone.

Padmashuri was already at work when we arrived that morning, along with Vijayakumar Agaley and Sandhiya Meshram, two full-time social workers. The three of them were scrutinizing in turn the clinical records and their hand-drawn map of the locality; an inoculation session was planned for today and they were calculating which sector was due for a visit. A sizeable refrigerator dominated the room, keeping the sera and medicines fresh. In the peace of the ante-room, two teenagers strained over their maths homework, passing Virabhadra's calculator back and forth between them. The operation, although set in temporary quarters, had a calm, established feel. But this was a relatively recent development.

After arriving in India, Virabhadra and Padmashuri had devoted a few months to research. Visiting some of the projects already operating in Maharashtra, they had gradually developed their plan of campaign. By the time it became evident that the Dapodi land negotiations had entered a legal quagmire, they had realized that there was no need as yet for specially constructed facilities. Their first task would be to get to know the local people, and let the people get to know them. Because of the 'Buddhist connection' they already had a number of friendly contacts in the locality, and so set up their bits and pieces of equipment in borrowed rooms and on patches of open ground between the huts.

They had started with a simple survey, weighing and measuring the children, and giving them medical checks. As expected, there was a high level of malnutrition, an often invisible malaise responsible for stunted growth, retarded mental development, and low resistance to diseases like dysentery, measles, and tuberculosis. Vitamin A deficiency was rife, obviously causing sight defects. Diarrhoea, with its associated dehydration of the body, was a frequent killer. In most instances the victims of these debilities did not require drugs, operations, or even vitamin tonics; they just needed to eat more and eat better. The main thing Virabhadra and Padmashuri had to offer, they realized, was knowledge.

There were a number of doctors already practising in the Dapodi area. Many of the locals went regularly to Ayurvedic healers, or to what could only be called 'magical' doctors. They were attracted to allopathic medicine too, but with an almost superstitious faith. For their part, the allopathic doctors frequently took advantage of their mystique, prescribing the inordinately revered, and costly, injection, or an expensive tonic, when all that was required—apart from a better water supply—was some more green vegetables in the diet, or a simple, and cheap, rehydration solution of water, salt, and sugar.

Virabhadra and Padmashuri took on a couple of full-time social workers and approached the hutment dwellers, asking them to talk more fully about themselves, trying to find out what they themselves most wanted. The survey made it clear that, above all, parents wanted help in preparing their children for life at school. In the villages and hutments, thousands of children went without any kind of education at all; hundreds of thousands more left school at the age of ten or eleven because their families needed the miserable pittances they could earn as scavengers or dogsbodies. Those lucky enough to get to school, or to remain there, had to live with the inflexible ruthlessness of the exam system. It was not education but paper qualifications that would pull them—and thus their kith and kin—out of the poverty trap. And yet, children born into the hutment world had no cultural preparation for education. Their parents were often uneducated, their mothers usually illiterate. Many Buddhist parents, mindful of the example set by their great 'Babasaheb', knew that education was a priceless key, but lost hope when they saw their children being intellectually swamped by those from more sophisticated homes.

The little team, now known as *Bahujan Hitay*—'For the Welfare of the Many'—therefore took on a couple of unused shacks and a patch of empty ground, and created a series of *balwadis*, or kindergartens. By spending a few hours in these places each day, the toddlers would be able to get a feel for classroom discipline and the learning process, and even make a start on that process itself.

Sandhiya Meshram, a serious, quietly spoken woman in her early thirties, took me on a tour of the balwadis. As we walked through the hutment lanes, she took pains to point out the obstacles and pitfalls ahead, at the same time answering a volley of questions about me from the people we passed. At length we entered a wooden hut, fifteen feet by twenty.

I was received without ceremony, and allowed to sit and watch while twenty two- to four-year-olds laid pebbles onto the outlines of Devanagari characters chalked on the concrete floor. They were not yet learning to read and write, but were at least developing some familiarity with the complicated lines and swirls of their alphabet. I felt quite jealous: I was struggling with those hieroglyphics myself!

Many of their mothers attended a similar class in the evenings. Few hutment women could read enough even to be sure they were catching the right buses. Sandhiya told me she spent a lot of her time escorting women to hospitals and bureaucratic institutions in Poona. Without her help they would have had a job finding their way around. At the 'women's literacy classes' they not only learned to read and write, but were also given advice about filling in forms, finding out about government benefits, and dealing with officials from large institutions.

The second balwadi, a solid cement and brick construction built, he claimed, by Virabhadra himself, nestled in the shadow of a colossal, pink cinema. Inside, a class was in full swing, and an elderly woman, seemingly composed entirely of sharp angles, led the children through chanted rounds of numbers, hours of the day, days of the week, and months of the year. Jutting her chin in my direction, and pointing at me with her elbows and arms, she broke off from her work to bark a series of cheerful questions at Sandhiya. Behind horn-rimmed glasses, her eyes flashed, pierced, and twinkled. While Sandhiya patiently answered her, the children took advantage of the break to start wrestling.

We moved on, across another invisible borderline, into the neighbouring locality and entered another balwadi. A line of sewing machines reposed along the walls; in the evenings the room was used for sewing classes. Now, however, twenty-five children sat in a circle, singing songs under the leadership of two middle-aged women. Like the supervisors in the other balwadis, one of these had been sent on a course by Bahujan Hitay, and was now a trained kindergarten teacher. The other was a local lady who helped out in whatever way she could; perhaps in time she would take a course too.

I did my best to merge into the background, but it soon became obvious that something was wrong. As they fixed me with round, unblinking eyes, and mouthed the words of their ditties, the kids were dissolving into tears. When the song faded out completely, Sandhiya explained that Virabhadra and Padmashuri had recently been here for an inoculation session. Most of these children had suffered the needle and now, seeing my white face and camera bag, were afraid I had come to give a repeat performance.

Among his friends in England, Virabhadra had a reputation for the luxuriance of the bushel beneath which he concealed the light of his medical knowledge. He was, as a rule, the last person to whom one thought of talking about the pains afflicting one's back, or the strange lump that had appeared on one's wrist. Anyone bold enough to approach him for medical advice would receive his now legendary prescription: 'I should see a doctor if I were you.'

I was therefore thrilled by the prospect of attending the afternoon clinic. I was finally going to see him at work! After all, he must have done something since he had been in India, for he was now known universally, and exclusively, as 'Doctor'.

If he kept rather quiet about his medical skills, he was also exceptionally quiet in respect of another talent: his Marathi. Although he had been here for just three years, he spoke almost fluently, and was the only Englishman who didn't seem to feel the need to shout in order to make himself understood.

We arrived at the balwadi in Bhim Nagar just after lunch. For fifteen minutes Virabhadra sorted through his cards and Padmashuri prepared her needles and vaccines. Mr Agaley sallied forth to find a kerosene stove for heating water while Sandhiya went off to tell people in the selected area that the clinic was about to open. Soon the place was a bedlam of screaming, shouting children, and their talkative parents. At the door, a ghoulish crowd of older kids hung about waiting for the fun to begin, eyeing Padmashuri's devices with awe and delight.

The procedure was simple. First, Mr Agaley would hoist a child into the rubber weighing harness which hung, via a massive white dial, from a beam in the rafters. Then, standing the child against a colourful 'Weight for Height' chart, he announced the vital statistics, which Virabhadra jotted into his records, noting whether the child was in the 'red', the 'green', or the 'yellow'. This provided an immediate indication of whether or not the child was suffering from malnourishment. Virabhadra then made a brief examination, asking the parents about the diet at home and the medicines used in times of sickness, trying to find out as much as he could about the general conditions in which the child lived. If an inoculation was due he alerted Padmashuri, who—with whatever help was forthcoming from the parents, or from Mr Agaley—plunged her needle into the exposed bottom and squeezed the fluid home. Coming now to the end of the line, the child was committed into the hands of his or her parents, and comforted in whatever way they thought best.

This was the procedure, so far as I could tell, but as the room continued to fill, and as bottlenecks formed, the clear, logical order of things was soon lost in superficial chaos. A squeaky toy had been unearthed and two girls now fought for possession. Over by the door, a mother was helping her son to swallow a spoonful of polio vaccine by clamping her hands over his nose and mouth while he performed a creditable impersonation of somebody drowning. Screams, laughter, and loud chatter filled the air. To his own obvious satisfaction Mr Agaley, a short, slight, and cheerful man, managed to get his wards in and out of the harness without dropping a single one—while they did everything they could to spoil his record. Padmashuri displayed remarkable skill, keeping her needle inserted, always to the right length, while the reluctantly proffered buttocks shuddered and bucked before her.

Each set of parents had its own post-operative comforting technique. A powerfully built fellow, with muscles that seemed poised to burst through the seams of his 'Dalit Panther' T-shirt, snatched his daughter out of Mr Agaley's hands once the injection was over, and set to bouncing her in his arms, resonantly slapping the afflicted cheek, whilst almost deafening her—and the rest of us—with a volley of 'Ka! Ka! Ka!'s and 'Ho! Ho! Ho!'s. Twenty-five seconds later she was laughing, her trauma quite forgotten. Across the room, a mother sat on the floor with her howling son, smiling warmly on him and stroking him tenderly, before fetching him a savage clout on the back of the head. After ten minutes of this treatment—the alternations growing faster by degrees—a breakthrough was still to come.

Virabhadra entered details on his record sheets in a flowing Devanagari script. He could have kept his notes in English, but it was the policy of Bahujan Hitay only to set things going, rather than run them in perpetuity. Marathi records would be easily accessible to whoever took over when the time came to move on.

'Nurse!' Virabhadra's voice cut through the hubbub, 'I think I've got an expanded spleen over here!'

Soon, Virabhadra had Padmashuri and I feeling our way around a baby's lower abdomen, locating the slightly hard, unnatural ridge that lay beneath. This was possibly serious; it would mean a blood test at least, and perhaps a hospital visit. As Virabhadra explained the problem to the boy's parents, Padmashuri returned to her syringe.

'It's just this one, and the bald one over there now, isn't it?' she called. She had so far given about thirty jabs, and the vaccine was running low, but Sandhiya was now back with us, her rounds completed.

At this stage the team could offer little in the way of direct medical treatment, but their policy was nevertheless bearing fruit. They had been able to do something about the children who were still living on breast milk alone in their third and even fourth years and, although one woman withdrew her daughter from the weighing sessions on the grounds that the scales were causing her to lose weight, they had been able to challenge some of the superstitious beliefs about illness that passed for medical knowledge in the locality. Night blindness, for example, was commonly believed to be caused by placing the foot on an eggshell on a Saturday, or by stepping over papaya seeds, and was to be treated by an elaborate begging and fasting ritual. Until they arrived, very few people seemed to know anything about the effects of carrots or green vegetables. As time went by, the team was managing to instill a higher level of basic dietry knowledge. Although this development came too late for some children, whom Virabhadra and Padmashuri had to watch as they died, many local babies were now gaining weight; the fatal effects of diarrhoea and measles were being overcome; there were many lives that had been saved. The programme was a success.

A little way off, the medical centre was rising from the ground. By chance, the legal problems involved in the land purchase had been cleared just as fund-raising efforts in the West were making considerable amounts of money available. Once the new centre was complete, the team would have a thorough understanding of the situation, and enough familiarity with the Dapodi people to put it to good use.

Even so, I still wondered whether it was really necessary for Bahujan Hitay to be doing this work when the Indian government was carrying out its own social welfare programmes in the hutments.

'Well, if the government ever does do something here in Dapodi, we'll probably be wiped out at a stroke!' Virabhadra was in a dry mood.

'So what would the people here lose if that happened?'

'In a way they probably wouldn't notice much of a difference at all— to begin with. But the thing is, government agencies tend to offer a blanket approach to the symptoms. They organize vaccination sessions, maybe pour in tonics and vitamins by the ton. But they can't take the same interest in the specific problems of a particular community as we do. Actually, a government vaccination team did come here just before we arrived, but we discovered that only twenty percent of the kids got their jabs. They don't place any emphasis on education either. Our programme tries to help people learn how to feed their kids in a more healthy way.

'Then there's the problem of corruption. The crudest cases I've heard of are when doctors from government clinics have been charged with diverting government supplies to their private practices. Then there are the times when government sponsored clinics in hutment areas become transformed into places where only the better-off go for treatment. Obviously this isn't the government's fault, but it does underline the need for programmes which concentrate on the very poor, run by agencies which can reach them. Then again, many doctors work in private practice where the need to find patients may lead to a tendency to advise unnecessary treatment. So, at their clinic sessions, they may tell the hutment patients that they'll only get proper care if they go privately. All kinds of unnecessary operations get done that way. A favourite is the Caesarean section. It's easy for a doctor to tell a pregnant woman she's in for a risky time without one. What can she say when it's a doctor giving her advice?

'But the main loss would be the Buddhist connection. People here trust us because we're Buddhists. They tell us about their lives, even let us into their homes. They feel we're part of the family. They'll talk to us about family planning, or their debts, things they'd otherwise keep very private. 'Then, because they know we're Buddhists, and know that a lot of the money for our work is coming from Buddhists in the West, they begin to realize that the Dhamma is effective; it gives them tremendous confidence in Buddhism; it points the way to what they could be doing for themselves.'

I decided to pick up on this point when I took another walk with Sandhiya. How important was it to her that she was working with Buddhists? She almost choked on the question.

'Of course it's important! If I was not a Buddhist I would not be doing any of this at all.

'When I was young I got on well at school, but I never had any idea that I could make something of my life. For a few years I didn't even have a job. But when I started reading Dr Ambedkar's books, I realized that I could go further. It was only then that I thought of going to college. I studied social work entirely because I wanted to do something to help his work along. It was some way of showing my gratitude for what he had given me.'

As we talked she was leading me towards a low, brick and corrugated-iron hut, one of the more substantial buildings in the colony. I had been asked to interview a member of the Dapodi community for the charity's magazine, and Sandhiya was going to introduce me to Sarika Barathay.

She was out when we arrived, so I was left sitting on the bed while Sandhiya went off to retrieve her from the water taps. The house measured ten feet by twenty, and was divided into two distinct environments by a set of rough wooden shelves. One half of the 'house' was all but filled by the bulk of the huge iron bed. The other was a cooking and 'bathing' area, dominated by a battery of water pots. I tried to work it out, but couldn't imagine where the children slept. The mud-rendered walls were bare, but for a single dingy print of Dr Ambedkar. Sarika had lived here for twelve years, since entering the place as a fifteen-year-old bride. Her husband, being of the Barathay line, was an established member of the locality, and owned his house and the land on which it was built. By contrast, most of the huts in Dapodi were illegal squats, less than twenty years old, belonging to the area's immigrant community.

Sarika arrived, looking tired and, at first glance, middle-aged, though she was no more than twenty-seven. She explained that she was still recovering from a sterilization operation. Only later did I discover that she had had the operation three years ago.

Lethargically stroking the head of her daughter, she described her daily round. There was nothing especially terrible about her life, no awful dramas, no heart-rending tales of disaster: just a simple catalogue of unmitigated drudgery, of fetching water, heating water, preparing fuel, cooking on just one bucket stove, trying to make the money stretch. . . . From six in the morning until nine at night she performed her chores, more or less without a break, doing as much as she could with other women, so that she could chat while she worked.

She counted herself lucky because she got on well with her husband. They were cousins and had been close friends throughout childhood. Kindly elders had arranged what turned out to be a good match. At the water taps she would listen as other women complained about their husbands' shortcomings, but could do so without having to join in. To her relief 'He' did not drink or gamble, beat her, or withhold housekeeping money. They had an old radio, which sometimes worked; some friends in a nearby locality owned a television set, so on Saturday nights they got to see a movie. She even got a 'holiday' each year, when the family decamped and spent a month with her sister's family, on the other side of Poona. That way she had company, and less work to do since the chores were shared.

Her husband was one of the better-off Dapodi men. He worked as an electrician in Poona city, and brought home five hundred rupees a month. Few families in Dapodi had a total income of more than three hundred, and some men earned as little as a hundred. As a rule, he gave his parents a hundred rupees each month, though they often needed more—which he always tried to find. He had once been given the chance to take a two-roomed apartment in Poona as a perk of his job, but his parents vetoed the option. They felt that his place was in the ancestral locality, living on a part of the family plot. They obviously feared that if he moved out he would not be on hand to help them, practically and financially.

Sarika was upset when the Poona possibility fell through. She had once hoped that her life might turn out differently. There had been arguments: she with her husband, her husband with his parents; but in the end they had stayed. Now she was used to her life, and had made her peace with it. She was already hoping that her own two sons would stay at home as long as possible, and never move too far away.

She was one of a handful of Dapodi women who could read and write. When her daughter was old enough to need less supervision she would try to get a menial job in a local hospital. Meanwhile she was cultivating her ambitions for the children. She looked forward to the library and study facility that Bahujan Hitay was going to build since it would give her sons somewhere to do their homework. She was also proud that her daughter was attending the balwadi, and nurtured an obvious hope that the girl would make something of her life. . . . Perhaps more than she had?

I took my pictures and said goodbye. Mrs Barathay set off back to the water taps, about fifty yards away. After an hour's talk she looked exhausted.

Later, I took a stroll with Padmashuri through the compounds and winding lanes of Dapodi, past an extensive, roped-off enclosure where the library and social centre would be going up, and finally into a mixed Hindu-Buddhist locality. It was noticeably shabbier than the others I had visited. There were no trained flowers gracing the huts, as there had been—here and there—in Jai Bhim Nagar. The smell was stronger too. Some of the Hindus were from the Koli community, the fisherman caste, and clearly brought something home from their work, if only a sickening stench.

Padmashuri exchanged a flow of greetings as we walked. Everyone was obviously familiar with her sari'd figure, and treated her with affection. Earlier in the day, Virabhadra had tried to make a case for launching her as a new Mother Theresa.

'Well, she's young; she's got good looks, *and* she's got class! We could make a fortune!'

As we strolled past a tiny hutch, just six feet by four, made of sticks, sacks, and mud, a man hailed us. He sat in the dirt at the shelter's entrance, giggling and shouting, all the time miming exaggerated rowing motions. He was drunk to the wide.

'He's one of the Kolis,' said Padmashuri, 'He does the fishing and his wife sells the stuff down at the bazaar. But there's a very sad story there.

'He and his wife thought they weren't able to produce a child and went to the temple to ask for help. The priests said they would perform the appropriate rites, but only on the condition that, if they had a daughter, they would give her to the temple when she was old enough to serve.

'Sure enough, they had a daughter, but she was born deaf and dumb. She's a lovely little thing. She always comes and hugs herself to my legs when I visit them. She's about eleven now, which means that in a couple of years she'll have to go away to the temple, and work as a prostitute.'

My tour ended at the construction site, where the concrete bones of the clinic and office complex were rising from the hard ground. Catching sight of me, Sopan Kamblay rushed up to say hello. He was an Ambedkar Society man, a regular face at the morning meditations. He knew no English, so we had never been able to talk, but he greeted me with such warmth that I felt like his brother. Formerly a clerk with the Post and Telecommunications Department, he now worked full-time with TBMSG, and was doing excellent work as site manager on the project. Even so, he begged Lokamitra to replace him every time he saw him, since he suffered from an acute lack of confidence. Lokamitra was adamant however. Sopan *could* do the job, so it was best all round that he stayed on. Perhaps, when the site supervisor at Lohagaon finished work on the students' hostel, Sopan would be relieved, but for the time being he would continue.

A few days later I was visiting Lokamitra, when the Dapodi project architect appeared with some sketches of the complex in its completed form. In time there would be a medical centre, a gymnasium, a library and community centre, facilities for study, a Dhamma centre, and a job-training complex. The pictures showed a surprisingly futuristic set of buildings, as if from a science fiction fantasy.

I sincerely hoped I would get back to Dapodi some day; it would be fascinating to see how those concrete marvels blended with the huts, shacks, and hovels.

* * *

Lohagaon was another suburb of Poona. Unlike Dapodi it was surrounded not by industrial new towns, but by the bare expanses of an air-force base. This was where Bahujan Hitay was building its first students' hostel, or 'Educational Resource Centre', as the publicity brochures had it in the West.

Even when parents did not need a son's contribution to the family income, or a daughter's help in the house, the smokey, crowded, unlit environment of a village or hutment household was hardly conducive to the amounts of homework required by the Indian education system. In poor areas I would often find children squatting on pavements, reading and reciting their lists of facts and figures by the light of flickering streetlamps; there was simply nowhere else for them to go.

The first project undertaken by Ambedkar's 'Society for the Benefit of the Excluded Classes' was the building of a string of hostels for schoolchildren: places where they could live, eat good food, and enjoy the facilities they needed for pursuing their studies beyond school hours. The benefits of such facilities were still so obvious that Bahujan Hitay soon found itself entering the hostel business.

By now I had visited patches of land in Aurangabad and Ahmedabad where, in time, hostels would be going up, and I had overheard a number of highly complicated phone calls relating to the project at Ulhasnagar, where a hostel was due to open within the year; but I had not yet been to see the one nearest base—and the one closest to completion. This was at Lohagaon, where one of two main buildings was already functioning and where twenty-five boys had been installed for some months. After some hard bargaining with Lokamitra, Bodhidharma was freed up to take me there on the back of his scooter.

'I love going to this place!'

Bodhidharma had to yell to make himself heard above the whine of his scooter and the far louder roar of a fighter plane that was clawing its way into the azure above our heads. 'I always get a thrill to be here with the kids. You'll like it so much!'

Lohagaon was just twenty minutes from Yerawada, but it had something of a village atmosphere. It was hardly a big place: just a couple of dirt roads, the usual rows of open fronted shops, barber's stalls, and cafés, plenty of temples, a large school, and now, dominating its own end of town, the clean, modern lines of a Bahujan Hitay structure. As the scooter bounced to a halt on the rubble-strewn path between our two buildings we were immediately greeted by Mr Mhende—another Dhammavijay regular who was supervising the construction work here—and Dipak Agaley, the hostel warden. We entered the smaller, completed building, and sat down for tea at a monumental desk in the main ground floor room.

For the time being, all the hostel's activities were taking place in this and a similar room upstairs. A tall stack of mattresses revealed that the room was used as a dormitory at night, the Buddha-shrine in the corner meant that it also served as shrine room, and the blackboard and wall posters indicated that this was where extra study sessions took place before and after school.

The boys attended the Sri Santa Tukaran School, just five minutes walk away. They began their classes at ten forty-five in the morning, and finished just before five. As we sipped our tea, the streets outside resounded with noise as seven hundred children freshly released from their daily labours made their ways home. Soon, our own boys began to arrive, filtering into the room to see who their visitor was. Mr Agaley lined them against the wall and bade me ask questions.

Aged between nine and sixteen, the boys hailed from almost every corner of Maharashtra, from the hutments of Poona, Bombay, and Nagpur, and from more remote villages. They were mostly, though not exclusively, Buddhist. But for the hostel, not one of them would have been at school any longer. One way or another they would have been out trying to earn some money: carrying water, cleaning floors, labouring in the fields, or perhaps even begging.

The boys told me their names, their 'standard', or year, in the school, what their parents did for a living, and—if they felt courageous enough to tempt fate—what they hoped to achieve in life. It did not come easily to kids from their background to announce that they were hoping to become lawyers, engineers, or architects. For the time being, most of them seemed more than content to have got even this far.

I really don't know what I had expected to find, but what really surprised me—and almost overwhelmed me—was the undiluted cheerfulness of the hostel. In all, I lived through an entire twenty-four hour cycle there, and wondered at the end whether I had ever been in such a happy place before. Even though I knew that some of the boys came from the most pitiful and degrading backgrounds, it was quite impossible to work out which boys these were. They all seemed able to live completely in the moment, giving themselves to it without restraint; and because this moment of their lives was a happy one, they were happy.

Much credit went to Dipak, the warden, an exceptionally mature man for his twenty-seven years. He had himself shown great promise as a child. When he outgrew the possibilities offered by his village school, a kindly uncle in Poona took him in, feeding and clothing him while he attended school there. For a few years he had high hopes of qualifying as a mechanical engineer, but when sickness forced his father to retire early, Dipak's education came to a summary halt and he became the family's breadwinner.

He got a job as a clerk in his old village school. The work itself was no problem, but he found it painful to watch low-caste children missing out in life because they had no grasp of 'exam-technique', or because they had no idea how to apply for jobs or how to display themselves to good advantage in interviews.

He took to giving extra tuition outside school hours and, before long, the sessions became so popular that he found himself facing classes of eighty or more. He persuaded some of the teachers to help him, and soon had a kind of alternative school on the go.

While doing this he was also trying to find out about Buddhism. Since childhood he had felt a strong sense of devotion to Dr Ambedkar, and constantly found himself wondering whether the great man's conversion to Buddhism could have been more significant than his friends and elders had led him to believe. He sought out monks and Buddhist politicians, but his somewhat sceptical mind found no satisfaction in their answers.

Then, one day, at the end of 1981, he went to Poona for a wedding, and saw a poster advertising a talk to be given that night by one 'Ven. Maha Sthavira Sangharakshita'. On an impulse, he opted out of the wedding altogether, and instead came along to one of the first talks of our tour.

He was deeply impressed by the talk and immediately began to attend every TBMSG activity he could get to. Now, three years later, though not yet ordained, he had just given up his job in order to work full-time with the movement. He was the natural choice for the warden's post, and jumped at it the moment it was offered, even though it would involve a considerable drop in salary.

'I am getting seven hundred rupees per month here. Outside, I know, I could perhaps be getting twelve hundred. But I get satisfaction out of this, and the work is very worthwhile. I don't think I would be happier than I am if I was earning seven *thousand* a month!' When the new building was complete, his wife would be joining him in a room on the top floor. For now, as he put it, he had brothers and sons all around him.

The hostel's day began at five o'clock, when Dipak patrolled the building ringing his little bell to rouse the boys. While they washed and dressed, he wrote a 'fact' and a 'thought' for the day on the blackboard, while another boy rushed into the streets to hammer a crude gong, calling local Buddhists to the morning meditation.

The meditation session was voluntary, but most of the boys appeared downstairs all the same. Their bright, fresh eyes contrasted accusingly with the bleary, sleep-haunted faces of the dozen men who turned up over the next ten minutes.

Upstairs, with daunting vigour, a few more boys put themselves through a set of physical jerks. They were joined half an hour later by the meditators, who bent, stretched, and squatted, with even more enthusiasm, making up for lost time.

By the time they had completed their exertions, school was still four hours away. An atmosphere of silence and concentration now descended as they bored into their books and did their best to prepare for the day.

Except on Sundays, when the boys looked after themselves, a local woman did the cooking for the hostel in a nearby hut donated for the purpose. Even so, the morning study period was broken by a brisk session of vegetable chopping—Dipak being keen that the boys should play an active part in the running of the place.

The boys were organized into committees which dealt with most aspects of the hostel's day-to-day life. Dipak sat on most of them, and had the ultimate say in the way things were run, but did all he could to help his wards take responsibility for the situation—and thus acquire confidence in their ability to run their own lives. The Purchasing Committee monitored the food store and the hostel's facilities, and saw to it that the shopping was done with the money Dipak provided. A Public Relations Committee received guests and ensured that they were well cared for. A Health Committee was responsible for learning and giving first-aid in cases of accident. The Cultural Committee organized plays, gymnastic displays, and any other cultural events for special occasions. There was even a Study Committee, whose job was to keep an eye on the boys, and find out who was working hardest, who was slacking, and who was indulging in 'idle chit-chat' during homework sessions.

As well as attending committee meetings, the children belonged to work teams, responsible for cleaning floors, washing, and Sunday cooking. The system had taken a while to introduce, but Dipak was pleased to report that his own job was getting easier all the time. What pleased him most was to know that the boys really did care for the place, and were developing a kind of capability and a sense of responsibility which would stand them in good stead even if their academic achievements were disappointing.

At ten-fifteen, after a substantial meal, the boys set out through the streets and disappeared into the jaws of their school. They had marched off looking fresh and alert, but I was already feeling ready for bed. While they had been poring over their books I had been out in Lohagaon being led from one Buddhist household to another, and I'd eaten three breakfasts.

The first port of call had been the home of Mr Kamblay, a local postal officer; the second was that of Dharmanand—the Order member primarily responsible for our contacts here—and the third was the fine and rambling abode of Chandrakant Ohal. Along with Dipak, they described themselves as 'The Four Muscateers', the four most devoted Buddhists in town. Certainly, there was no resisting the infectious bond of friendship and loyalty that sparkled between them.

Chandrakant, a chunky, wild-eyed, forty-year-old, was clearly the most successful member of the team. As a government engineer he had a fair sized house, a good income, and a company jeep. He sat Dharmanand on his knee and held him in a warm embrace while explaining his debt to him.

'I was a terrible drinker man, you see. Every night I was coming home tipsy! My good friend Dharmanand hit me and hit me about this drinking, and my eating of meat, and taking rest all of the time. But he had little success, because, you know, I was *very* happy in my life at that time!'

Laughing uproariously, he slapped himself, slapped Dharmanand, and anyone else within reach.

'Now I will tell you one thing: I was once touched by Babasaheb! Yes! At a meeting, when I was a child just nine months old, he took me and held me for a while, or so they tell me. Well, because of this, I recited the Refuges and Precepts every day, *every day*. But you see there was arguing in the house all the time because of my drinking, and my losing of money at gambling. In the end I started to think about this. There was a gap between this drinking and the fifth Precept. "No," I thought, "Two parallel lines do not meet!" You understand? And all the time Dharmanand, knowing that I was a good man underneath, kept on chasing me and hitting me.

'In the end, I went to one of these retreats he was talking about. I enjoyed *very* much, and afterwards I made sure that I continued the meditation. After some months, I felt a sudden lifting in myself! I was a reformed man!'

He beamed, fully aware that he was something of a cliché—and liking it.

'Of course,' he continued, 'my wife was still keeping some Hindu gods in the home. We started to have big arguments about that. Finally, I ordered her to go on retreat too. When she came home she threw the gods away herself! Now she is reformed!

'All of my family have been on retreat now: one by one by one. And this little son of mine,' he wrapped huge hands around the toddler's head, 'he knows no Hindu things at all. Just Three Refuges, Five Precepts: just Buddhist things! Nothing else is in his head!'

Chandrakant loved the hostel and had an obvious respect for Dipak. As a boy, determined to get himself educated, he had walked ten miles to and from school every day for four years. It gave him immense pleasure to see a few boys getting a better deal than he ever had. He spent every moment of his free time there, talking and playing games, chatting with Dipak, or simply sitting around spreading lunacy and mirth. 'If I am not working, eating, or sleeping, you will find me there!' he said. And I did.

As we weaved our way back to the hostel, we met a grey-haired woman in a simple orange sari. Dipak answered her questions about me, before explaining that it was her husband who had left TBMSG the land on which the hostel was being built. I made as respectful a salutation as I could, but she returned my salute with an even fuller gesture of gratitude. She was content that such good use was being made of her husband's legacy. It was not uncommon for land donated to charity to lie idle for years on end, while arguments raged over how it should be used.

A few paces further on we happened upon the building contractor, a languid, Westernized young Parsee, dressed in blue jeans and sporting the ultimate status symbol, an American baseball cap.

'How's it going?' I asked.

He sighed with cool resignation, 'Well, I'm happy, but your people aren't.' Bodhidharma had been giving him a hard time over the schedule. There were now forty labourers clambering about the site, and floodlights kept the work going through the night. The official opening date had now been fixed, the dignitaries invited. There could be no slip-ups. Bodhidharma was away seeing the *Sarpanch*—the traditional village head-man—about a dispute over the siting of a drainage pipe.

The boys popped home at lunchtime for a light snack, then disappeared again. Their afternoon was to be a fairly light one, since the entire school would be out on the 'parade ground' rehearsing its drills for the coming Republic Day celebrations.

While they were practising their dances and gymnastic exercises, I paid a brief call on the school's headmaster. Dipak had assured me that he was a good and intelligent man, spoke English well, and had great respect for the hostel. I was consequently a little surprised to find myself being greeted with cold formality, by a man who claimed to speak only Marathi and Hindi. We sat, rather formally, on opposing sides of his desk, surrounded by a steadily growing team of would-be translators.

It was not to be an easy conversation. I had gone along hoping for a lively, in-depth encounter with a liberal educationalist, a man who might regard the hostels as something of a shining hope for the Scheduled Castes and for India in general—the fruits of which would make good copy for the charity's magazine. Instead I found myself plodding doggedly—and embarrassingly quickly—through my list of questions as one supremely minimal response followed another.

'Are there many children here from the backward classes?'

'Ten percent.'

'Are there any hostel children in the school, other than ours?'

'No.'

'Do you think that education can help a backward child to make progress in the world?'

'Boys only. Not girls.'

I sipped at my tea, wondering how this man might be drawn into a conversation, an argument, or anything.

'Do hostel boys make better students than the others, or worse?'

'No different.'

'So our boys compare reasonably well with the rest?'

'Very poor. Very bad background. Very ignorant. The hostel atmosphere is good, but they must study. Extra coaching is required. They must work hard.' His voice was disdainfully matter of fact.

'What do you feel is the purpose of education?'

'Service only! Work. Food!' He extended a hand across the desk, rubbing the thumb and index finger together, to illustrate his point.

'What do you think about Dr Ambedkar's views on education?'

He paused, sighed, re-extended the hand, fingers aflurry: 'Just money.'

He posed stiffly while I took the promised photograph to accompany an interview which would never see the light of day. I thanked him and made my exit. Actually, he was not a bad man, and I was sure he was quite typical of his sort. He meant no harm to our boys, but he was not going to go out of his way to help them either. They would have to do that for themselves.

At five-thirty they rushed home again, looking as lively as ever, ready for a session of games out in the fields. While they played, I took pictures, concentrating on Suresh Chavan, a tribal boy from a village near Poona. His father was unemployed, but got occasional work drawing water from the wells for the richer villagers. His mother worked as a field labourer, and provided the family's only reliable income: fifty rupees a month.

Until Bahujan Hitay offered Suresh an opportunity to continue his education, he had been working with his father as a water bearer. He was fifteen, and already suffered from severe stomach and chest cramps, for which he needed medical attention. In the holidays, if he went home, he would be put to the same work. Dipak was doing his best to fix things so that he could stay at the hostel instead.

Suresh was not the poorest boy in the hostel, but looking at him and his friends as they played their games, ran off with my silly straw hat, or teased Dipak, I had to keep reminding myself of the hells from which they came.

After a short rest period the books came out again, and the boys re-applied themselves to their studies. While the younger boys worked upstairs, Mr Mhende, the site supervisor, took over the room below to give some of the older ones, and a group of local girls, a dose of that necessary 'extra coaching' in maths and English. The end of year exams were not so far away; failure would mean returning to their old lives, and none of them were in any hurry to do that.

With obvious regret, Dipak confided that one or two were likely to fail. He knew he would be very sad but firmly believed that anyone who had to leave would be taking something with him from this experience which would stand him in good stead for the rest of his life. Those who were more successful would become important leaders in their localities—at the very least. Dipak's vision of their potential contrasted encouragingly—and crucially—with their headmaster's. Although successful Buddhists had a tendency to turn away from their old 'backward' world, ex-hostel boys did so very rarely, and figured prominently on the social welfare scene throughout the state.

After another meal it was time to rehearse the play for Republic Day. The hostel was planning its own event for this occasion, and some of the boys would be seeing their parents for the first time in weeks. In the hostel's early days, parents who didn't live too far away came visiting almost every week, but Dipak now encouraged them to stay away for as long as possible. Experience had taught him that the boys seemed happier and more stable when left to themselves. It was another testament to his qualities that the parents trusted his judgement, and limited their calls.

At nine-thirty the gong resounded in the streets once again, and a small party of locals trickled in to join the evening *puja*, a short round of chants, readings, and recitations, led by Dharmanand. Although the hostel was still relatively new, it was clearly part of the local scene. When the new building opened, more space would be available, not only for another twenty-five boys, but also for this aspect of its work. There would be a community meeting room, a good library, and perhaps more Dhamma classes. These would be valuable features in themselves, but would also serve the function of helping the boys to feel part of a broader, friendly world, rather than inmates of an institution.

At ten o'clock I lay on my mattress in the dorm, surrounded by a sea of dark bodies and lively mosquitoes. Tired out, I waited . . . and waited, expecting the lights to go out. But some of the boys were still reading, reading until they quite literally fell asleep over their books. It was midnight when I was finally able to creep across the room—picking my way over their snoring forms—and quench the harsh fluorescent light.

s e v e n t e e n

A perfect dawn was breaking, spreading gold over the eastern sky. The tree-tops scintillated like jewel fountains.

Walking past the church, I caught my first sight of the bungalow. The brilliant flame of an ochre robe flickered from one end of the balcony to the other. I drew close; the robe came to a shimmering halt, half hidden in the leaves of the bodhi tree.

A rich Yorkshire voice split the air.

'What on earth are *you* doing here?' Then 'No, no! Not that way! *Here*, round this side, through this gap in the fence. But what are you *doing* here?'

Aurangabad. Journey's end. Jyotipala.

He had been living here for most of the time since I left India in '82, staying with 'Ol' Paw Dongray', as he still liked to call him, and with Mahadhammavir.

He sighed, as if fending off terminal gloom, 'Oh well, seeing as you're here, I suppose I'll have to put the kettle on. But you're going to have to wait for biscuits. I haven't got any biscuits in yet. I'll be getting biscuits in when I go to the bazaar for my shave.'

I sank into a wicker armchair, touched by the joy my arrival had brought into the world, and asked where the others were. Mr Dongray, he thought, was in Bombay, visiting a wife I'd never known him to have, and Mahadhammavir, 'the old rogue', had not been seen for a few weeks. He had gone off on his wanderings, letting his children and grandchildren look after him a bit, and no doubt pouring more of his fire and brimstone sermons over Marathwada.

'So it's just the two of us then, is it?'

'Yes. It looks like I'm going to have to put up with you all by myself. When are you going back? Did you say?' Reaching out to grasp my shoulders in his hands, he burst out laughing. He had been feeling lonely.

I spent five miraculously enjoyable days with him, sitting on the veranda late into the night, hearing about his life as a Catholic monk, and his reasons for quitting it ('Sex' and 'Sex'), his more positive, and so far more successful encounter with celibacy as a Buddhist *anagarika*, about his attempts to come to terms with the 'desperado and killer' in him, and catching up on his latest news. In the day time, we visited his friends, and went along to a few locality programmes—something which would not have been possible even two years before.

There had been a breakthrough in Aurangabad. Partly because Jyotipala had spent so long in Aurangabad, and partly because a local man—Nagasena—had been ordained during Sangharakshita's last visit, the movement was no longer seen as something from 'outside' the local community. Doors were opening, and most weeks Jyotipala and Nagasena would be down in the hutment compounds, giving talks and making contacts. Now, wherever we walked—and he saw to it that we walked everywhere—Jyotipala was a familiar figure, obviously known and liked.

We went to a class for 'regulars' at Milind College, led by Nagasena, a couple of locality talks in the reeking hutments, and, as the high-point, a real 'village programme', a twenty-four hour round trip to the village of Managon, just forty kilometres from Aurangabad, but a world away from anywhere I had ever been before.

That day began as usual with meditation and breakfast: an impossibly violent mixture of curried vegetables and lentils, prepared by the lady who lived with her family in a slightly oversized dog-kennel down in the garden. Once upon a time she had been Mr Dongray's hired help, but a few years ago had declared UDI, and then squatter's rights. For a consideration she cooked for Jyotipala, but would not, he assured me, lift a finger for poor Mr Dongray. For hours after eating her handiwork—and despite a concluding banana—my lips burnt, stung, and seemed to hum. Once, I even caught myself glancing in a mirror to see whether I was exhaling smoke.

'Stop being such a cissy and get it down you. There's no telling when you'll eat again.'

It was Jyotipala who had met me at the airport on my first visit to India. Within minutes he had imparted his three cardinal rules, which together constituted all one needed to know in order to survive India:

'Eat, piss, and shit when you can, and not when you want. Got it?'

Clearly, he still observed these rules, and expected others to do likewise. I therefore did my best to struggle through the meal, while he scattered scraps of left-over chapati about the place. The morsels that he threw onto the roof of the porch below were for the mynah birds, the crows, and for the tiny little things whose wings flashed blue, like drawn swords, as they flitted through the trees. The scraps which he placed on the balustrade were for Boxer, the next door neighbour's dog, with whom I'd fallen deeply in love—much to Jyotipala's disgust. Although a mongrel, Boxer's brown and white body was exceptionally sound; he had all his hair, and four legs; not even a limp disfigured the cheerful manner of his coming. He was, one had to admit, a terrible coward, running for cover when any of the local dog gangs seemed to be heading our way. But for all that he had a ready smile and hidden depths, which I felt Jyotipala failed to acknowledge. I was to be surprised.

Boxer was very much on his mind as we set off for the bus station at eight o'clock.

'I don't know why I think this, but there's something distinctly Russian about Boxer. Do you know what I mean?'

'I *do* know what you mean!' I replied readily, 'It's as if, when he's around, there's something, shall we say Slavonic, in the air? The hum of deep, bass voices; perhaps the faintest odour of a samovar?'

'Yes. I don't know why, but there's something distinctly Russian about him.'

'Something even aristocratic? The wild dash on horseback across the frozen steppes? The flurry of a mazurka?'

'Yes! No, I don't know why it is, but I always get a feeling for something Russian hanging around that dog.'

We pondered on in this foolish way, traversing the burnt expanses of the maidan, heading towards the main road. How, we wondered, could a Russian count have so arranged things as to get himself reborn a mongrel dog in a Muslim household in Aurangabad?

At length a rickshaw appeared.

'ST stand! ST stand! Yes? ST stand!' announced Jyotipala.

Languages, he frequently admitted, were not his strong point. Self-repetition, clearly, still was.

The driver peered at this apparition through hooded, grudging eyes. 'Yes, Baba. ST stand. Get in.'

At the ST stand—which was the Indian term for 'bus station'—Jyotipala bustled about, buying tickets, trying to find out from which bay our bus would leave.

He had trained himself to do everything he could for himself, and to pay his own way whenever possible, rather than let others look after him—which was the more common procedure where monks were concerned. But he also knew for a fact that there were few people in India more able than he in the art of getting onto a bus. He was a genius at it—which was something you could be in India. He knew where to place himself ten minutes before the bus was due to arrive, how to take up a good position in the crowd when there were just five minutes to go, how to edge forward without causing offence as the bus reversed into its berth, and how to slide, as if two millimetres thick, through the other front-runners, and climb the steps, leaning back ever so slightly—but with dignity—on the people behind, thus gaining a fast entry.

Today, as always, he was the first aboard, and from the back of the crowd I caught a glimpse of him pacing the dark interior, like a game-keeper inspecting his traps, choosing the best seat. Outside, the rest of us congealed into a seething mass.

An age later, I groped my way through the jam-packed bus, climbed over a few people, and sat down at the place he had saved. Sidewards, he gave me a look of paternal contempt. There was still something of the killer in him.

I should mention that at this point in the proceedings I had almost no idea where we were going, nor what was going to happen when we got there. Jyotipala was never very forthcoming about that sort of thing, rather like a father who couldn't be bothered to explain to his child what a circus was, but knew he'd enjoy it once he got there.

By mid-morning we were in Jalna, perhaps the untidiest place I have ever seen. The street layout was impenetrable, the people dressed in tatters, the traffic a maelstrom; even the animals seemed unkempt. The whole place reminded me of the kind of dream in which nothing could possibly go right. There were bullock carts everywhere, choking the alleys and blocking the streets: great convoys of them, each loaded to a dangerous height with monstrous sacks of cotton. Here and there, as our bus threaded its way towards the town centre, we passed stockyards where teams of women stood atop glistening mounds of pure white cotton wool, raking fresh consignments into place.

From the bus station we took a rickshaw out to the edge of town, and strolled into a well established hutment colony. Red and black flags fluttered here and there, and people raised their hands to Jyotipala paying their 'Jai Bhim's. From one hut a bent old lady appeared, scuttling out and prostrating herself at his feet.

'Is this where we're doing the programme?' I asked.

'Oh no, there's still quite a way to go. We've been invited here for lunch.'

We entered a shack: one main room and a tiny kitchen area to the back. Again, a dung floor, bare brick walls, a big iron bed, and a picture of Dr Ambedkar, freshly garlanded in honour of our visit. Within minutes Jyotipala was bullying the man of the house, flirting in a playful way with his wife, and taking over their son, bouncing the two-year-old on his knee and tickling the underside of his chin, while his parents proudly looked on.

'This is Nanda, Nagabodhi. I gave him that name. Say "Jai Bhim!" to Nagabodhi, Nanda.'

As we ate a bowl of sweet milk rice, our host, Mr Gaikwad, explained the afternoon's plan. We were to take a bus out of town for a few kilometres, and then proceed to Managon by bullock cart.

'Oh my word!' exclaimed the Namer of Children, putting down his bowl and stroking his heart, 'Oh dear! Oh dear!'

'What's the matter?' I asked.

'Have you never ridden in a bullock cart?' he retorted, 'Gaikwad, how far will we be going in the *bhal-gadi*?'

'Ten kilometers only. No more.'

Too stunned to speak, Jyotipala clutched his head in his hands. I was beside myself with joy. I had never ridden in a bullock cart, and it was something I'd always wanted to do. This was going to be a really comprehensive taste!

'Oh you poor, deluded fool!' he spluttered, 'Have you any idea what it's like to ride in a bullock cart? It's painful. And it's agonizingly slow. You'll see. You'll see!' He was in terrible pain of the soul, and threw himself face down across the bed.

'Agonizingly slow! There might be other ways to describe what a bullock cart's like. You can try and think of them, but I honestly don't think you're going to improve on "Agonizingly Slow". Tell him, Gaikwad! Tell him what a *bhal-gadi*'s like.'

Slightly perplexed, Mr Gaikwad looked down on Jyotipala's prostrate form. 'Slow. Yes. Very slow.' He laughed uneasily.

'*Agonizingly* slow!' corrected Jyotipala, 'Oh God!' He clutched at the hair-stubble that carpeted his skull and drew his face up to mine so that his eyes bored into me.

'AGONIZINGLY SLOW!' Exhausted, he collapsed and said no more.

By now Mrs Gaikwad and her daughters were peering round the partition, wondering what was going on. Seeing that it was only Jyotipala, they laughed a little and disappeared.

It was still quite early in the day, and I didn't have much of an appetite. I was therefore just allowing myself to enjoy the pleasant illusion that our bowl of milk rice had been the meal, when a Mr Vankaday placed his head in the doorway to announce that 'lunch' was ready.

Jyotipala and I were led round the corner to another, similar hut. Here, two narrow carpets had been laid on the floor, upon which we took our places, more or less in silence, and waited for the food to appear. In the kitchen, Mr Vankaday exchanged whispered instructions with his wife and daughter, while in the 'dining room' I had to deal with the fact that I was placed directly opposite a huge treadle sewing machine, its barrel emblazoned with the golden letters of the word 'Durex'. I simply couldn't bring myself to believe that such a company would feel the need to diversify in this of all countries.

As Mr Vankaday passed between us with a flask of water and a bowl, bidding us wash our hands, his wife appeared with two *thalis*, each mountainously laden with rice, chapatis, vegetables, bhajis, dal, curried potato, and yet more of the sweet rice mixture. Stunned, we contemplated our fate.

'Oh no,' whimpered Jyotipala, 'Please. Bring empty *thali*. Too much!' For a few minutes we transferred food from our plates onto the empty one, cutting our meals down to size in the only way that etiquette permitted. Mr and Mrs Vankaday looked on, smiling indulgently. Well, they had almost got away with it.

It seemed appropriate to ask Jyotipala whether people here appreciated his sense of humour.

'Well, you see, the bhikkhus have got them to adopt a very strict approach to people in robes. There's no laughing; they must prostrate in exactly the right way, be sure to sit so that they are on a lower level to the monks, all that sort of thing. So I make a special point of keeping things friendly, and having lots of fun. It can really throw people, because I always try to sit lower than anyone else, and make lots of jokes with Nagasena, if he's with me. But that way I try to show people that the spiritual life is something enjoyable, and that the sangha is about friendship.'

An hour later, crammed into a rickshaw, groggy and uncomfortably full of food, we headed back into town. Mr Vankaday was with us now, and Nagasena was waiting at the bus station. Our party was complete. Another hour later, an overheated bus left us on a stretch of empty road, surrounded on every side by fields of sugar-cane and cotton. Miraculously, the one man-made object in that deserted landscape was a tea stall.

We sat drinking, wondering what was going to happen next, until, from out of nowhere, a cheerful, well-rounded gentleman appeared among us, saying that our conveyance was ready, and had been these past two hours. This seemed strange, for we had seen nothing. Stepping out from under the tea-stall's canopy, and taking a good look around, we caught sight of the cart and its team, almost buried in a crater-like depression just a few yards away.

Eager as a child on holiday I circumnambulated the vehicle, admiring its robust bodywork, the simple arrangement of poles and yokes, the rough construction of the wooden wheels. Two white bullocks waited patiently, nuzzling each other as they stood together in harness.

'Now you'll see! *Now* you'll believe me!' snorted Jyotipala as we climbed aboard.

We began to load the cart with ourselves and our baggage. That was when I noticed how little room there was. Actually, it was quite impossible to find anywhere to sit without being placed on top of a gap between the planks, or without feeling the end of a spar digging into one's back. A rough, uneven mud track led away from us, disappearing into the fields. . . .

The driver began to cluck and moo to his beasts, and gave the one on the right a hard stab with the handle of his whip. We were on our way. As we lurched out of the crater, two boys appeared from the road, and set off down our path, hooting with laughter at the sight of us. The track was very uneven, and hard as iron. As we shuddered and crunched along, I couldn't help noticing that the boys were proceeding quite a bit faster than we were. This was going to be very slow . . . and agonizing.

Jyotipala said nothing, but huddled himself into an angular ball up at the front, a yellow T-shirt wrapped around his head to protect him from the sun, and us from the miserable severity of his expression.

Beside him, Nagasena had managed to settle himself so comfortably that within minutes he was asleep. He had been working since early in the morning, and was taking just half a day off to act as Jyotipala's interpreter. As often as not these days, he gave his own talks, but liked to work with Jyotipala whenever he could. He was a short, serious man, his face so scarred with pock-marks that it resembled the far side of the moon. At his Milind College Sunday class I had heard him give a talk about the principle of 'Dependent Origination'. Obviously I had not understood a word of his Marathi, but I was still struck by the quality of his voice, which seemed to come from somewhere very deep within him. He was a secondary school teacher, but was thinking seriously about retiring early, in his mid-forties, to work for the movement full time.

Agonizingly slow it was; but there were compensations. It was a glorious day, and the fields, undisturbed by our lumbering passage, shone and rippled as light and wind caught the sugar-cane. The mangoes were in blossom, and sometimes I could pick up the scent from a single tree a hundred metres away—a scent that was all the more dizzying for being so enchantingly subtle. Down in the fields, sugar-cane harvesters chopped and hacked, and boiled up immense shallow pans of cane juice, from which they were making *jagaree*, a rough, country sugar. They shouted at us, inviting us to drink juice with them; but we, apparently, were in a hurry, and so lurched on.

We passed a milestone: 'Managon: 10km'. This was going to be hard. To boost morale, Jyotipala and I ran through our repertoire of suitable songs: 'The Surrey With a Fringe on Top', 'Oh What a Beautiful Morning', the theme tune from 'Rawhide' . . . Mr Vankaday stared down at the track, shaking his head, the driver turned to look at us, rolled his eyes and grinned dangerously, revealing scarlet, pan-stained teeth.

I had always imagined that once he'd got a bullock cart moving along a simple, straight track, the driver would have little to do but doze contentedly on his bench while the beasts did all the work. Not a bit of it. Our driver maintained an almost uninterrupted repartee with his team, shouting at them, coaxing them, encouraging them, jabbing their sides, and yanking their tails. Sometimes he would get up and stand on his seat, his whip arm raised heroically high above his shoulder so that his shadow fell directly in the bullocks' line of vision. Or, leaning forward, his hand holding the whip like a scalpel, he would scrutinize the animals' backs, searching with total concentration for the exact spot where a strike would have maximum effect.

For a few kilometres we made our way up a long, gradual incline. At the top, almost buried in mango trees and banana groves, lay a small village of crumbling stone temples and scanty wooden homes. Old men squatted in the dirt, fashioning hand-brooms from sugar-cane leaves, a tailor worked his sewing machine out in the sun beside his house. A troop of monkeys ran screaming from us and darted into the trees, a half-crushed dog lay stinking in our path. Not a soul stirred as we passed by, but all kept their eyes fixed on our cart and its bizarre cargo, in frank disbelief.

A paradise of meadows, mango trees, acacia trees, and banyans now opened up before our eyes. The sun was westering, and clothed the entire panorama in a veil of misty dust-smog. In the distance we could make out the temple-tops of our destination: a village little bigger than the one we had just passed, out of which seemed to grow a number of curious grey and brown mounds. Mr Vankaday, who had been hanging onto my case throughout the journey, saving it from falling off the end of the cart, gave an encouraging smile. We would be there in forty minutes. In all, our ride would have lasted two hours—and we were going to have to do it all again on the way back tomorrow morning!

Two white-dhoti'd figures materialized at the point where our track entered the village. Jyotipala stood up to arrange his robes, which had come somewhat adrift by now. Stumbling and tottering, he finally lost his balance and crashed down cursing—as quietly as he could. We were on duty now.

'Jai Bhim! Jai Bhim!'

The greetings were serious, even tinged with urgency. Our hosts quickly took positions at the front to guide us through the narrow, winding lanes of the village.

The place could have been—and probably was—a thousand years old. Although one or two of the dwellings were built of wood, most of them were made from clay, and sprouted roofs of thatched sticks. The earth was of clay too, as were the dome-like hummocks that rose here and there about the village. In places it was impossible to tell where the land ended and the habitations began, hard to decide whether one was looking at a house or a heap of earth. Potters sat in the dust, spinning crude wheels with their feet, throwing pots and flasks. We passed a few temples: one big Shiva shrine, the rest just simple little huts. Peering into the gloom beyond their doors, I could just make out the ugly, ochre-stained forms of their misshapen denizens. Candles flickered beside them, accentuating the timeless, private darkness.

We were the centre of everyone's attention. A crowd of children ran along behind and beside us, helping the cart round the tighter corners and out of the deeper pot-holes. At length, coming to the very edge of the village, we took a sudden left turn and arrived at a sort of stage. This grew from the back of the last building in the place, and faced out towards the open plains. An even bigger crowd was waiting here, ready to help us climb, jelly-legged, from the cart.

The driver freed his team and set them munching at mounds of hay in the shade of a venerable banyan, while we were led up onto the stage and offered soft mattresses. Jyotipala gasped and groaned, burrowing into his mattress like a dog settling down for the night, while the older boys and the men came to sit with us on the stage, watching with friendly curiosity while we gulped down glasses of brackish water. There wasn't a woman to be seen.

Five minutes later, two shallow cups of tea appeared, one for Jyotipala, and one for me. Our servers waited beside us as we drank, taking the cups as soon as we'd finished. Five minutes later they reappeared with tea for Nagasena and Mr Vankaday. These were probably the only two cups in the Buddhist locality.

After yet another five minutes, two more men appeared bearing the largest papaya I had ever seen and proceeded to cut it into cubes which they arranged on a large metal plate. The sight of all that oozing, succulent fruit was so enticing that I only just managed to stop myself from snatching a piece out of the man's hands when he finally offered it to me.

Our audience talked quietly among themselves, pointing towards us and chuckling, no doubt commenting on the show so far, while our blessed servitors plied us with chunk after chunk of papaya meat. It was an astounding papaya, a consumate papaya, combining something of the peach, the apricot, the melon, and even the banana in its gentle flavour. When we had taken as much as we could eat, there was still enough left to allow every man on the stage a good-sized chunk.

This idyllic hiatus was not to last, however. Deciding that we were sufficiently relaxed, rested, and ready, our hosts led us down from the stage just as a party of six young men appeared. Each of them bore a *lezhim*—a Maharashtran 'instrument' comprising a thick wooden pole some two feet long, its ends linked by a heavy metal chain onto which was threaded a series of small cymbals. Two drummers arrived as well, one bearing an enlarged tabla, the other a flat skin-drum. The final arrival was a clarinetist. We seemed to have the makings of a procession.

'Doctor Babasaheb Ambedkarantsa!' yelled a cheerleader.

'JAI SO!' came the response.

And we were off. The *lezhim* troop took the lead and, as the drummers burst into a heady, primitive rhythm, and as the clarinet player performed his audition piece for a Turkish Delight advert, they hurled themselves up into the air and down almost to the ground, giving their instruments savage tugs and jerks, making the cymbals crack and chink against the wood. Behind them came the band, and behind them walked some fifty of us, in a tight huddle.

The cheerleader kept up his work continuously:

'Bhagavan Gautam Buddchacha!'

'JAI SO!'

'Anagarika Jyotipala-ki!'

'JAI SO!'

'Dhammachari Nagabodhi-ki!'

'JAI SO!'

At the back, a throng of women joined in, at first diffidently, but then more boisterously, adding their own chants: 'Ek, Dom, Tin, Char! (One, two, three, four!)—Doctor Bahasaheb Ambedkar: Jai-Jai-Ka!'

For about forty minutes, while the setting sun bathed the village in a hazy glow of pink and gold, we danced and marched through the lanes, passing far beyond the Buddhist section and out to the different localities of the main Hindu village. Not for a moment did the *lezhim* players cease their war-like gyrations; it was as if we were surging through a network of canals in a war canoe powered by the strong arms of the young men at the front.

We were a raggle-taggle mob. No doubt people had dressed as smartly as they could, but these were simple country folk. Their whites were ripped and ragged, their turbans stained and grey, their faces could have been carved from rough stone, so strong they were, and so weather-hardened. Many of the younger men wore their hair down to their shoulders, which gave them an almost tribal aspect.

There was no way that anyone from the Hindu village was going to attend our meeting, but that was hardly the point. The Buddhists were showing us off, and, in the process, raising a little hell. Each time we passed a temple, the volume of the chanting increased and the *lezhim* team put even more fervour into its performance. By now they were running with sweat, and dancing as if possessed. This was a display of endurance. The Hindus squatted by their doors and shops, looking on through narrow, enigmatic eyes.

Jyotipala walked tall, dignified, and stern of countenance, throwing the occasional groan from the side of his mouth if I tripped over a boulder, or became entangled in weeds.

We arrived at a rather stately hut, set in its own courtyard. The *lezhim* team proceeded to the door of the building—which looked remarkably like a low slung mushroom—and formed themselves into an ellipse. Eight women now appeared from the door of the hut and entered the ellipse, bearing trays of flowers, candles, and incense. Jyotipala stepped forward from the other end to meet them.

The dancers danced, the drums grew louder.

Jyotipala stood—statuesque—in their midst while the ladies prostrated before him, waving their trays under his face, and generally making much of him. Meanwhile, the men shouted at the women, telling them what to do, and in what order, making them ever more nervous. Nagasena joined in, rushing up to pour a schedule of works into their ears as they performed their ritual.

Disaster almost struck. A lady on her way upwards after a prostration struck her head on the underside of a tray in the hands of a lady on her way downwards. In the event, just a few marigold blossoms fluttered to the ground. Calm, impassive, Jyotipala stood before them: 'Sukkhi Ho . . . Sukkhi Ho!'—'Be happy . . . Be happy!'

As soon as I had the chance, I asked Nagasena why there had been so much fuss. Why couldn't the men just let the women do things in their own way?

'Well, this sort of thing is very important for our people. Until just a few years ago these ladies were not allowed to perform any kind of religious ritual at all. None of us were. Now that we have got rid of caste restrictions, everyone wants to get things exactly right. If the ladies can learn to do things just as they should be done, they will feel very pleased and confident. But it will take time to learn.'

We were now on our way back to the stage and Jyotipala was beginning to enjoy himself.

'I mean, *look* at me. A miner's son! From *Barnsley*! How on earth have I managed to get myself caught up in something like this? Eh? I mean, if I was a millionaire I still couldn't get an experience like this, could I? There are some things you can't even buy. Not even with money!'

A fat full moon wallowed in the trees when we finally arrived back at the stage. It was six-thirty, and we had had a long, hard day. Without ceremony, Jyotipala and Nagasena threw themselves down onto the mattresses, and fell asleep in instants. As before, our hosts looked on with satisfaction.

The stage was really a large room, open to the world at one end. At its rear, liberally dressed with marigolds, a shrine stood beneath a portrait of Dr Ambedkar (here portrayed in his military incarnation). Wires had been hung around the loud pink walls, and a loudspeaker system was being concocted. Obviously, our hosts had not been sure that we were really coming, and had left the practical arrangements until we were physically present. A fluorescent tube, tied with string to a beam near the front of the stage, flashed on and off rapidly while someone fiddled with its starter. At last it remained alight.

Jyotipala murmured in his slumber: '*Fiat Lux.*'

I decided to try for a nap myself, and had just dropped off when I realized I was being kicked in the ribs.

'Come on. Grub.'

We were led round a corner and offered tea in the porch of a tiny, barn-like structure. Outside, gathered around little fires, the other villagers set to eating. Back at the stage, a smartly dressed young man from Jalna tortured the night, passing live wires over the terminals of an amplifier. The moon was bright, and threw a pale sheen over the fields.

These fields, I discovered, belonged to the Buddhists and were farmed by them. A generation ago, in Ambedkar's time, the Scheduled Caste community had given rise to four exceptional leaders. Inspired by Ambedkar's words and deeds, they had succeeded in unifying the local Untouchables in a struggle for their rights. In the end they forced the municipality to grant them the rights to the land.

It was good land, and they all seemed to be healthy and well fed. They were proud too: proud of their achievement in carving out this slice of freedom, and proud of their record as Buddhists. Although they lived in such a remote spot, they managed to organize some kind of Buddhist event, with a guest speaker, most full moon nights. They were also aware that in this respect they led the way for Buddhist communities throughout their region. Even city Buddhists rarely got so many opportunities to hear the Dhamma. While we drank, I could hear the tinkle of bicycle bells; people were arriving from neighbouring villages, and even from Jalna.

We were led into the heart of the house: a single room thickly coated with rich brown dung. A lone, chimneyless oil lamp offered yellow, dancing light as we worked our way through a simple meal of coarse chapati, rice, and lentils. The lentils were so powerfully curried that even Jyotipala growled softly while he ate. But we had to get through every mouthful. Even if these villagers were not going hungry, this was not a place where food could be treated lightly. Silence reigned throughout the meal, possibly because no one was capable of speech while those fires raged in their mouths and throats. Up on the wall, even Dr Ambedkar scowled painfully.

We ambled back towards the stage where the smart young man was now testing his equipment, sending a broadside of 'Hello's into the infinite. Raising the little finger of one hand, Jyotipala indicated that he needed to use a toilet. Apprehending the symbolism of this gesture, one of our hosts responded immediately, 'Make water only? Come!'

He led us out into the fields, helping us to avoid the ditches and tangles of gorse, and left us to do our business in a low depression. From here the illuminated stage, surrounded by the red glows of the camp fires, resembled a child's entry in the nativity exhibition at an English country church. Beneath the banyan tree in front, our two white bullocks gazed upon the silvery world with dreamy benevolence. Here and there, mounds of sacking indicated where a few people had already turned in, sleeping under the stars beside their fires.

The stage—which seemed to be the auditorium as well—was now packed. The women, many with babies asleep in their laps, chatted among themselves; the men talked to each other, sitting with their arms draped easily over each other's shoulders. The atmosphere felt uncommonly natural, deeply nourishing.

It would have been a lot more nourishing without that public address system. After much work and experimentation on the part of a steadily growing committee, it seemed that we had a choice: we could either have hum, or we could have crackle, or we could have hiss. Because Mr Vankaday worked for the local electricity board, he was tersely ordered to see what he could do.

After just a little fiddling, he made his decision. We would have hiss.

At nine o'clock, Jyotipala and Nagasena rose from the throne-like chairs they had occupied during the introductions, and Jyotipala launched into his talk.

He began by contemplating the question of what it is that makes a 'great man' great. Using Ambedkar's own criteria (outlined in a book on the reformer, Justice Ranade), he explained that a great man is someone who can combine sincerity with intelligence, and who always acts for the good of the great mass of people. He then proceeded to demonstrate how Dr Ambedkar met these criteria, and could be truly described as a 'great man'.

A noisy conference erupted somewhere near the amplifier.

The PA system was working adequately. Indeed, the PA system was quite superfluous since Jyotipala was more than able to make himself heard by our small audience without electronic aids. It was a chilly night, and those at the back had pushed the others forwards so that only a few people had failed to find room on the stage. Some were even sitting behind Jyotipala, tightly wrapped in heavy blankets. Even so, the 'sound committee' was not satisfied. The amplifier was attacked again and began to howl feedback.

Undaunted, Jyotipala continued, 'After all, look at us. We are all here tonight, together, listening to a talk on the Dhamma. Why is this? It is because Dr Ambedkar started the Dhamma Revolution!'

While Nagasena delivered a fast, slightly extended translation, a broad man stepped forward as if to shake Jyotipala by the hand. Instead, he removed the microphone. Jyotipala spoke on while the technician painstakingly dismantled the offending gadget, blew into it, reassembled it and, shrugging theatrically towards his companions at the back, set it on its stand.

'We could even say that Dr Ambedkar was a Bodhisattva!'

'Now, what is a Bodhisattva? A Bodhisattva is an ideal Buddhist. He is a *perfect* Buddhist. He is someone who works untiringly at his Dhamma life. And he does this because he wants to help others.'

The technician reappeared, took the microphone away again, and replaced it with the sort of thing through which Edward VIII must have announced his abdication.

'A Bodhisattva is someone who practises the Six Perfections. . . .'

The conference at the back was over. It was now possible to hear the sound of dogs baying at the moon, not too far away. An important looking burgher in the front row leapt to his feet and shouted orders to lieutenants at the rear—who rushed out urgently into the night. I waited, expecting the crackle of small-arms fire. Instead, a minute later, one of them reappeared with a glass of water which was passed hand to hand through the audience and set at Jyotipala's feet.

He began to list the Perfections, starting with 'Generosity'. After a few general words on the virtue itself, he proceeded to demonstrate the many ways in which Ambedkar had practised it.

'He gave his whole life to the uplift of his people. He gave them his care and his concern. He gave them the three Refuges, the five Precepts, and the twenty-two Vows: he gave them the Dhamma!'

As Jyotipala moved on to the 'Perfection of Morality', we were already suffering a new distraction.

A squadron of insects, each about one and a half inches long, with evil brown bodies and short, busy wings, had happened upon our gathering. They had a curious trick of seeming only to fall out of the air, rather than flying, and struck their targets with a sickening crunch. They fell onto people's heads, onto their laps, onto the sleep-drenched faces of the babes, and onto the floor at Jyotipala's feet. Having fallen, they would then unfold their major purpose in life, which was to look ugly, mean, and unpredictable. How they managed to give this appearance of falling without ever seeming first to rise eluded me. A wave of panic rippled through the audience, though the cramped nature of our circumstance allowed little room for manœuvre. Jyotipala was now addressing a subdued riot. Eventually, two boys at the front took out their pencils and began killing the things, rather brutally and inefficiently.

Jyotipala pushed on to 'Forbearance'—and the power failed. All light and all sound went dead. But Jyotipala kept talking, the natural tones of his voice contrasting sweetly with the din that had been coming from the loudspeakers. In the background could be heard a racket of desperate fumbling which bore fruit just as Jyotipala addressed himself to the theme of 'Energy'. Back came the crackle of the speakers, and back came the lights—to reveal that, in the black interim, the entire place had been rewired.

From 'Meditation' Jyotipala finally arrived at 'Wisdom: Seeing Things as They Really Are'.

'Dr Ambedkar saw the world. He saw it without any illusions. He saw that people needed the Dhamma. So he gave them the Dhamma. He saw that only the Dhamma would change the world. And yet his followers rushed into politics. They tried to get laws passed. They tried to form political parties. They tried to do all kinds of things. But all that energy should have gone into the Dhamma!

'With the Dhamma we can develop confidence. We can learn how to be generous, learn how to practise all the perfections. We can work on ourselves and become great beings, like Dr Ambedkar, and like the Buddha.

'We have Buddha images and Buddha shrines in our viharas and in our homes. This is because we are trying to develop respect for the Buddha, and because we are trying to develop the Bodhisattva spirit. It is not enough to be a follower of someone in a half-hearted way. If you are going to follow someone, then you must follow them all the way! You cannot be a follower of Dr Ambedkar and not be a Buddhist! And even that is not enough. No! Dr Ambedkar was a Bodhisattva! So if we are going to follow him then we have to become Bodhisattvas too! We have to practise the Perfections!'

Later, I put it to Jyotipala that he had become something of a hell-fire preacher-man since his days in Purley.

'Oh yes. Well, I can do it here, can't I? I'd be dead useless in England, but here I can get away with it. If I come on a bit strong or even a bit angry with them about Hindu gods, or drinking, they really like it. They know that I care, and that I mean what I'm saying.'

There was no doubt that this talk had gone down well. Even though it was now gone ten, all eyes were alert and happy, smiles and nods were exchanged as the applause rang out. Thoroughly inured to the kind of disturbances with which our talk had been fraught, nobody seemed to have missed a word.

It was now 'Guruji''s turn to take the microphone. 'Guruji' was the village teacher, and it was his job to thank the speaker and announce donations as they were presented. One by one, twenty villagers stepped forward, whispered in the teacher's ear, and prostrated, before slipping a *dana* offering into the mouth of Jyotipala's bag. As they did so, the teacher announced who it was that was giving, and how much. 'Mr N. R. Pandagalay is now giving dana of two rupees . . . Mrs Sujata Kadam is now giving dana of one rupee . . . Mr B. B. Gaikwad is now giving dana of three rupees. . . .'

Jyotipala, his eyes drooping slightly, decided to cut through what could become a very lengthy procedure, and suggested that people should buy books with their money instead. Nagasena, at last liberated from his translator's role, soared to the microphone to deliver an impassioned account of the publications he had brought along.

By eleven, the audience was showing no sign of fatigue. Over to one side of the stage, a man sat tuning his tabla; somebody else had appeared with a harmonium, and the sound man was arranging the microphone for the 'music programme', a rousing medley of Ambedkarite songs, which would go on until the early hours.

I began to feel anxious.

But Jyotipala was my salvation, 'Come on, let's find out where we're sleeping.'

We rose and passed through the audience. Almost nobody noticed us now, for the band had struck into its first number. The organizers intercepted us at the stage mouth.

'Yes. Come. There are beds.'

We were led round into a narrow lane and invited to enter what was either a one-roomed house or a barn—and which no doubt served as both. One half of the room was elevated three feet above the other. Along its length four mattresses had been laid out. The walls were of rough stone, planted and bound in clay. The floor smelt sweetly of fresh dung. We clambered aboard and chose beds, while the two organizers, draped in heavy blankets, squatted talking with Nagasena and Mr Vankaday in the lower half.

It now occurred to Jyotipala that there was no bedding, and that none seemed to be forthcoming. He therefore asked whether it might be possible for him to have a blanket or two. A man went off, returning some five minutes later.

'Country blanket!' he announced in a good natured, challenging tone, handing Jyotipala a roughly woven length of sack-cloth.

'Oh my goodness!' intoned the evening's star. I laughed savagely at his plight. All day he had been teasing me for bringing my sleeping bag.

'Oh, this is great. It's lovely in here,' I purred, wallowing in the softness of the bag, feeling its side scuffle harshly against the coarse edge of Jyotipala's blanket.

But he was becoming quietly philosophical, 'It's really amazing though, isn't it? I mean, they give us their food, give over a house, some mattresses and a blanket. They don't know us from Adam. We don't even know their names! It's incredibly generous really.'

'Yes. But, after all, you are a special guest. You have just given a talk.'

'I know all that. But even so, because we're here, some people are going without a bed, and someone is going without a blanket, just so that they can make us as comfortable as they can.'

The conference had come to an end. Our guardians said their goodnights and left. A minute later, one of them returned with an oil-lamp—nothing more than a flaming wick lying in a shallow bowl of oil. He set it in a rough alcove so that it threw nightmarish shadows around the earthy walls. Within moments, Nagasena was asleep, Mr Vankaday well on his way. Not very far off, the shrill noise of amplified music assaulted the bright night.

'If you're uncomfortable about this, how should I feel?' I asked, 'I'm the imposter here. I've had the same treatment as you, and yet I've not done a thing to earn my keep.'

'Oh *no*! It's not like that at all. You've *been* here. Just by coming along—coming all the way here from England—it's done wonders for their pride. It's something they'll talk about for years.'

Comforted, I applied my ear-plugs, drew the folds of my sleeping bag around me, and sank into a deep, rich sleep.

But Jyotipala never got a wink.

eighteen

I had no need of a sleeping bag last night; the summer has turned oppressively hot and humid. Today the sky is full of threatening clouds, the air thick with the wind-blown scent of damp earth. The monsoon is approaching, a monsoon I'll never see—for this time next week I'll be on a plane, bound for London.

I have been in Panchgani for three months, scribbling until my fingers jammed, typing myself almost deaf.

Already the pattern of things has changed since I began. Padmashuri is now back in England, hoping to get out again in a year's time, while Virabhadra is in Delhi with Bodhidharma, looking into what can be done about his own position in India and that of Lokamitra. An Indian woman doctor recently joined the Dapodi team, and Siddharth—having left his job at the Bombay glass factory—is working there too, as secretary. But Sopan Kamblay has moved from Dapodi to the administrative office at Ambedkar Society. Mr Mhende took over from him as site supervisor when work on the Lohagaon hostel came to an end.

I took a couple of days off work to attend the opening ceremonies. The hostel looked superb, though by the time a thousand visitors had oozed through its bright rooms, it was almost in need of a repaint. It was school holiday time, but I was relieved to see Suresh Chavan in the audience. He'd obviously found a refuge for the duration.

Here in Panchgani the lights have just gone out; the water disappeared from the pipes a couple of hours ago. But there have been other events of note. In the Parthay household, we have had a demonic possession, a wedding, and an unsuccessful bid by Vasant to win himself a seat on the Municipal Council. Actually, he was standing on behalf of his brother Madhu—who is engaged in a running feud with one of the other candidates—so it was the shame involved in losing that seemed to hurt most.

As Madhu reflected last night, this has been a bad year for the family: their father died just before I arrived, Subhash's buffalo fell to its death from a nearby scarp, the election was lost, and the man who promised to buy their holiday bungalow welshed on them. I thought of pointing out that, had he not done so, I would have been deprived my lodgings, but I didn't wish to cause offence; I've come to like them all far too much for that.

Three months is a long time to spend in a small Indian town. The strawberry vendors and sweet-corn broilers now let me pass unmolested, and direct their attention to the haughty flocks of Bombayites who promenade main street between visits to the video-parlours and 'viewpoints'. These days, I rarely go into town without meeting at least a few people I know. Some of them take me by the hand, and lead me into the Apsara Hotel for a cup of tea, addressing me as 'Mr Terry'. They are of the Parthay faction. Others make hasty salutations and offer their 'Jai Bhim's. The Buddhists all know me, and know that I am writing a book about their leader. Other locals watch me from a distance, with reserved curiosity. They've seen me with the Buddhists, going into their localities, joining their festival processions. Perhaps the word has even got round that I've been giving talks.

Sanjay Kamblay—now a regular companion on evening strolls—told his friends about me immediately after our first meeting. A few days later Kishen Kamblay, a janitor at Sanjay's school, paid a visit along with Gauruanna Kharat, a respected elder in the Buddhist community. We chatted for a while, and then they led me down the rocky path to Kishen's house, where a clutch of boys and girls chanted their evening *vandanas* under my admiring gaze. Asking Sanjay to translate, I gave an impromptu talk on the purpose of devotional practice. The kids themselves seemed little moved by my performance, but Kishen, Gauruanna, and Sanjay decided to put me to work, and soon had me lined up to speak at Bhim Nagar, and then at a village some miles out of town. On the anniversary of the Buddha's Enlightenment we climbed fifteen hundred feet down the hillside to the village of Chikilee where I gave a talk to two hundred locals, in their surprisingly beautiful Buddha Hall.

Writing to Lokamitra, about all this I jokingly enquired whether I might be eligible for TBMSG funding. Rachel replied on his behalf, stating that they will support me once I start selling their books at my meetings. 'One thing', as she put it, 'does seem to lead to another'. Now that I have seen for myself how true that is, I can understand why Sangharakshita never gave up hope of doing something in India, and why Lokamitra has found it impossible to resist the pull of this world.

Many people try to dismiss the Buddhist revival as an entirely cultural phenomenon. It is an easy mistake to make, but mistake it is—even though the vast majority of Buddhists have little knowledge of Buddhism, nor even much more than a residual, culturally acquired desire to learn something about it. The fact remains that they do come to the talks, they listen, and they really do appreciate whatever scraps of Buddhism come their way.

When we first met, Sanjay hardly knew anything about Buddhism and had never tried very hard to find out about it. Now he is meditating every day, reading all the books I can lend him, and trying to get himself registered at a college in Poona so he can be near a TBMSG centre. I cannot predict where it will lead him, but I do know that his involvement with the 'Dhamma Revolution' has become individual and authentic. It was his 'Buddhist culture', not I, that planted the seed.

Shortly before moving here, I joined twenty men from Poona for a week's retreat at the Bhaja centre. Each day a couple of hours were left unscheduled so that we could go off in pairs for walks. Again and again—until I could virtually finish their sentences for them—I listened while one man after another told me the same story. They had heard about 'Babasaheb' throughout their childhoods; sooner or later they had read—or had had read to them—at least some of his books. Many had got themselves involved in politics and had become disillusioned. Then they had decided to learn something about Buddhism and, after searching for teachers and teachings, had ended up with TBMSG.

Perhaps I should add that every one of them considered himself an exception. Most of their friends, they admitted, were trying to build lives of material comfort, immersing themselves in their families and careers. But even if each of the men on that retreat was a 'one-in-a-hundred' phenomenon, it would mean there are sixty-thousand like-minded people in Maharashtra! If even a tiny proportion of them become 'Dhamma workers', willing and able to go out to the towns and villages to teach—as they most surely will—then it won't be long before they have a profound effect on their entire culture. Ambedkar's dream could still come true.

As we strolled about the fields and pathways surrounding the centre, we had only to raise our eyes to see the Buddhist cave temples, tucked into the ghats above. Two thousand years ago people practised the Dhamma there, keeping it alive through their efforts. Their time is long past, but the Dhamma has survived and travelled to other lands, other cultures, and into other ages. Now it has come full circle. Each evening, at sunset, the polished stupa in the main Chaitya Hall would catch the sun, and flash brilliantly. It seemed an auspicious sign.

When it was published, a little while after his death, Ambedkar's 'Buddhist Bible', *The Buddha and His Dhamma*, was given a mixed reception. His critics asserted that he had gone too far in his attempt to highlight the social dimension of the Buddha's message.

Ambedkar was working on that book on the very night he died. It is not a finished work but, although the final draft would have been more polished, I doubt whether Ambedkar would have shifted his basic approach to Buddhism. Unlike countless scholars, interpreters, and monks before him, Ambedkar could see that Buddhism offers a practical path leading to the fullest development of human potential and can therefore be applied as a catalyst in the radical, non-violent transformation of society. To have distinguished, upheld, and committed himself to this insight surely compensates for any limitations in his selective approach. Those of his followers who take up his challenge and practise the Dhamma for themselves will no doubt sort out the details.

Had Ambedkar died a Hindu he would still be remembered as a great social reformer, as an educationalist, and as a fighter for human rights. He would be honoured for the political, educational, and occupational safeguards he won on behalf of the Scheduled Castes. He would also be revered for the myth he embodied, the myth of a boy born in the mud of Untouchability who rose to a position of power and national influence without ever forgetting his people. But he did not die a Hindu; he converted to Buddhism, and in so doing, offered his people some even stronger myths: the myth of spiritual and social rebirth, the myth of the Buddhist revival in India, and the myth of the Dhamma Revolution.

These myths have acted as a rallying call and as a bond, boosting the self-respect and aspirations of an entire community. They have pointed to a path beyond hatred and resentment, one based on clarity, love, and creative action. I have walked so many times into huts, chawls, shacks, and worse, where the grinding poverty and deprivation should have bred nothing but misery, apathy, and brooding hostility. Instead, I met people with determination, hope, and even joy in life because they believed they had the power to make things better. And if those myths have not yet been seized and used to bring about the transformation that Ambedkar envisaged, they are still strong enough to put light and life into people's eyes. In time, his followers will pull through.

The myths have survived because they have taken root, not so much in the masses through whom they find their most spectacular expression, but in the hearts of each one of Ambedkar's followers. Somehow these great myths have merged and interacted with millions of individual patterns and personal myths, enriching them, directing them, galvanizing them, amplifying the urge to growth and further unfoldment which is innate in us all.

I think of Chandrakant Ohal in Lohagaon, now a 'reformed' and happy man because 'Babasaheb' once held him in his arms. I think of Prakash from Bombay, surrounding himself with heroes and rejoicing in his ability to emulate them. I think of Bodhisen, dragging his sacks of books around, poring over his accounts, mastering English so that he could act as Vajraketu's interpreter, and now going out to the Bombay slums to give his own talks. I think of the purposeful faces of the programme organizers as they walked in our processions, and I think of the policeman in Kopergaon who climbed onto the stage to offer Sangharakshita a posy in front of four thousand people. None of them, none of the thousands of people I've met here, could really explain what has happened to them. There was no one moment when they felt the myths catching hold of them and beginning to shape their lives. But the myths were and are there all the same, like jewels sewn into the folds of their coats.

A Hindu story relates that Indra, the king of the gods, possessed a fabulous net of jewels. The special quality of this net was that each jewel in it reflected the others, and was itself reflected in the rest. The Buddhists in Maharashtra are linked in a similar way by their myths. For all the wasted years and troubles, their myths, like hidden jewels, are intact and uncorrupted. As individuals among them take their practice of Buddhism to a higher level, then, in some way, the entire community will be affected, by the sharing of knowledge, by medical projects, by student's hostels, and by co-operative business enterprises; it will be affected—and strengthened—as new Dhamma centres and retreat centres appear, helping more people to redeem the value of their jewels.

I think too of men like Bodhidharma, Vimalakirti, and Chandrabodhi. They are followers of Dr Ambedkar, but they are now working in a far wider context than that of the Maharashtran Buddhist movement. They have begun to identify with the myth of the *bodhisattva*, the one who works tirelessly for the good of all beings, throughout time and throughout space.

Bodhidharma once told me, 'I no longer see my work as being just for the Scheduled Castes. Now I am working for the Dhamma. If you develop loving kindness, if you begin to feel a love for all, then how can you only identify with your own community? You identify with the whole world.'

* * *

In a week I shall be back in England. I'll be giving talks again, and teaching meditation at Buddhist centres there. I'll be offering the Dhamma to people who want a little peace of mind or a cure for insomnia. Some will have come along because they've just read a book about Tibet by Lobsang Rampa, others might be trying to work out the significance of an unexpected 'mystical experience'. It will be a very different world to that of the Indian Dhamma Revolution, but the jewels will be there all the same.

If I get any time off, I'll go up to North Wales to visit Vajraketu. He's living at a retreat centre, waiting to hear whether his second visa application has been successful, and in the meantime trying to catch up with his meditation. He'll want to know how his 'Bombay boys' are getting on. And I'll take my manuscript to Norfolk, and show it to Sangharakshita. He'll probably point out the mistakes, query my errors of judgement, and generally hint that I have a better book than this inside me.

But before I leave Panchgani, Sanjay, Kishen, and Gauruanna are planning to set me up with one last talk, probably at Bhim Nagar. If they manage that, Tuesday night will find us making our way to the 'vihara', a sort of stage-like shell, constructed on the spot where Sangharakshita once gave his talk. I'll take my place at the microphone—in front of two crude paintings of Dr Ambedkar and the Buddha—and Sanjay will stand beside me to interpret the talk.

I will tell my audience that my book is written, and I'll warn them—as I hardly need tell you—that mine is no scholarly work on Ambedkar, nor is it even a comprehensive account of his Dhamma Revolution. There are many more tales to be told than I have told, though few, I suspect, that end so hopefully.

I will affirm my belief that Ambedkar was a great man, and add that his full greatness has yet to be revealed. If his followers take the Dhamma Revolution seriously, and *practise* Buddhism, then the Buddha-Dhamma really will live again in the country of its birth, and India will again be transformed by it. Then the name of Dr Babasaheb Ambedkar will resound from one end of the earth to the other. Of all the many gifts he gave his people, perhaps the most selfless of all was custody over his ultimate place in history.

Well, anyway, I'll say something like that. I've still got a few days to think about it. . . .

But I think I do already know how I'll end the talk. After all, I heard Sangharakshita using a formula rather like it, every night for three months.

So, as you read the following words, try to imagine the warm evening air on your skin, the scent of woodsmoke, marigold garlands, and cow dung, and picture the trees and ramshackle huts outlined against a moonlit sky. Not very far away, dogs are howling and some donkeys have started to bray. From a little way off comes the occasional tinkle of a temple bell and the whine of motor scooter. Try to imagine these things, for what I will be saying to my audience on that night, I am saying to you now:

I have enjoyed being here in Panchgani talking to you. It is always good to talk about the Dhamma, always good to remember the life and work of Dr Babasaheb Ambedkar.

I hope you have enjoyed listening to me, and I hope that you will remember some of the things I have said. May they be valuable to you, and may they be of some use in your lives. May you become more free, more happy, and ever more inspired to make a better life for yourself and for those around you.

Now it is time for me to go. Let's hope that, one day, we shall all meet again.

Jai Bhim.

acknowledgements

This book is credited to a single author, but without the help and support of a great many people there would be no book—and no author to credit. Whether they gave time, money, advice and encouragement, or simply groaned and wept in appropriate places when regaled with readings, it is they who have made this book possible.

In particular, Rosy Anderson, Judy Child, Marlene Halliday, Chris Krupa, Hugh Mendes, and Dhammacharis Dhammarati, Subhuti, and Shantavira enabled me to make two extended visits to India by sharing a number of my responsibilities. Allan Miller, Woolf and Jean Pilchick, the Windhorse Trust, and Dhammacharis Bodhiruchi and Satyapala generously sponsored my travels. As the project neared completion, Virabhadra tracked down some important errors and omissions, and Shantavira checked, corrected, and prepared the manuscript for publication.

Lokamitra offered a warm welcome at all times of day or night, information and advice, a key to every door, and more of his time than I should ever have hoped for. Sangharakshita provided inspiration, a large part of my story, and the encouragement to tell it.

I cannot hope to thank personally those hundreds of people in India who shared their lives, memories, and aspirations with me. For months on end they gave me shelter and food, drew me into their world, and offered—among so many other gifts—that of their friendship.

Things have progressed apace since I wrote those first drafts in Panchgani. New public centres, educational projects, and 'right livelihood' schemes are being established all the time; thousands more people have become involved with the 'Dhamma Revolution'. Bodhidharma, Vimalakirti, Chandrabodhi, Chandrasil, Mr Agaley (now known as Maitreyanatha), and many more of the people whose stories and lives aroused and nurtured my enthusiasm are now substantial, leading figures in a movement that has become very much their own. May they and their work flourish.

Terry Pilchick (Dhammachari Nagabodhi)
Padmaloka, Norfolk

Summer, 1988

Also from Windhorse Publications:

Ambedkar and Buddhism
by Sangharakshita

On 14 October 1956, B. R. Ambedkar launched his movement of 'mass conversion'. Over the following months, India shook as hundreds of thousands of her most disadvantaged citizens threw off the stigma of 'Untouchability'—by renouncing Hinduism and becoming Buddhists.

Sangharakshita knew Ambedkar personally, and has himself played an important part in the movement that Ambedkar set in motion. In *Ambedkar and Buddhism* he explores the historical, religious, and social background to that movement. He also examines Ambedkar's interpretation of Buddhism, and assesses the considerable contribution made by Ambedkar to the spiritual tradition in which he placed his trust.

181 pages
Paperback. Price £5.95
ISBN 0 904766 28 4

Also from Parallax Press:

Being Peace
By Thich Nhat Hanh

Nhat Hanh was a spokesperson for the largely Buddhist Third Force
during the Vietnam war. *Being Peace* is a short, sweet, and deeply
affecting statement of his pholosophy, and it is something more. It is an
attempt to embody, or at least foreshadow, an emerging *American*
conscience based in part on Buddhist teachings as they've been
understood and adapted in this country over the last 20 years.
—*New Options*

For spiritual seekers and social activists, this is the book that best
describes the interface between the two. Simply the best statement yet,
the bible of Engaged Buddhism, by a man who lives it.
—*Inquiring Mind*

115 pages.
Paperback. Price $8.50
ISBN 0 938077 00 7

For a full catalogue of Windhorse books, please write to:
Windhorse Publications, 136 Renfield St, Glasgow G2 3AU, UK
For information about Parallax books, please write to:
Parallax Press, P.O.Box 7355, Berkeley, California CA 94707, USA